Sara VanDerBeek

HATJE
CANTZ

Sara VanDerBeek

Edited by Gloria Sutton

Horses, 2006

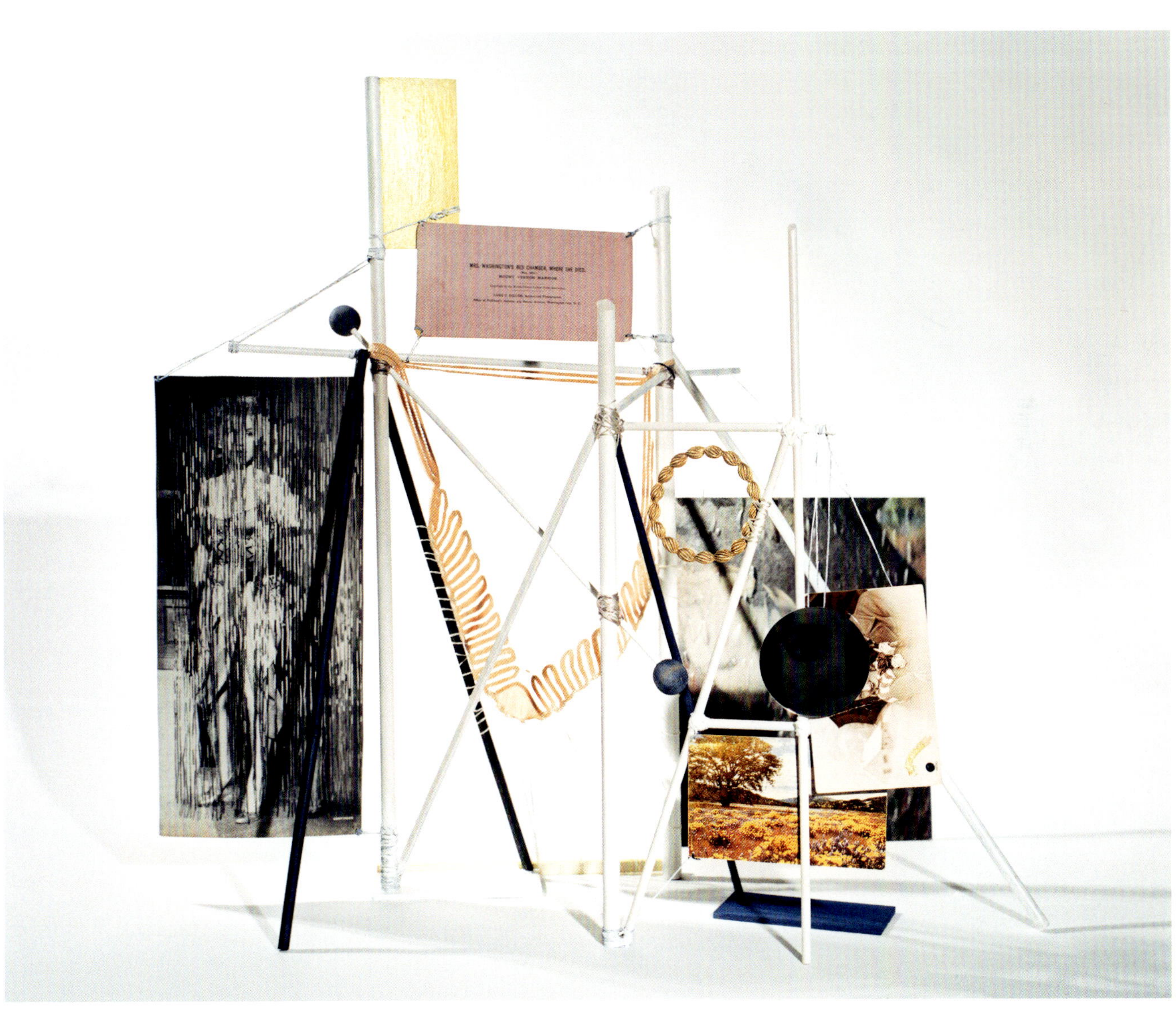
MRS. WASHINGTON'S BED CHAMBER, WHERE SHE DIED.
MOUNT VERNON MANSION

A Different Kind of Idol, 2006

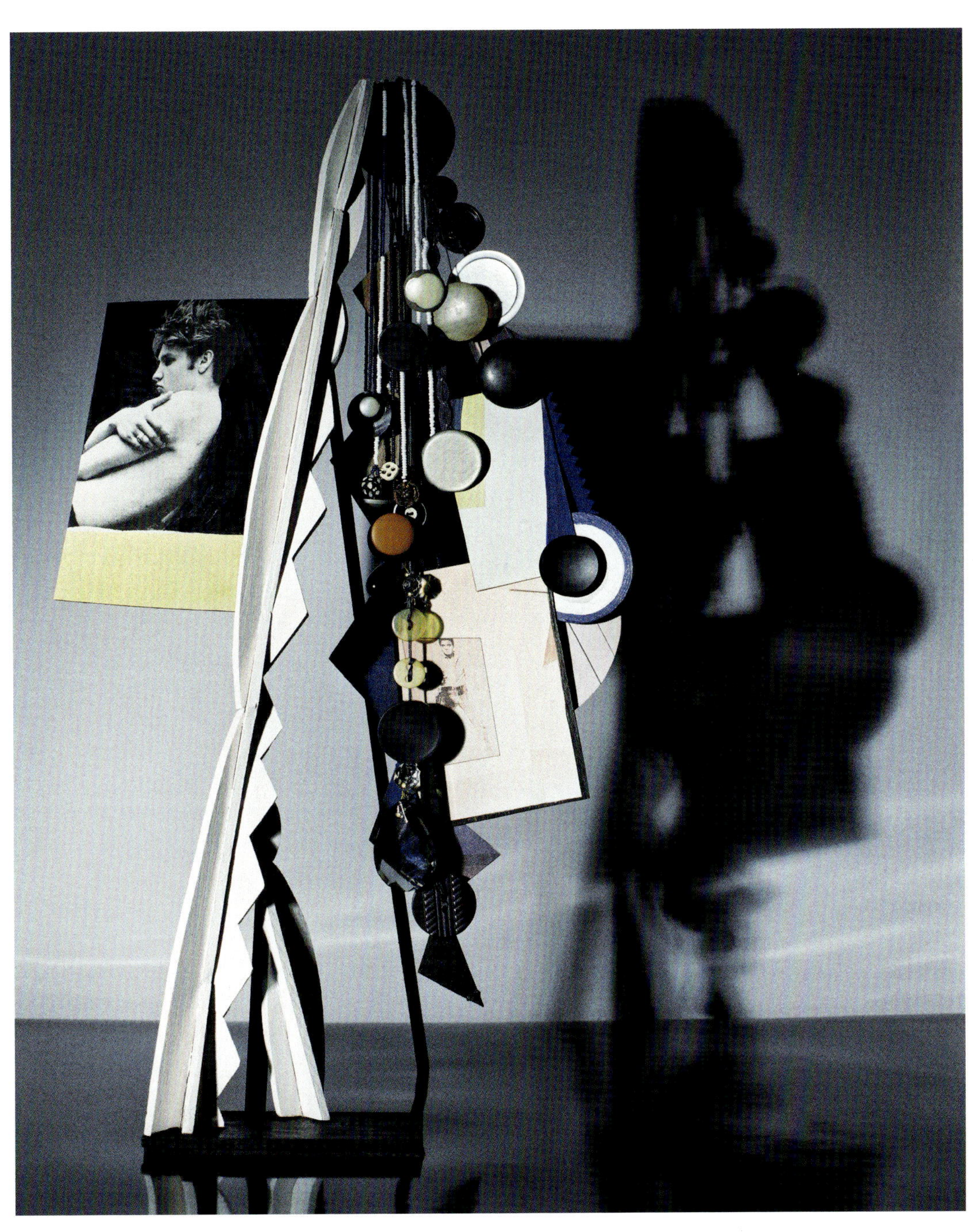

Ziggurat, 2006

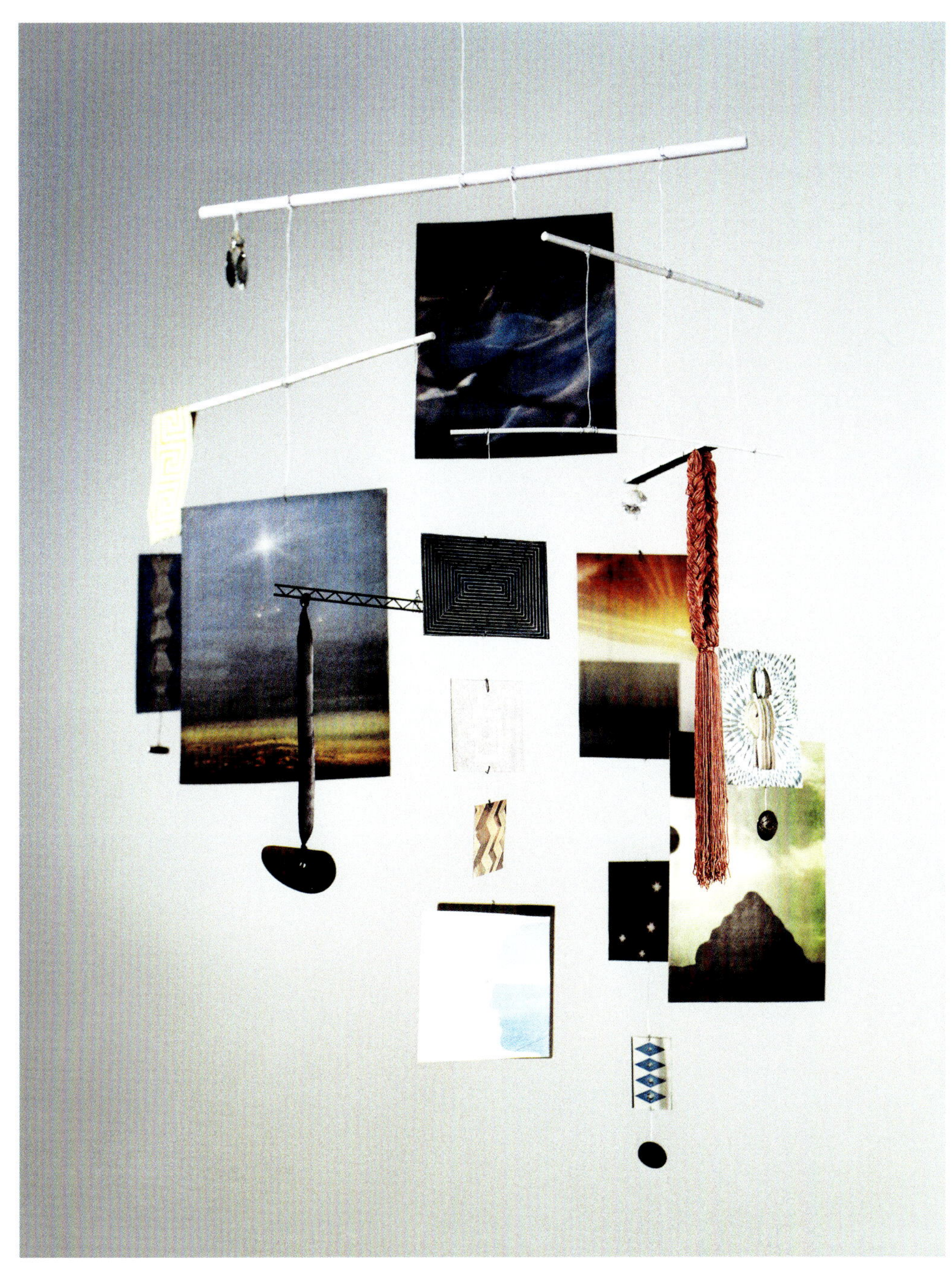

Decorations in a Notebook, 2006

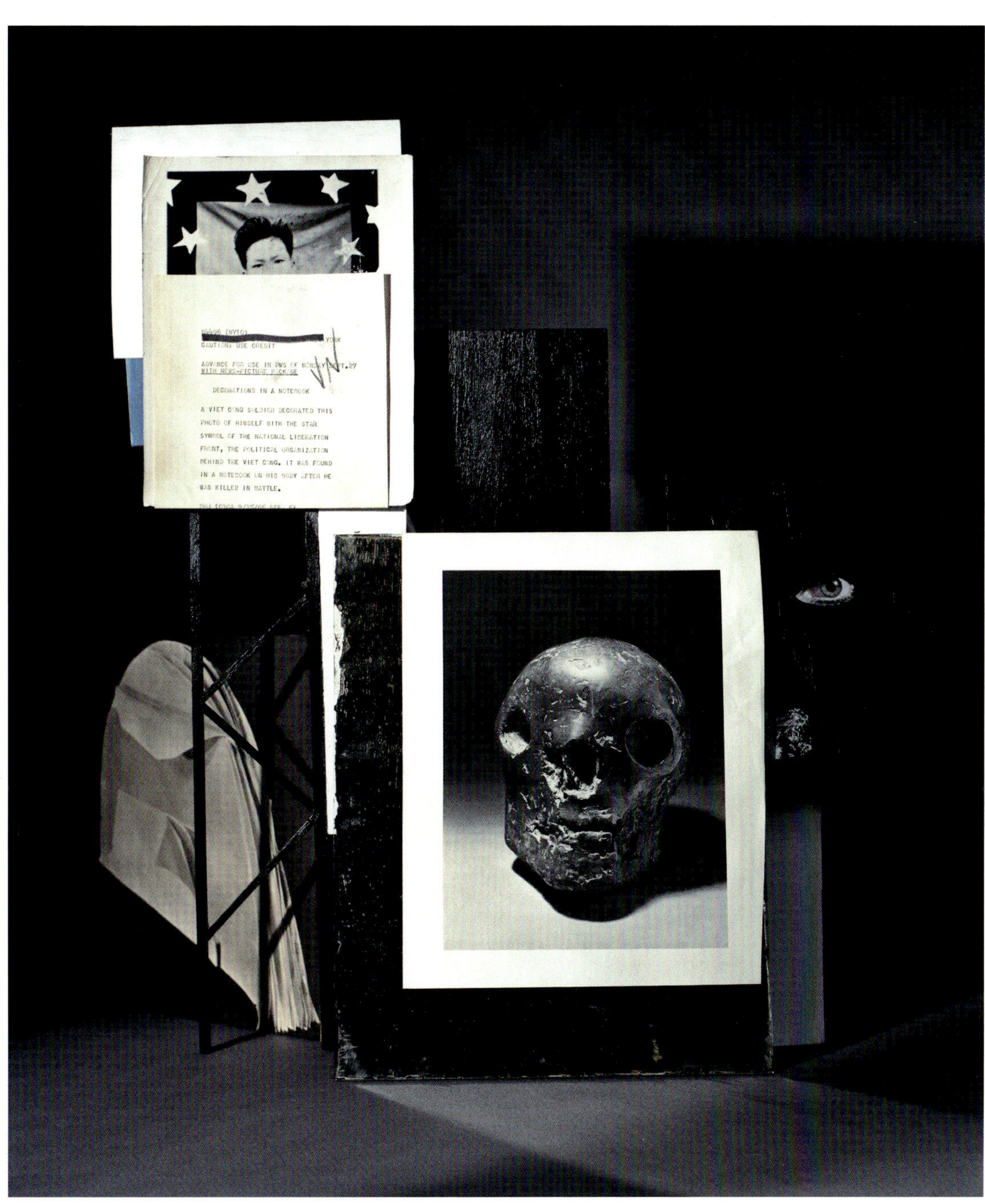
(NY10)
YORK
CAUTION: USE CREDIT
ADVANCE FOR USE IN PMS OF MONDAY SEPT.27
WITH NEWS-PICTURE PACKAGE
DECORATIONS IN A NOTEBOOK
A VIET CONG SOLDIER DECORATED THIS
PHOTO OF HIMSELF WITH THE STAR
SYMBOL OF THE NATIONAL LIBERATION
FRONT, THE POLITICAL ORGANIZATION
BEHIND THE VIET CONG. IT WAS FOUND
IN A NOTEBOOK ON HIS BODY AFTER HE
WAS KILLED IN BATTLE.

A Reoccurring Pattern, 2006

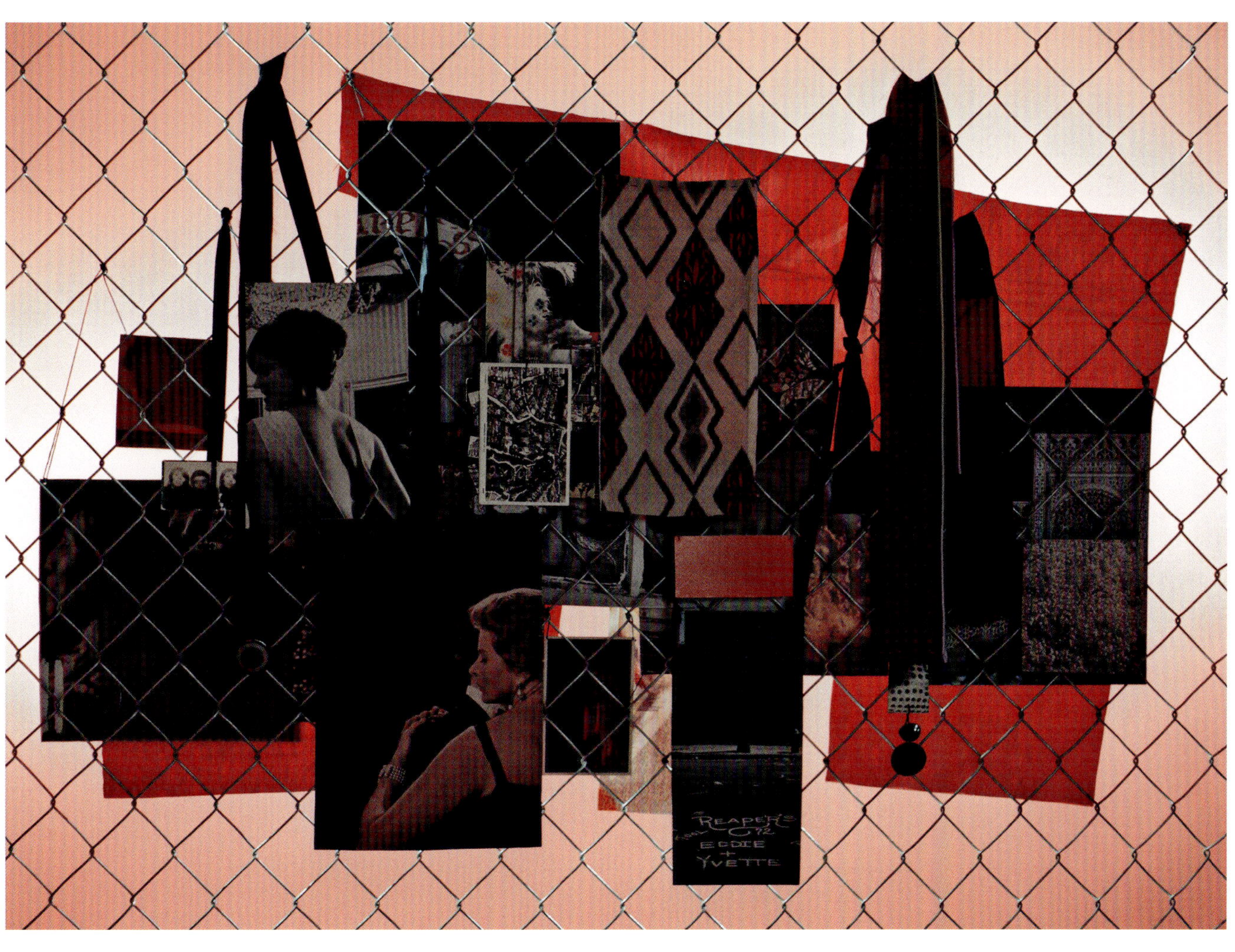
REAPER'S
'72
EDDIE
+
YVETTE

Walpurgisnacht, 2007

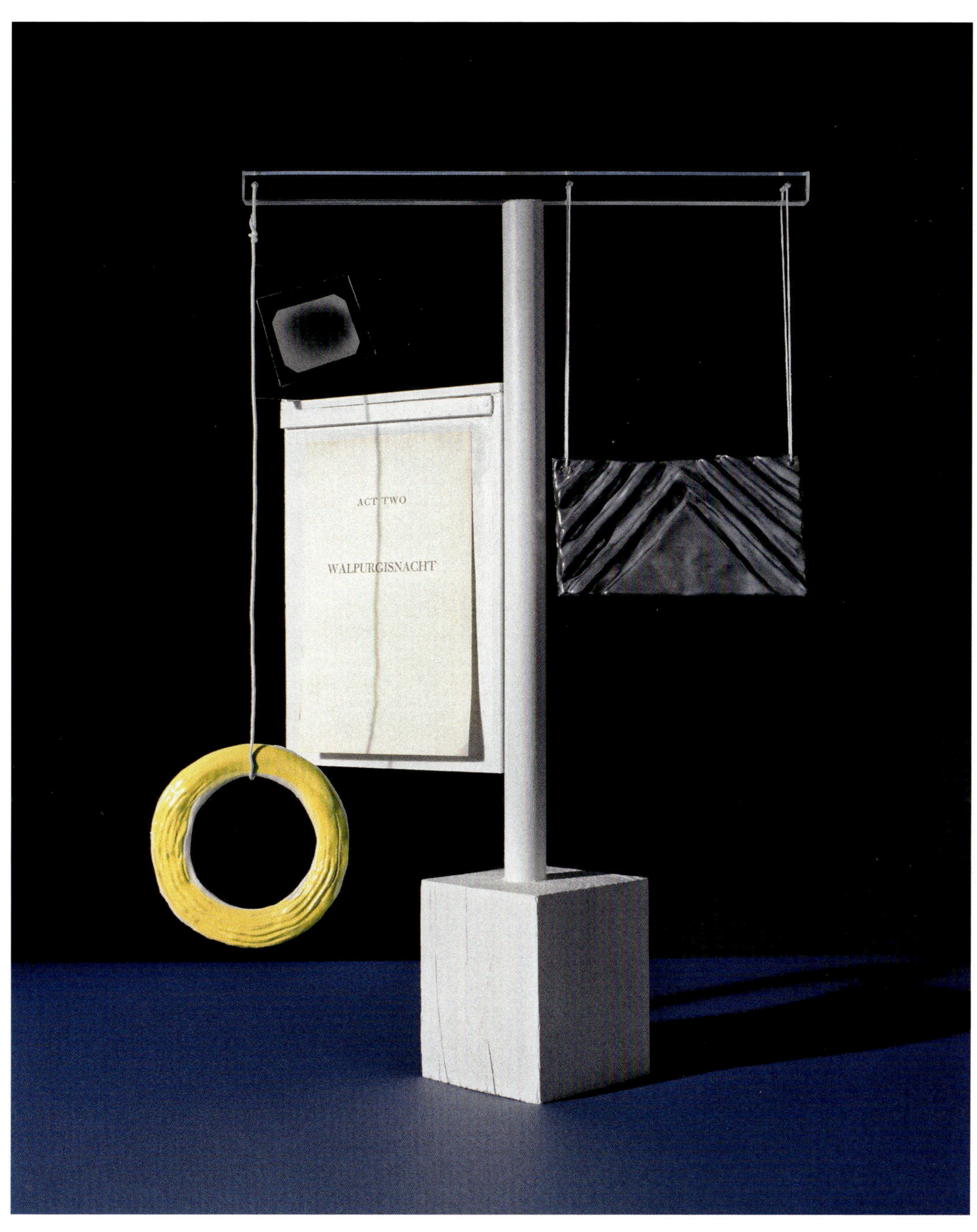
ACT TWO
WALPURGISNACHT

The Principle of Superimposition II, 2008

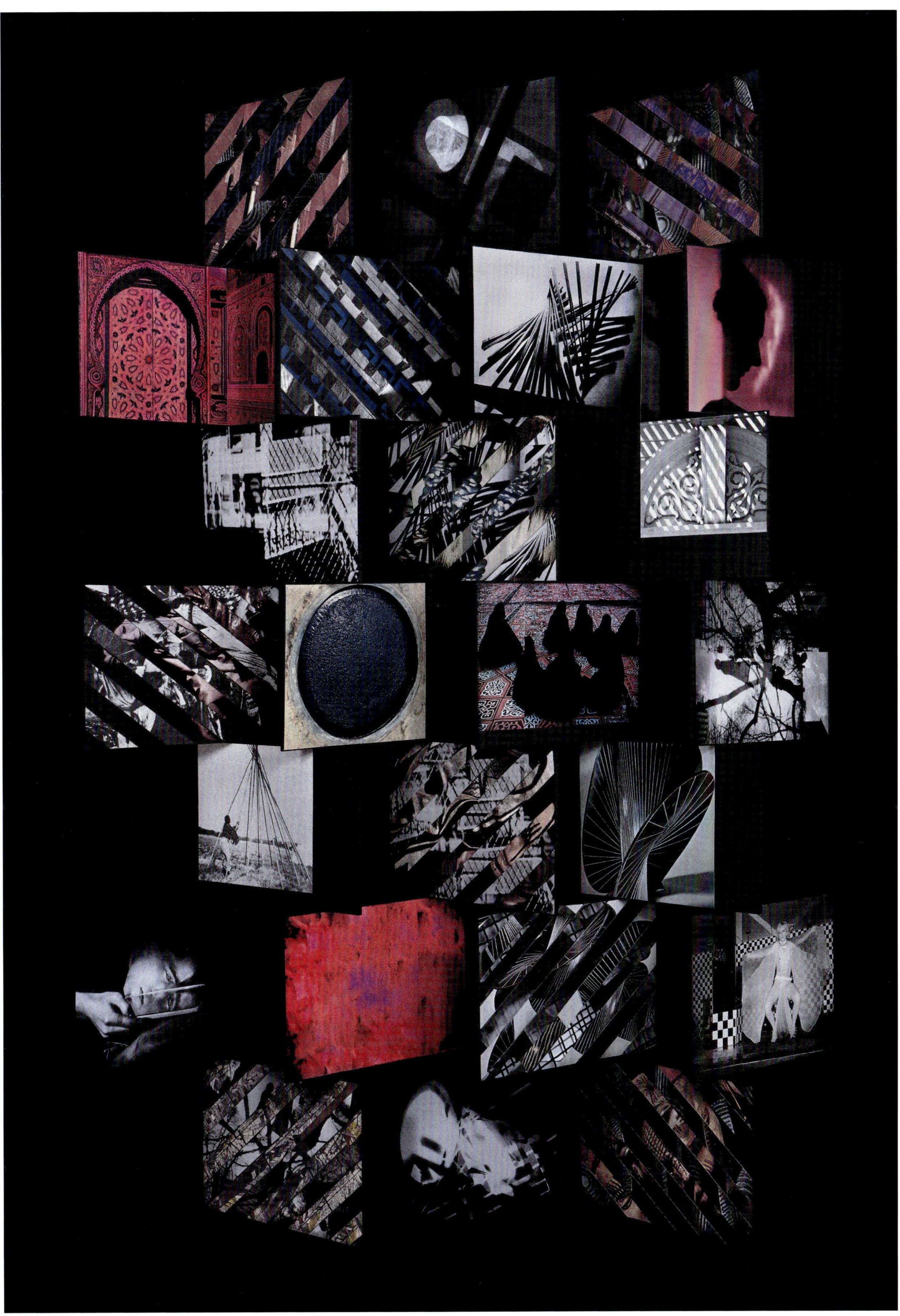

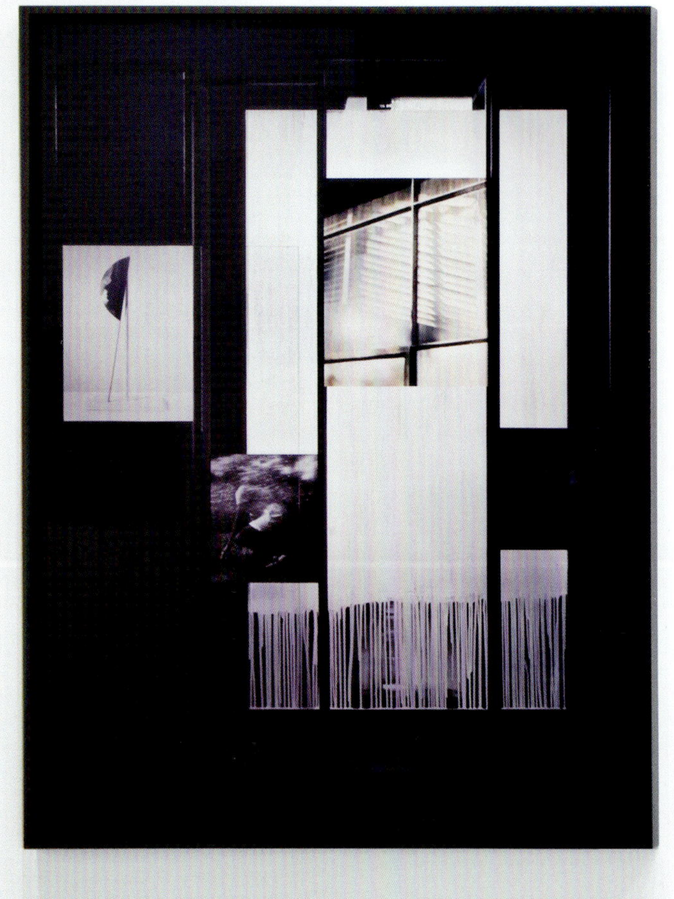
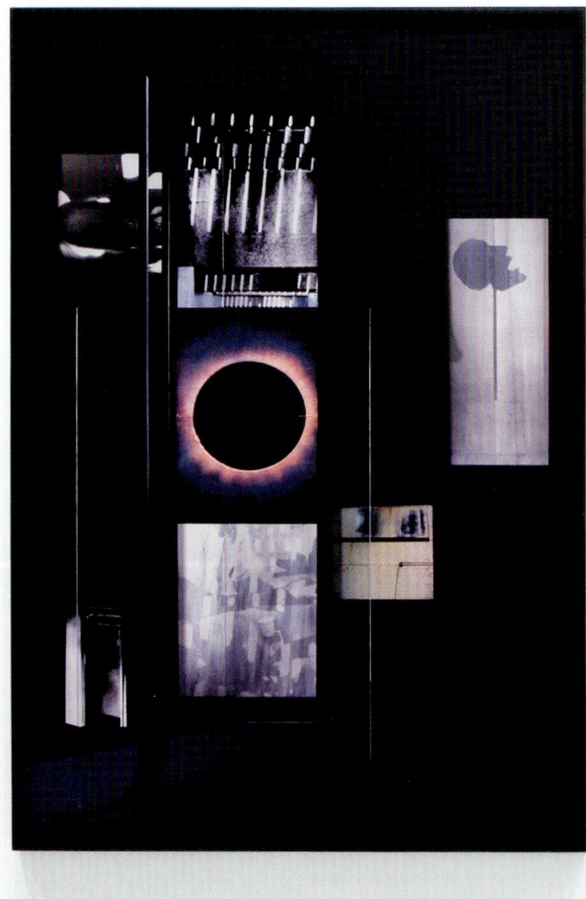

 A Composition for Detroit, 2009, installation view, *New Photography,* The Museum of Modern Art, New York, 2009

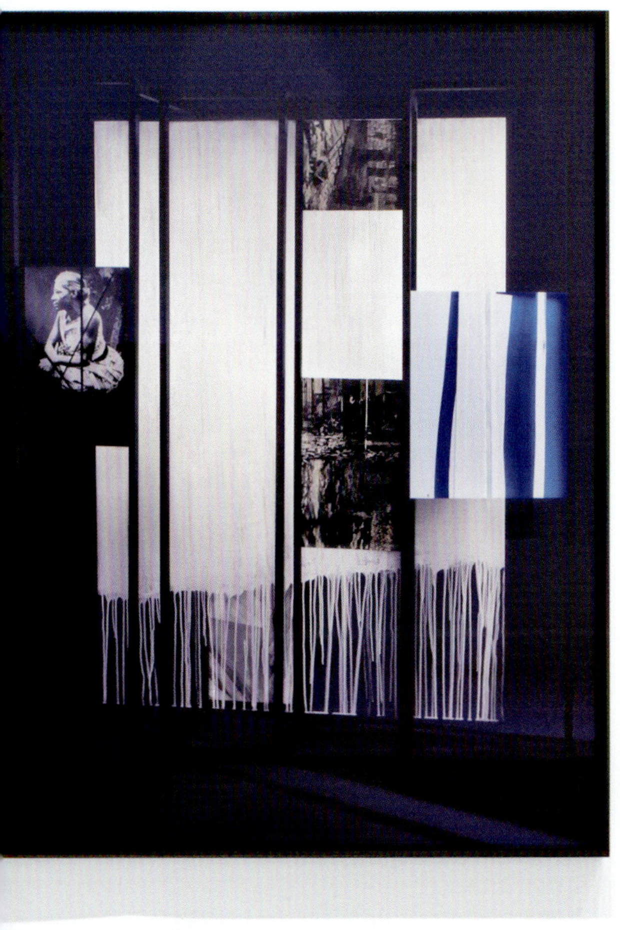

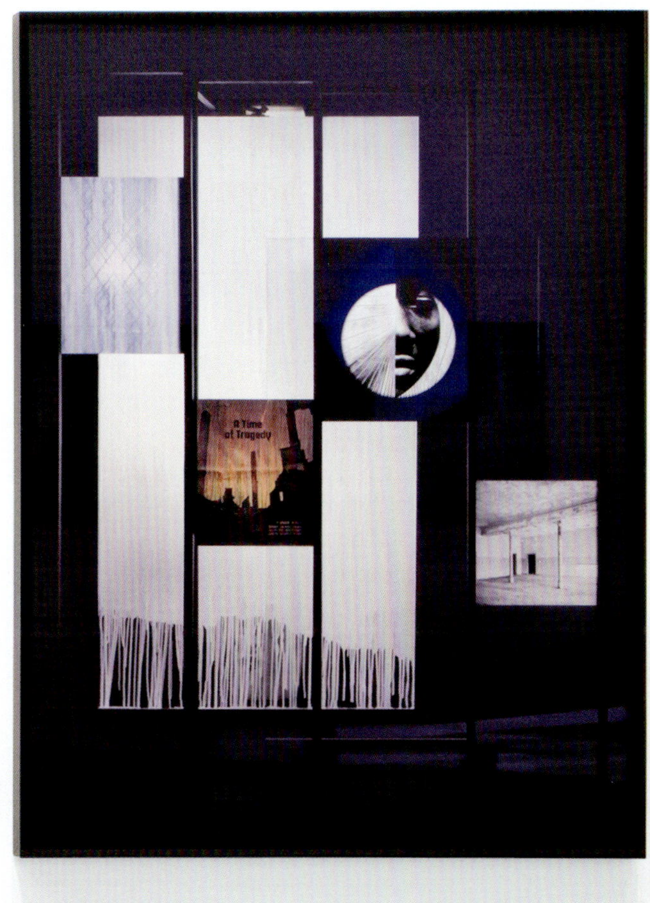
A Time
of Tragedy

Blue Eclipse, 2010

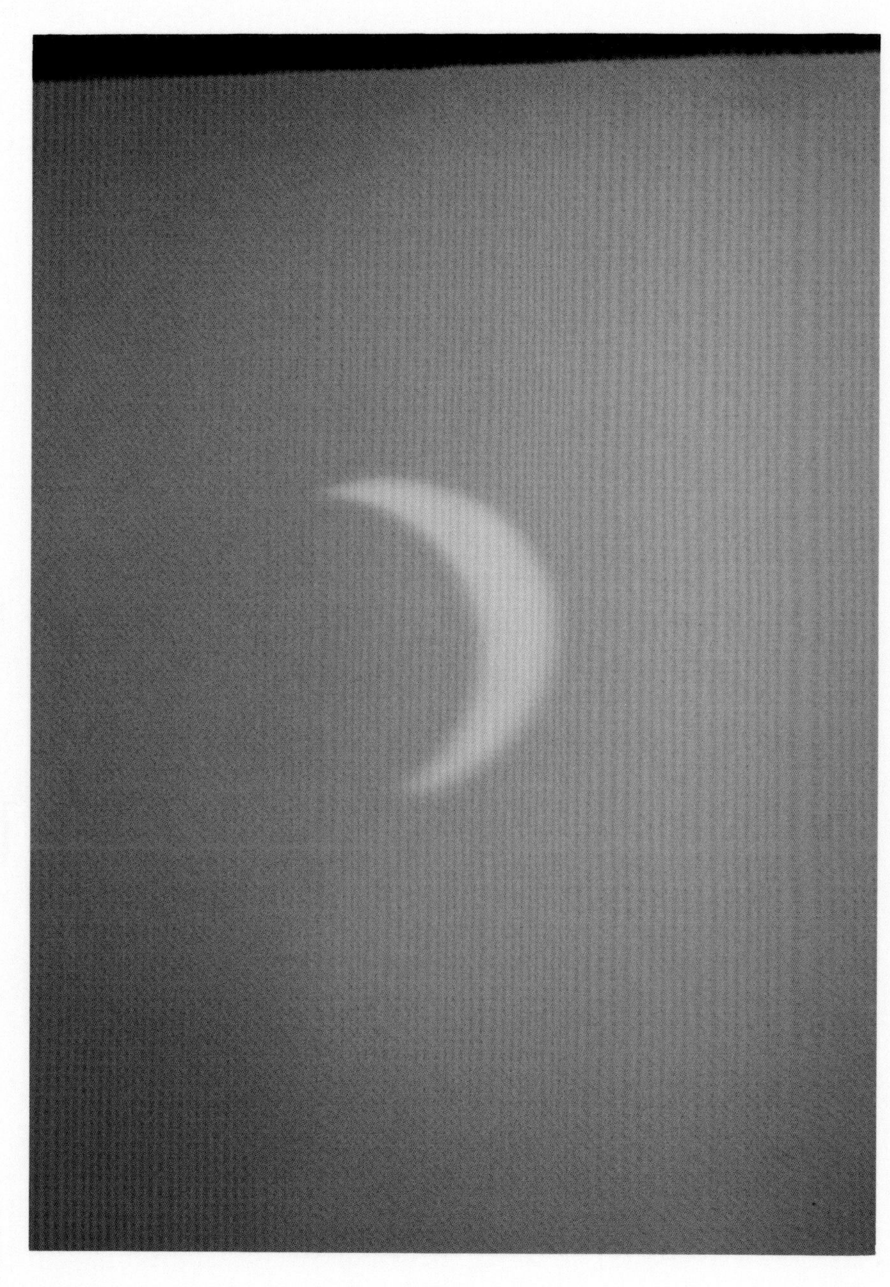

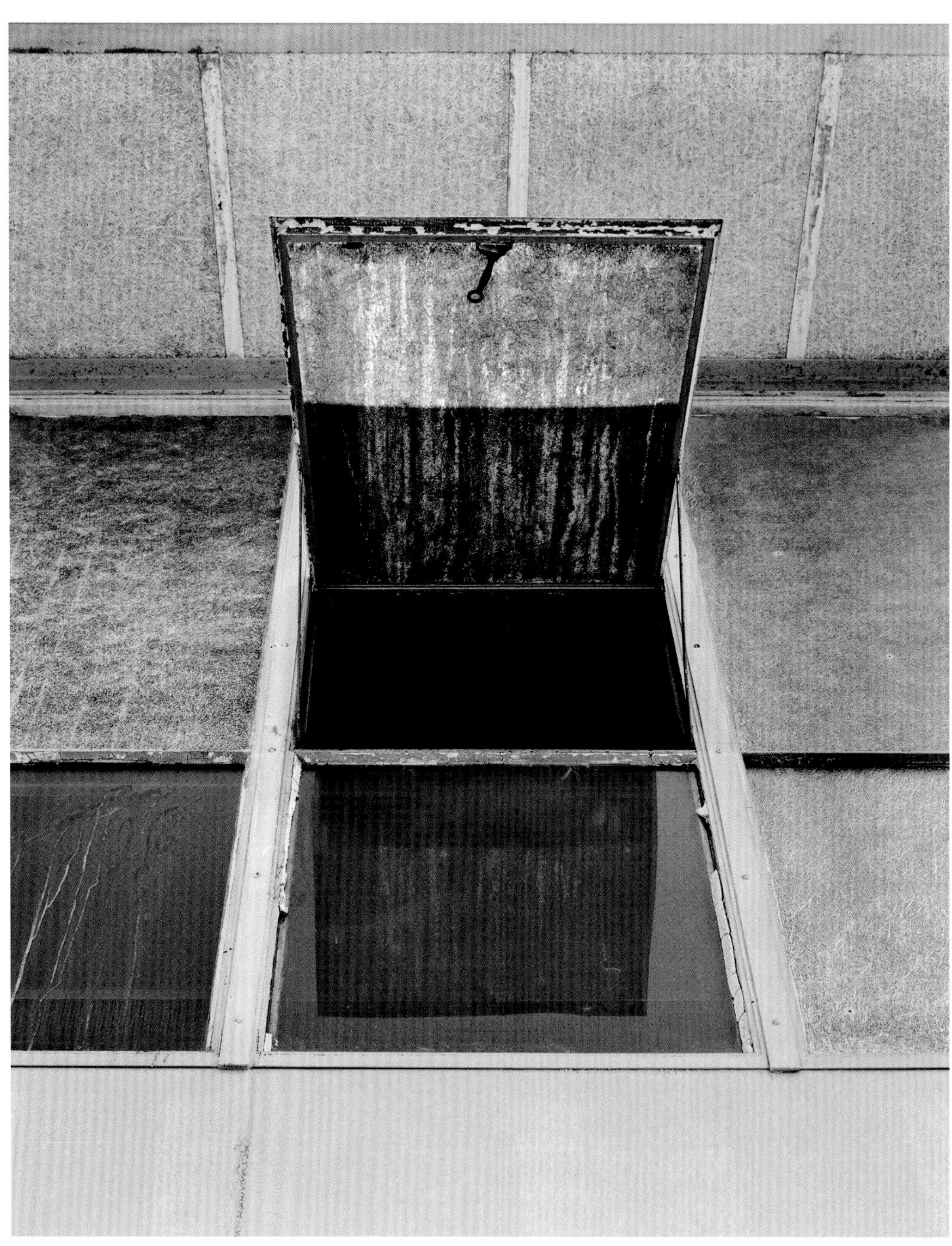

Treme School Window, 2010

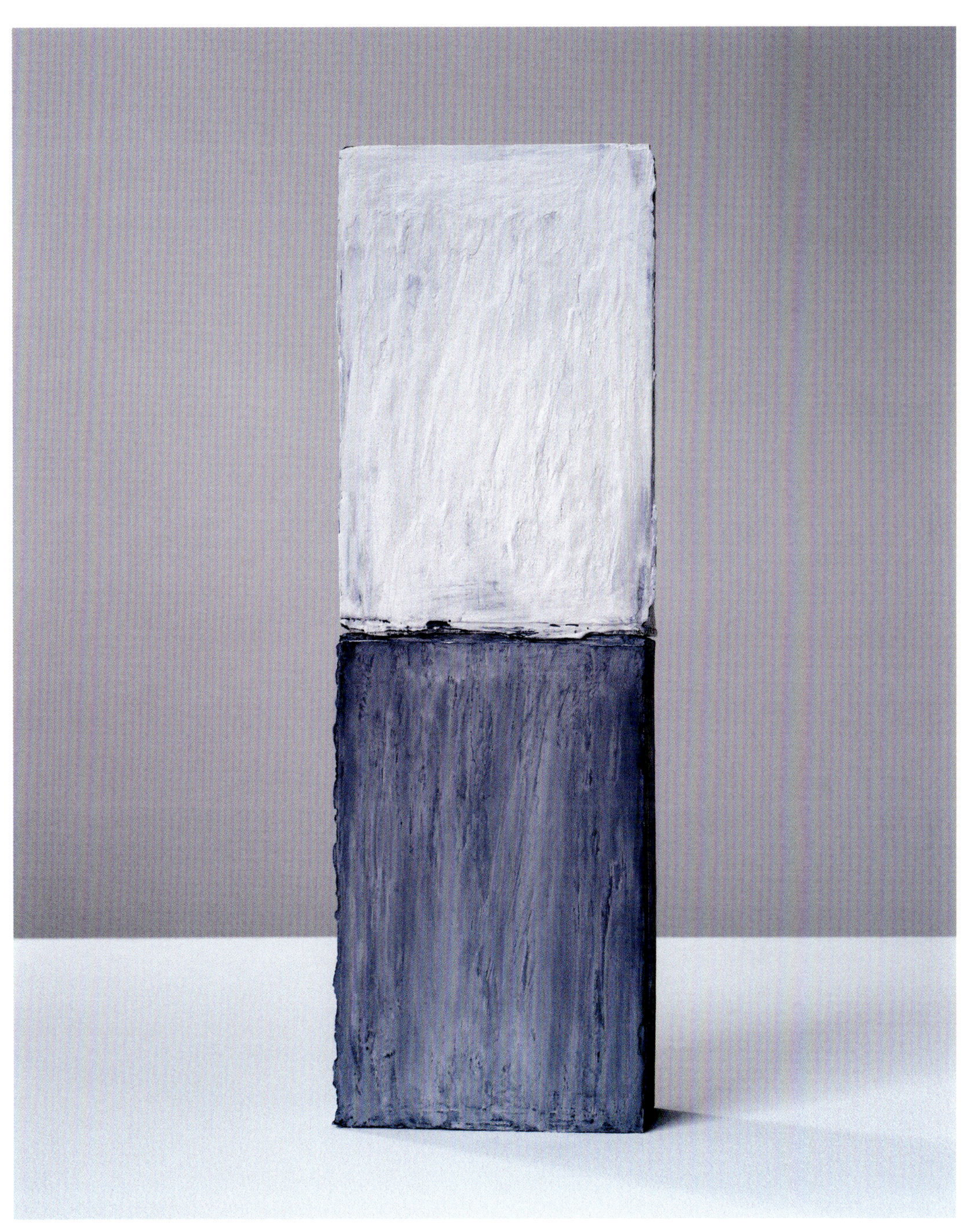

Treme, 2010

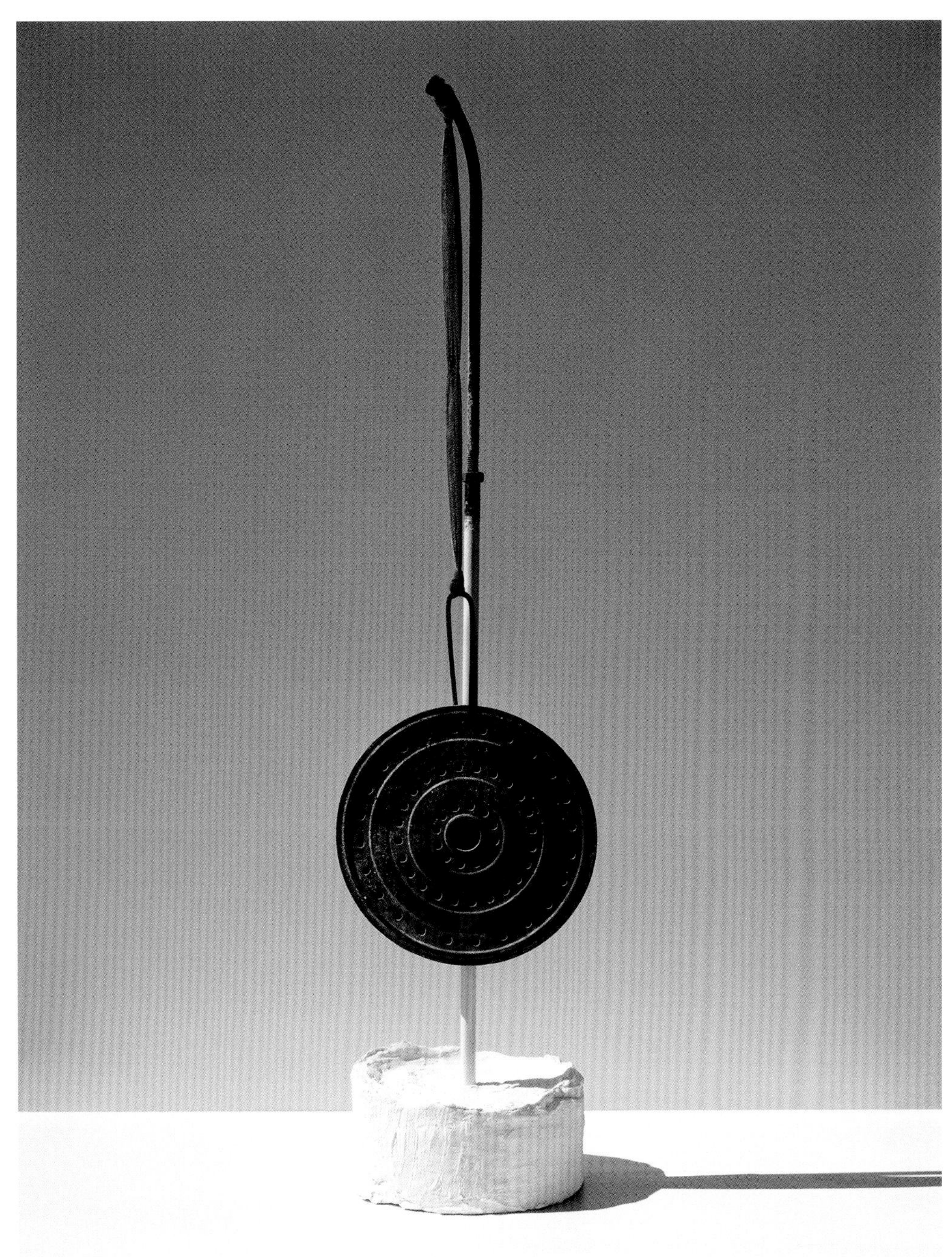

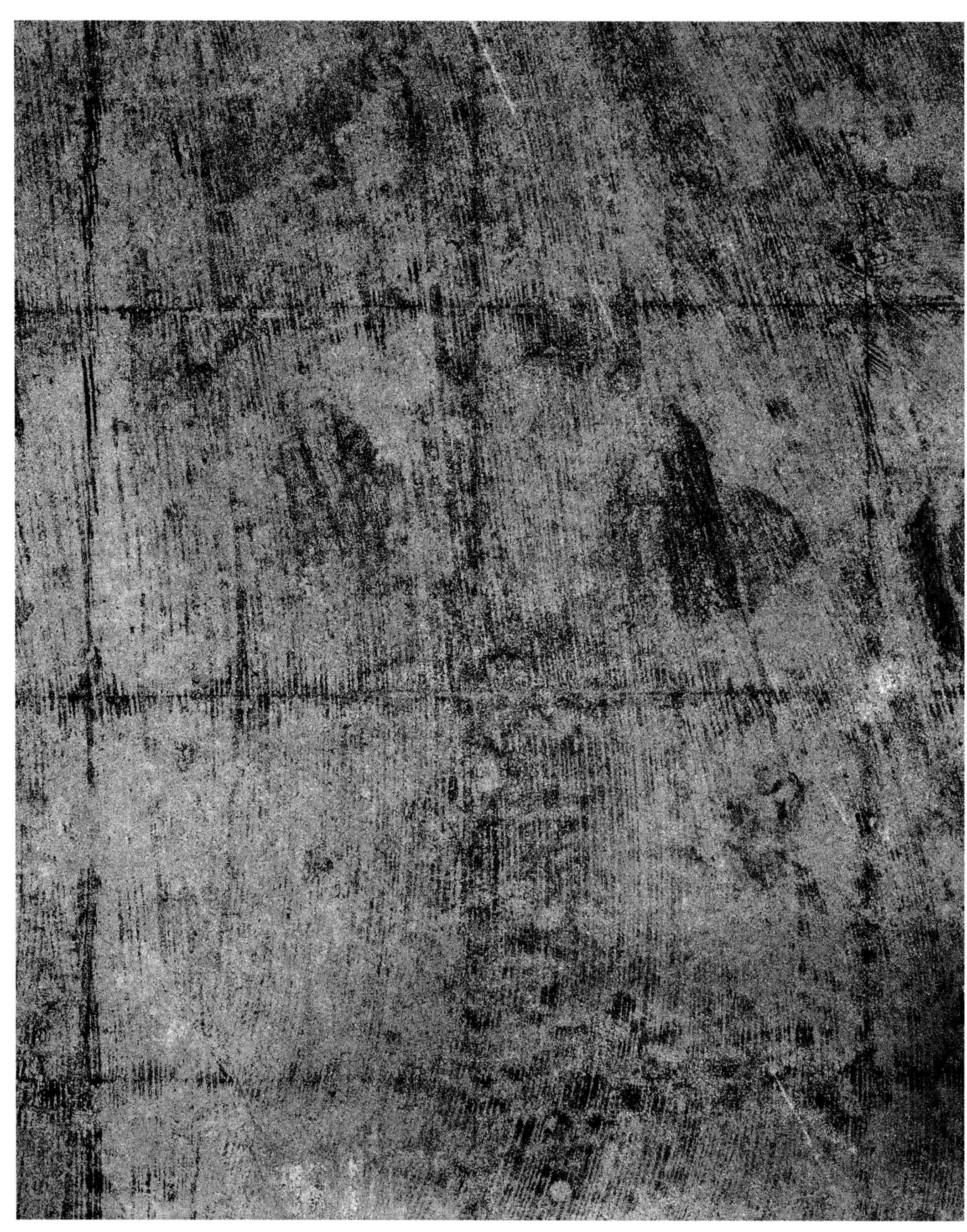

Foundation, Rocheblave Street, 2010

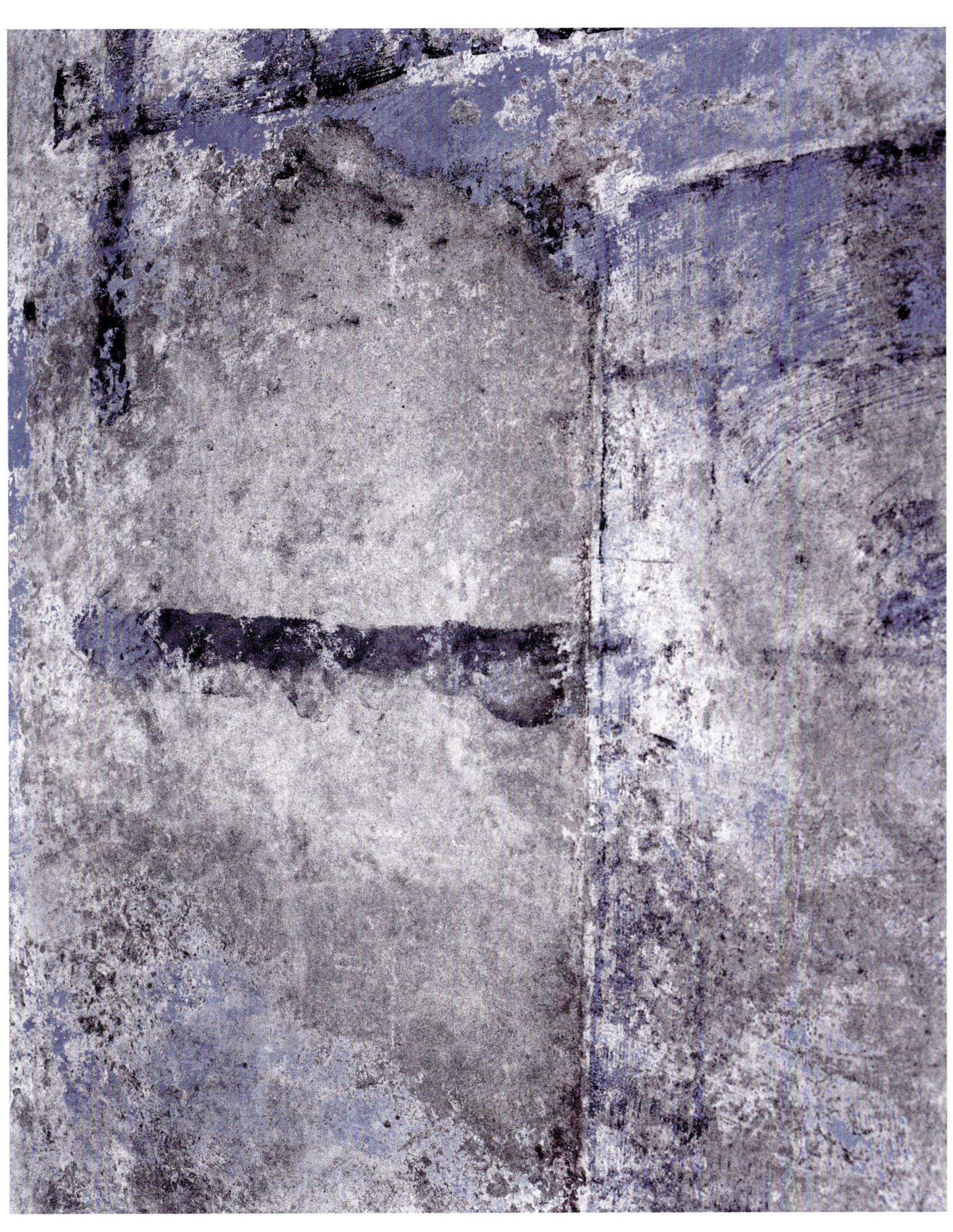

Foundation, Reynes Street, 2010

Temple, 2010

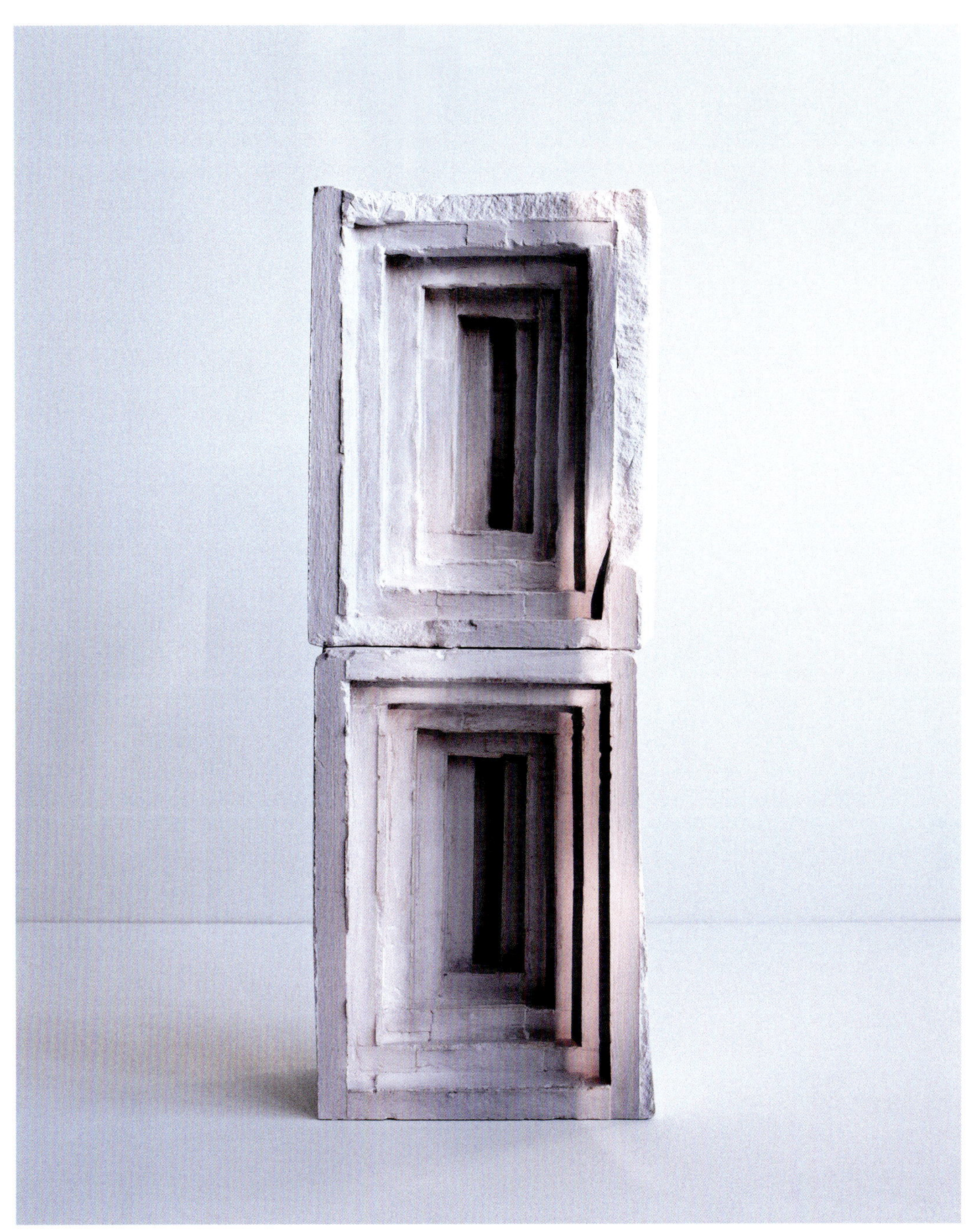

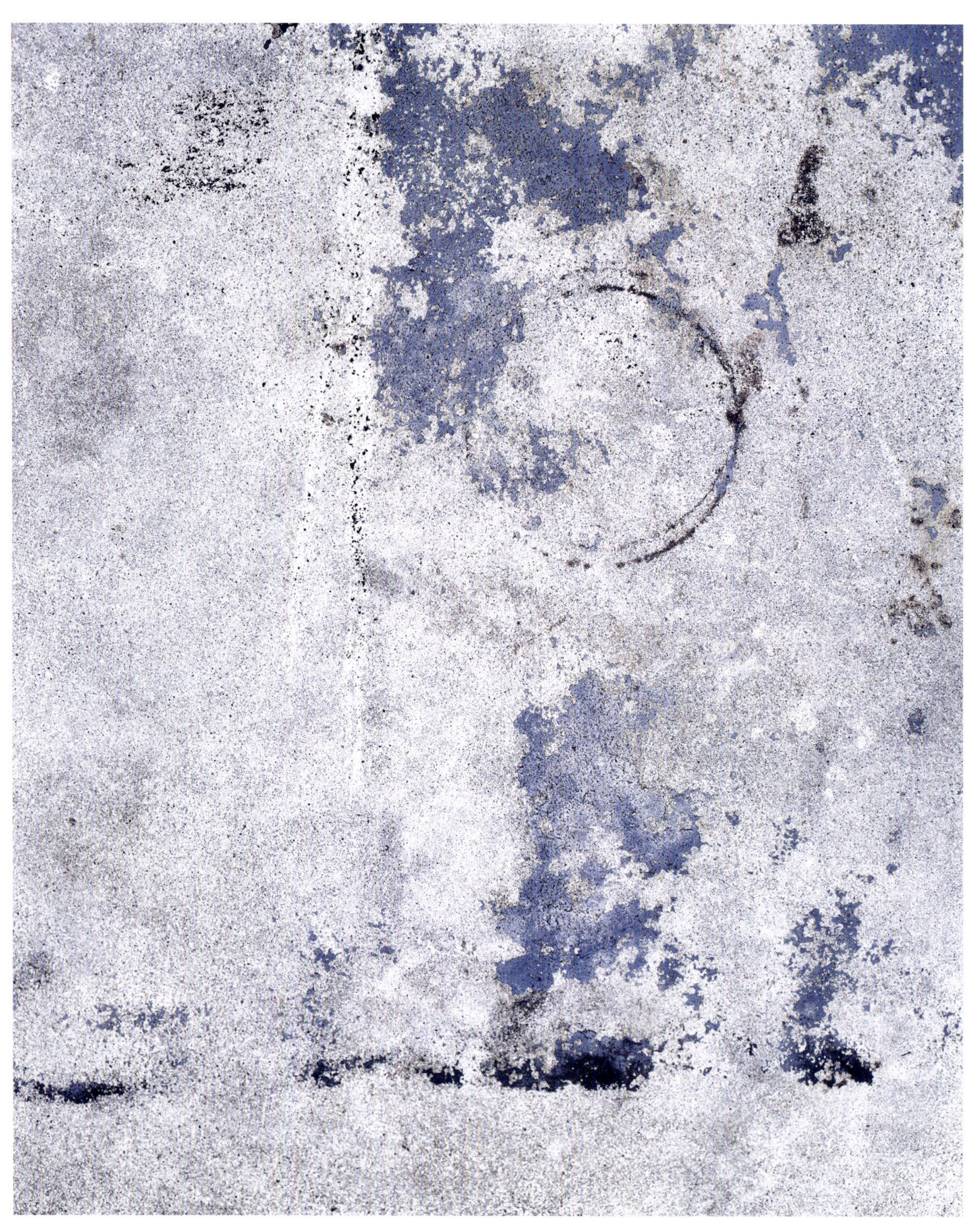

Foundation, Alabo Street, 2010

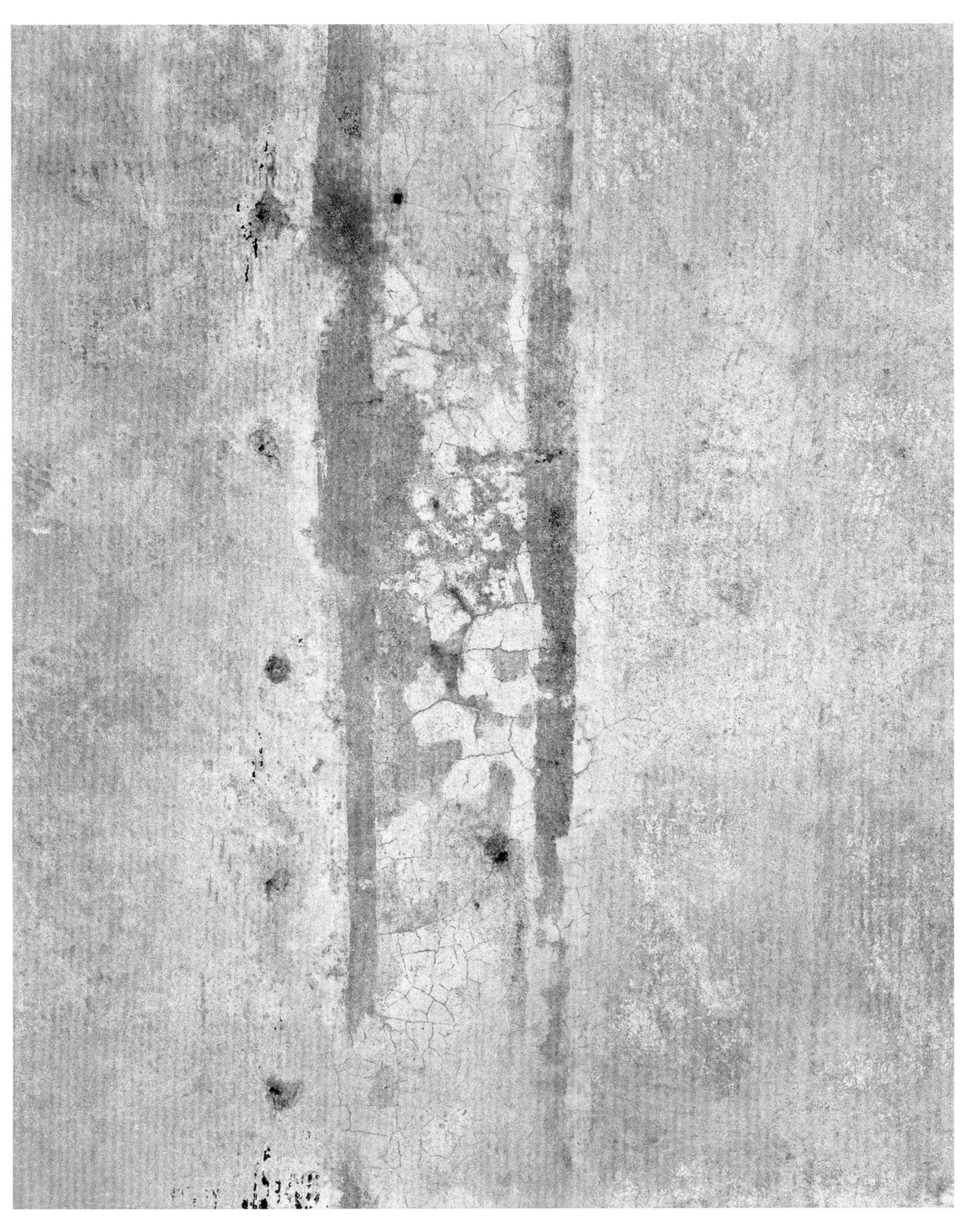

Foundation, Deslonde Street I, 2010

Blue Caryatid at Dusk, 2010

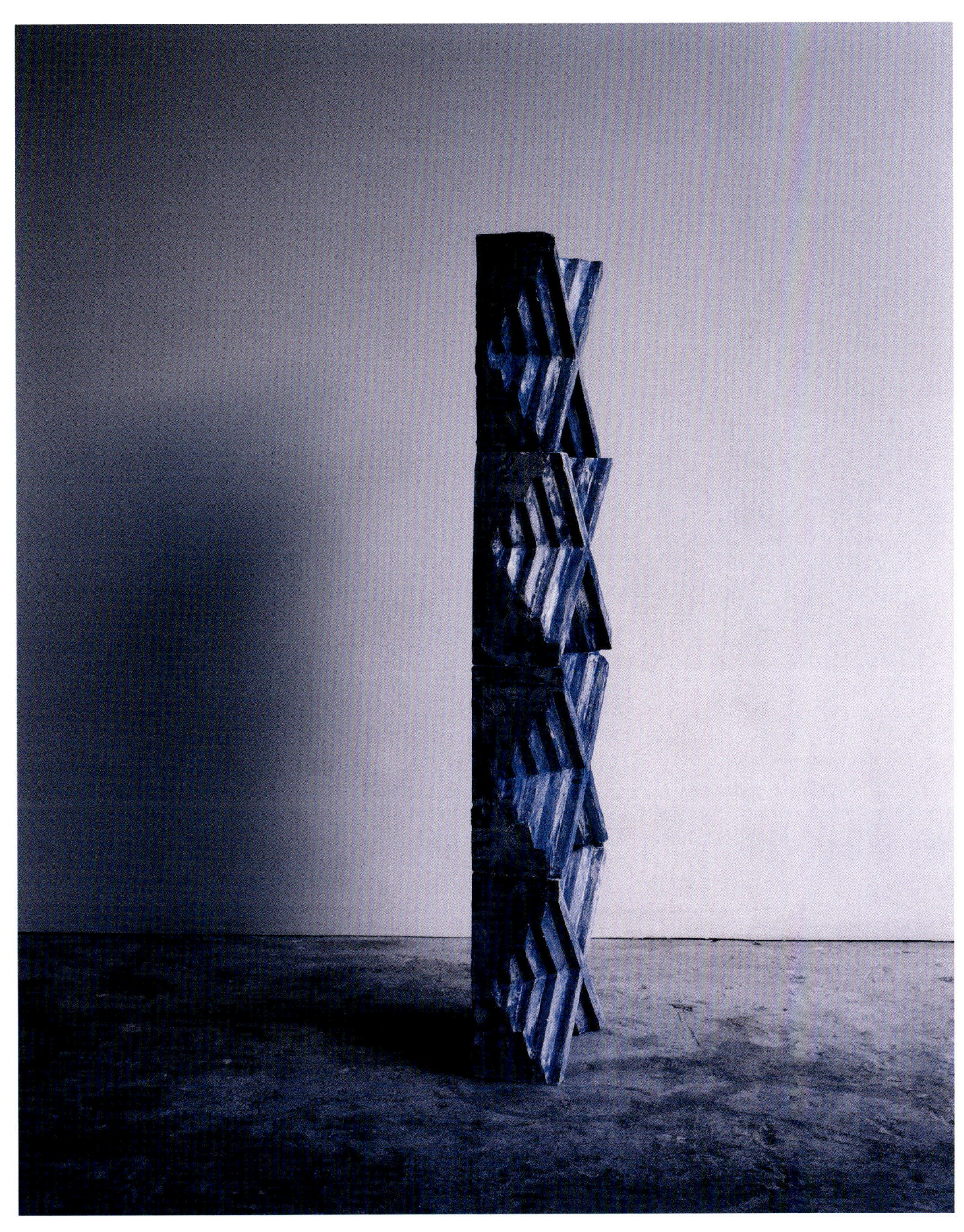

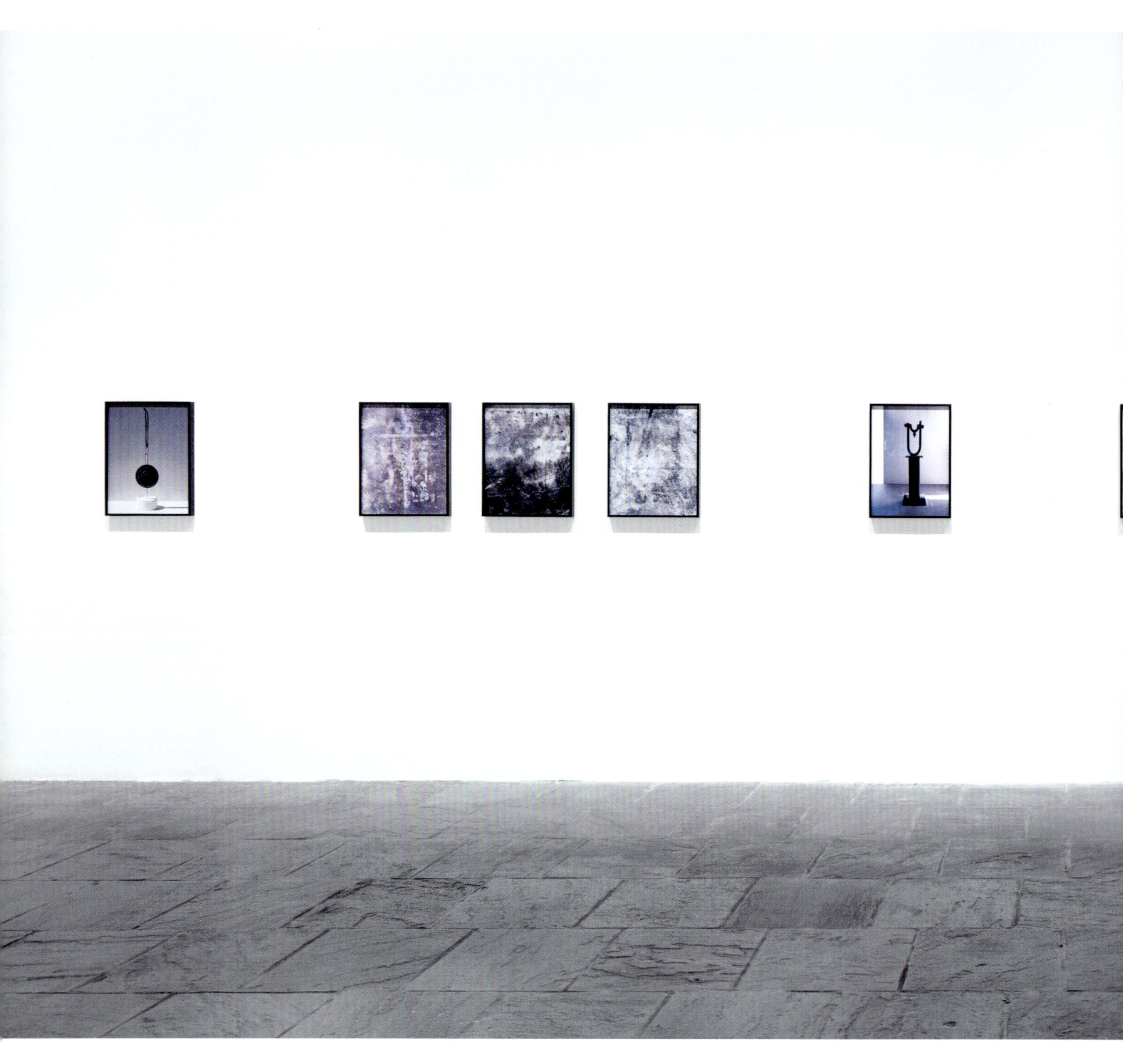

 The Sleepers, 2010, installation view, *To Think of Time*, Whitney Museum of American Art, New York, 2010

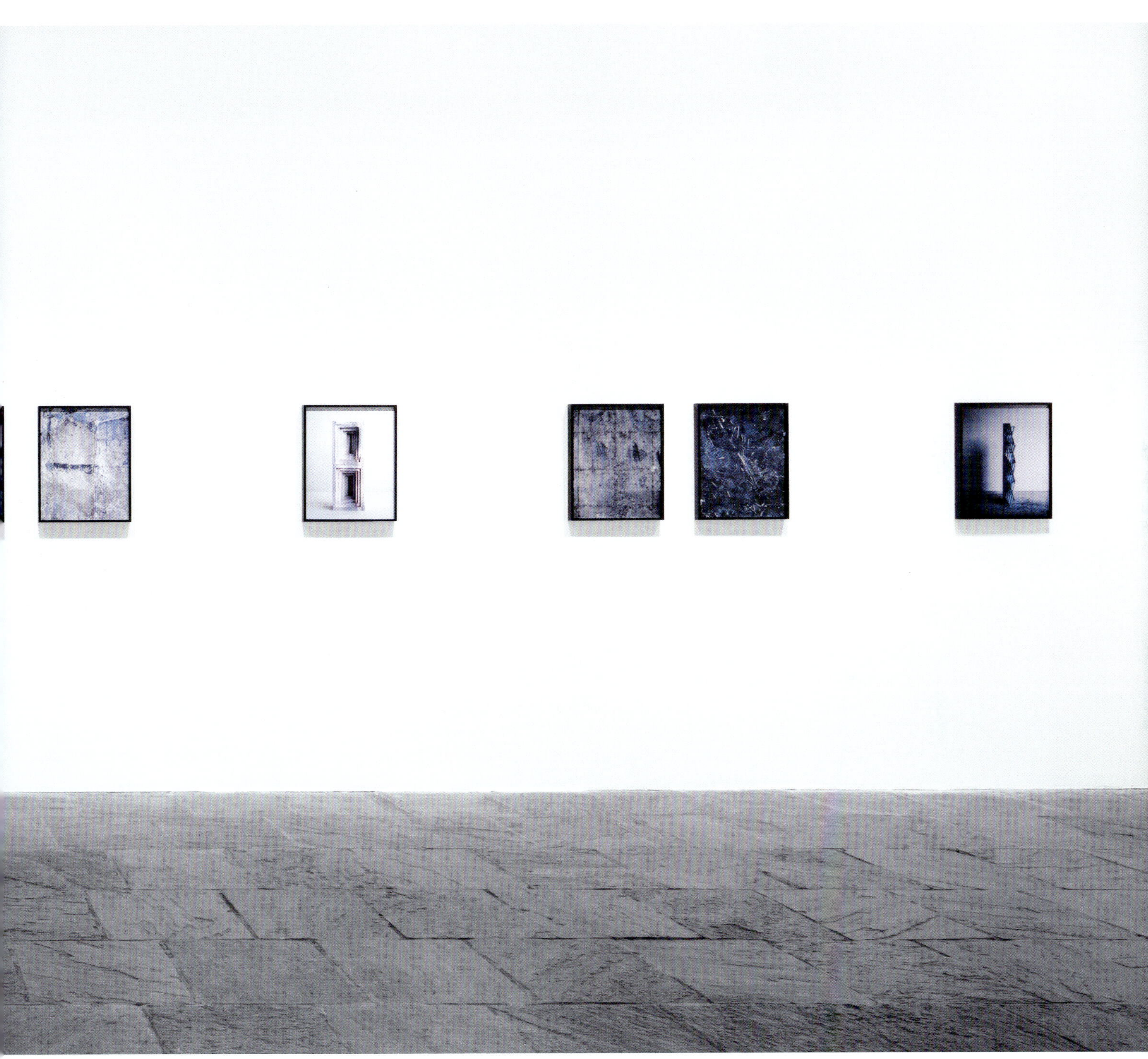

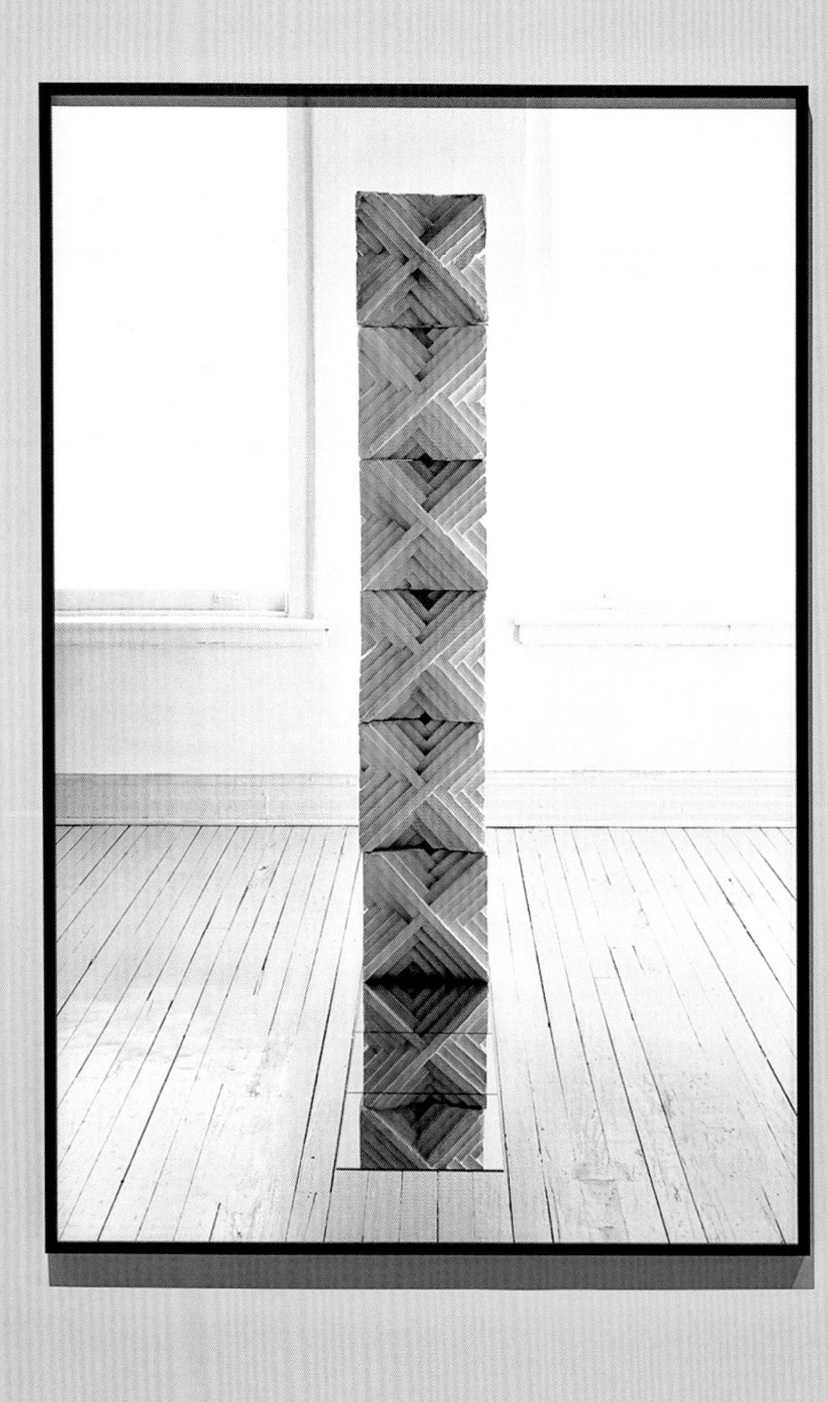

Sculpture, Photography, Surface

Ina Blom

On the media battleground of modern art, the legendary struggle is between painting and photography, the upheavals and transformations taking place as the images of preindustrial craft traditions were either displaced or remediated by images produced by a mechanical apparatus. Less fabled but no less significant is the battle between photography and sculpture. In a world increasingly given over to the ubiquitous yet fleeting imagery of photography, film, and television, the medium of sculpture—staid, immobile, three-dimensional *things*—would appear to have been left behind. Charles Baudelaire compared sculpture with the complex illusions of painting and found it "boring," and in a media age fixated on the constant capture of attention through dynamized sensation, it would appear even more so.[1] If twentieth-century sculpture did its best to stage itself as increasingly dynamic, serial, dispersed, placeless, and environmental, it could never compete with media speeds and media presences.

On the other hand, photography from early on seemed obsessed with sculpture while also serving the interest of sculpture on many levels. It documented three-dimensional artworks *in situ,* making them globally available for the new discipline of art history. Reducing them to a two-dimensional surface and a distinct point of view, photography also produced a play of light and shadow that fed the desire for illusion and interpretation. More broadly, this alliance between sculpture and photography is illustrative of the complex relation between images and objects in a capitalist economy. If Baudelaire also accused sculpture of being mere luxury objects, photography's ability to imbue isolated objects with depth and mystery was arguably *the* driving force in creating desires for brand-new shiny things among a burgeoning consumer class. Photography could only ever produce inferior reproductions of paintings, but it would add important new dimensions to sculptures and commercial goods alike. Photography was *for* the world of things. The unending celebration of the photographic practice of Irving Penn, to single out one example, seems to hinge almost entirely on his ability to turn anything and everything into a freestanding, sculpture-like commodity/object, attesting to the perseverance of this reality into the realm of late capitalism.

It is hard to avoid recalling this media history when confronted with the works of Sara VanDerBeek: her artistic trajectory seems to reproduce the

Caryatid, 2010, installation view, *Knight's Move,* SculptureCenter, New York, 2010

entire feedback loop between photographic images and sculpture objects. At the outset, she created sculptures for the sole purpose of subjecting them to photographic interpretation. As images, the sculptures were placed against neutral shallow backgrounds, framed and cropped in ways that supported their dimensions, lit so as to emphasize texture. Alternatively, they took center stage in actual rooms, engulfed in light and shadow. Generally the photographs would lean discretely toward the monochrome, underscoring the identity between object and image.

Yet, after this initial career as images, circulating in exhibitions, catalogues, and digital media, the same sculptures have taken on a new life as actual objects in installations. In this new incarnation, they have been framed by the walls of a white cube propped up on the outside by visible scaffolding, an ostensibly constructed space within a larger white cube exhibition space. More than anything, these spaces come across as photographic stage sets where sculptures are prepared for photographic reproduction as "exhibition pieces": they are, so to speak, physical reminders of the virtual museums of networked art appreciation, as exemplified by tendentious websites like Contemporary Art Daily that cater to visual skimming rather than reading. In these photographic (or photogenic) spaces, sculptures also

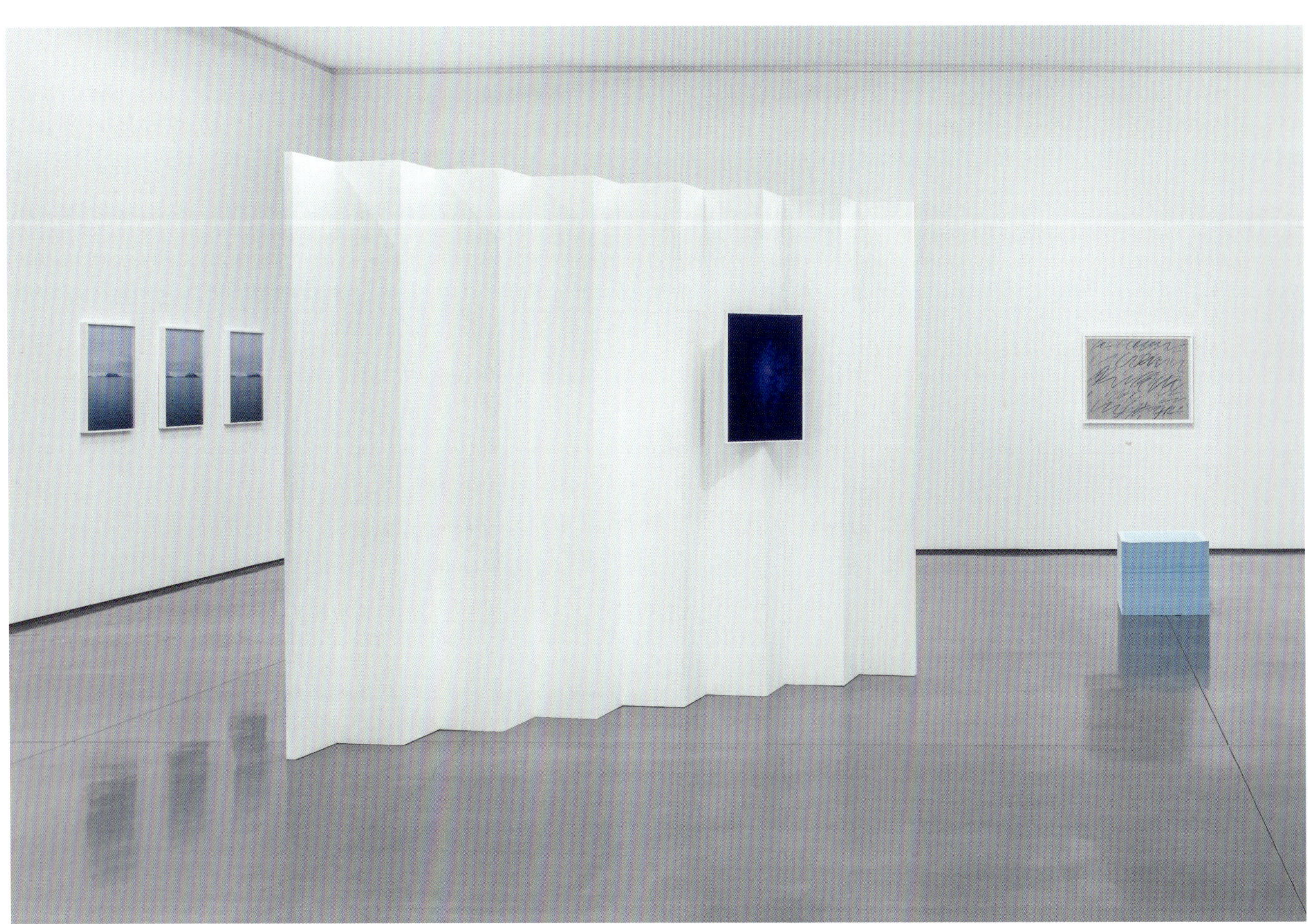

Turned Stairs/Stars, 2014, installation view, *The Blue of Distance*, Aspen Art Museum, Aspen, 2015

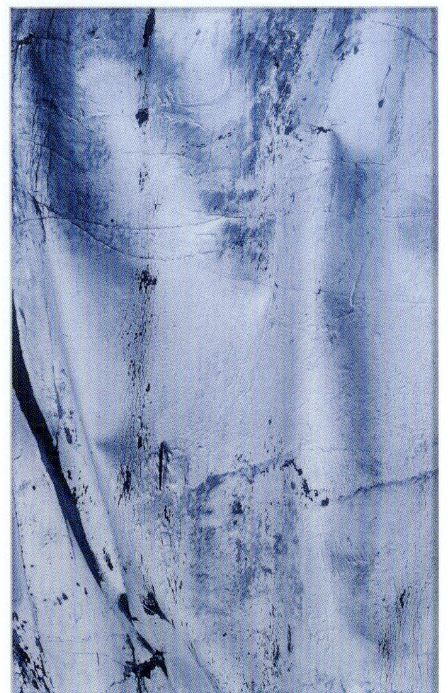

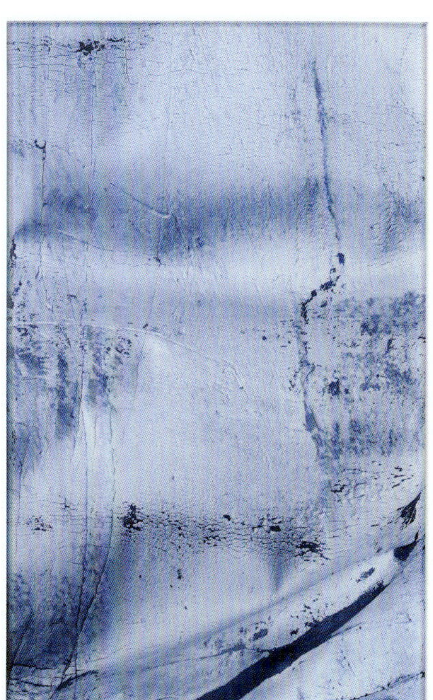

Alhambra I, 2014

compete for attention with framed photographs on the wall, object against object, so to speak. But then again, photographs also tend to be treated as objects *in* VanDerBeek's photographic works. Here they are recorded as elements in spatial arrangements that recall the way in which they are used in everyday life: for instance the way they are hung on fences or propped up on sidewalks and staircases in impromptu rituals of public mourning at sites of accident or catastrophe.

On first impression, her practice may recall that of Constantin Brancusi, who used photography to emphasize and extend the multiple reproductions of his sculptures, and further, as a way to explore the way they might function as purely optical effects, inscribed in plays of light and shadow or figure versus ground.[2] This is even more so since Sara VanDerBeek's sculptures often seem to intentionally reference the repetitive geometric forms of Brancusi's plinthless columns and column-like plinths. Still, to see the Brancusi-effect in her work is also to gauge the distance that separates her media feedback loop from these earlier encounters between sculpture and photography. This distance comes across above all in her emphasis on surfaces, underscored in close-up shots of anything from Greco-Roman architecture, ancient Native American ceramics, to the poured concrete surfaces of contemporary cities. This is significant in the sense that surfaces not only implicate objects, architectures, and images alike, but also are increasingly understood as a useful term through which to understand the dynamic existence of materials in the realm of digital technologies. In her recent book, Giuliana Bruno uses the concepts of surface and screen as a way of addressing an entire architecture of mediatic transformations. Due to the

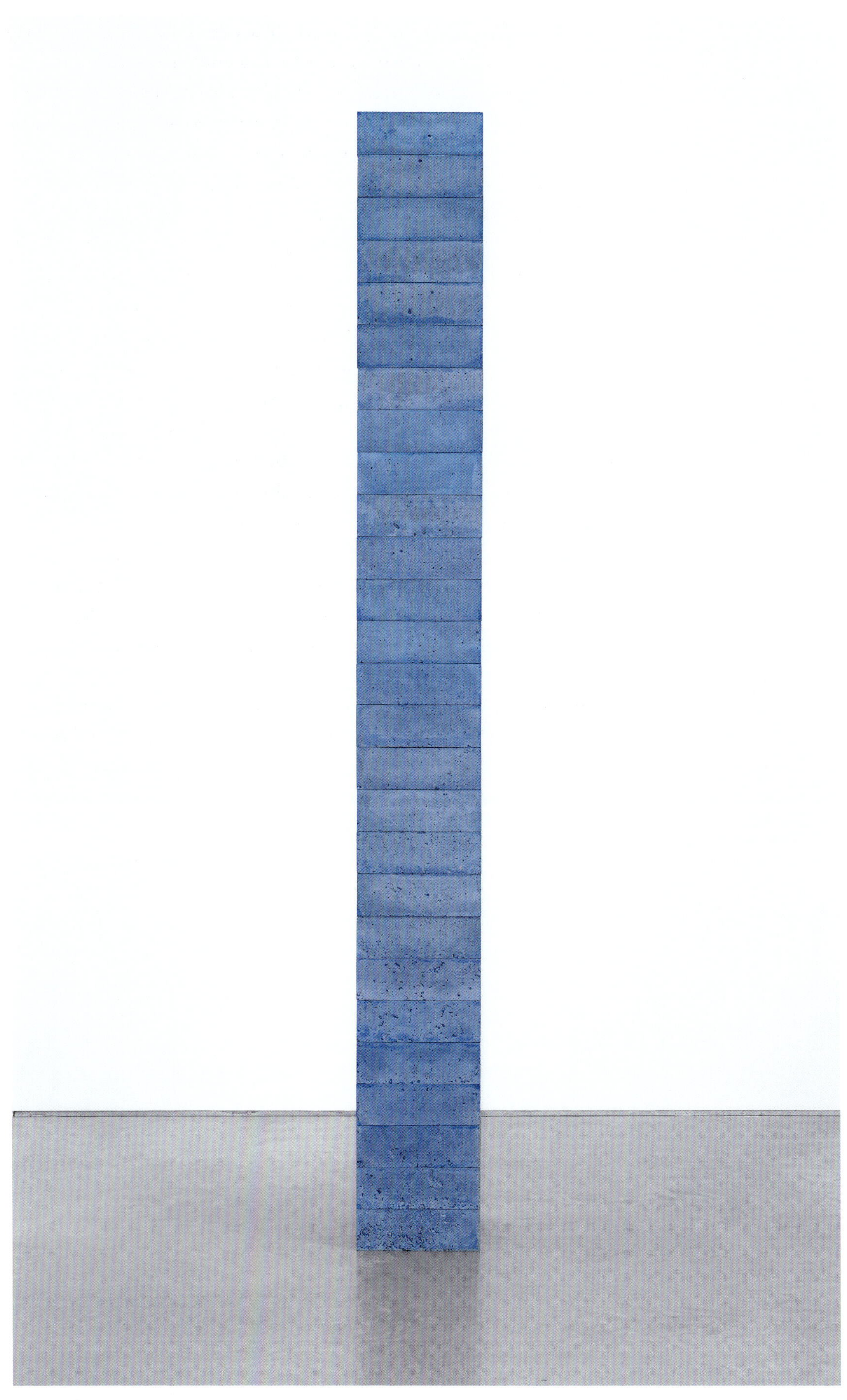

Setting Sky, 2014

variety of time-critical operations enacted through screen surfaces, they can no longer be contained by optical metaphors such as "windows" and "mirrors" but function more like membranes or connective tissues that turn architecture and art into pliant planes of moving images, or the enfolding of space.[3] As VanDerBeek's photographs constantly zoom in on the mottled surfaces of buildings and sculptures and out again to the various architectures of image/object display, we are implicated in precisely such pliant screen realities. Even classical sculpture—the Greek and Roman busts that were among the first love objects of photographers—is given a new life as screen effects. While nineteenth-century photographers like Henry Fox Talbot and Roger Fenton dryly captured such sculptural specimens for the purposes of art-historical registration, late-twentieth-century photographers like Patrick Faigenbaum staged them with dramatic lighting and close framing in order to invest them with the psychological qualities of real persons.[4] In VanDerBeek's photographs, in contrast, they seem to float inside demonstratively artificial layers of monochrome color, products of a modulation of surfaces that cares less about historical origins and points of identification and more about new material contingencies and points of contact. Here is a body of work that articulates some of our keenest contemporary intuitions: notably that screen realities are physical realities that extend far beyond the realm of the interface/surface in the limited sense of the term.

Ina Blom is Professor at the Department of Philosophy, Classics, History of Art and Ideas, University of Oslo, and author of *The Autobiography of Video: The Life and Times of a Memory Technology*.

1 Paul Paret, "Sculpture and Its Negative: The Photographs of Constantin Brancusi," in *Sculpture and Photography: Envisioning the Third Dimension*, ed. Geraldine A. Johnson (Cambridge, 1998), p. 104.
2 Ibid.
3 Giuliana Bruno, *Surfaces: Matters of Aesthetics, Materiality and Media* (Chicago, 2014).
4 Geraldine A. Johnson, "Introduction," in Johnson 1998, pp. 3–6.

Installation views, *Hammer Projects*, Hammer Museum, Los Angeles, 2011

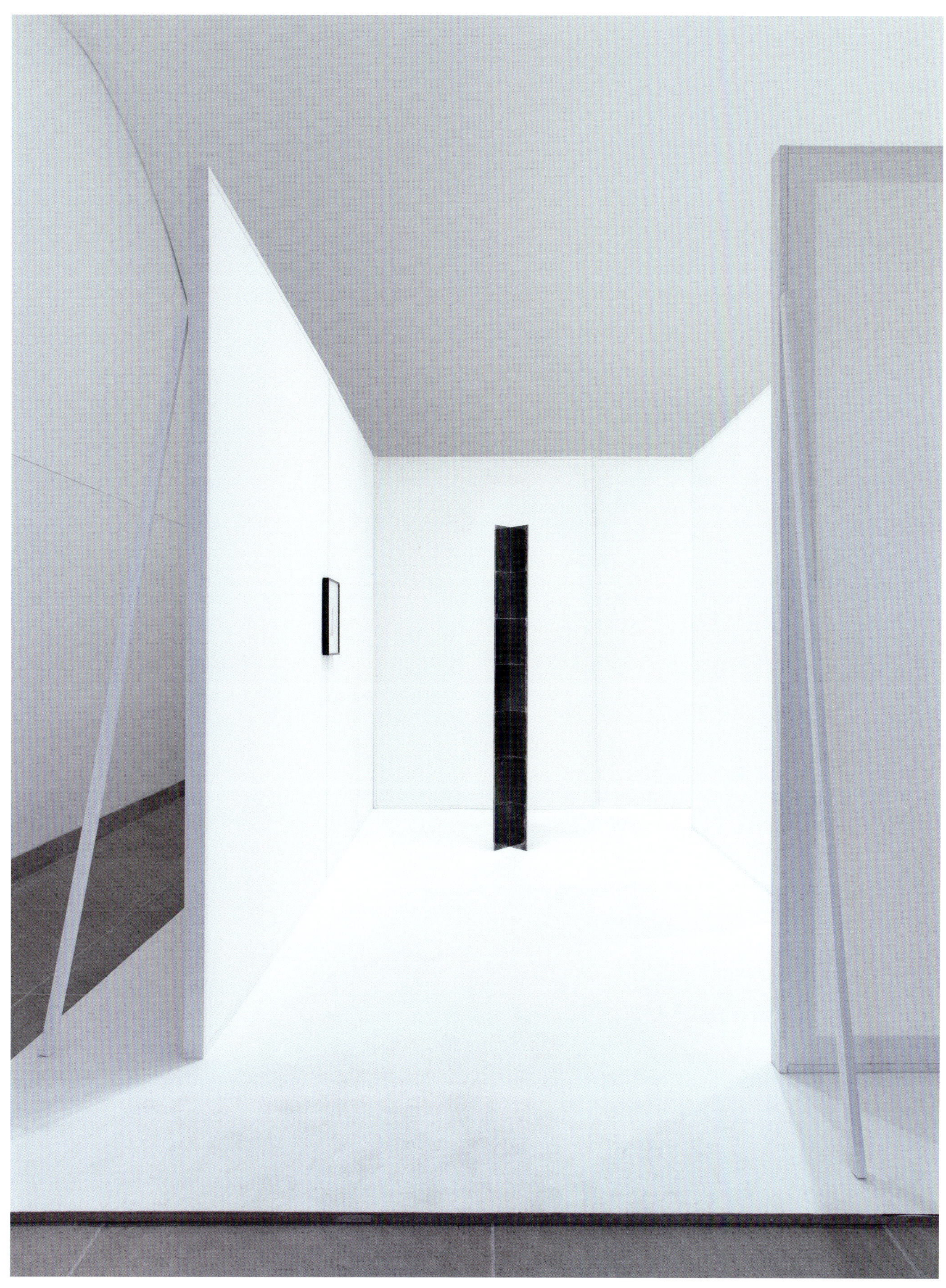

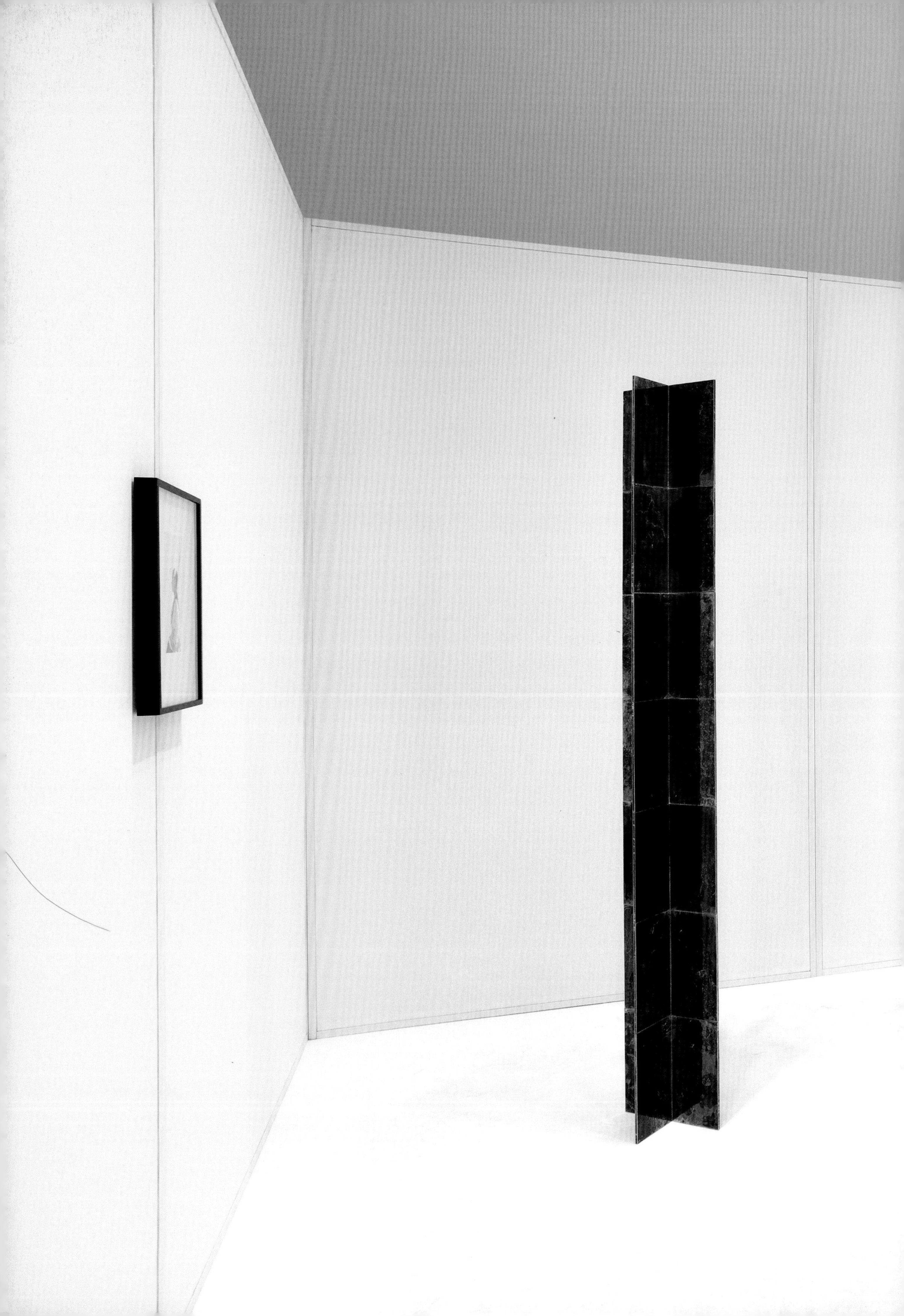

Western Costume, Aurora, 2011

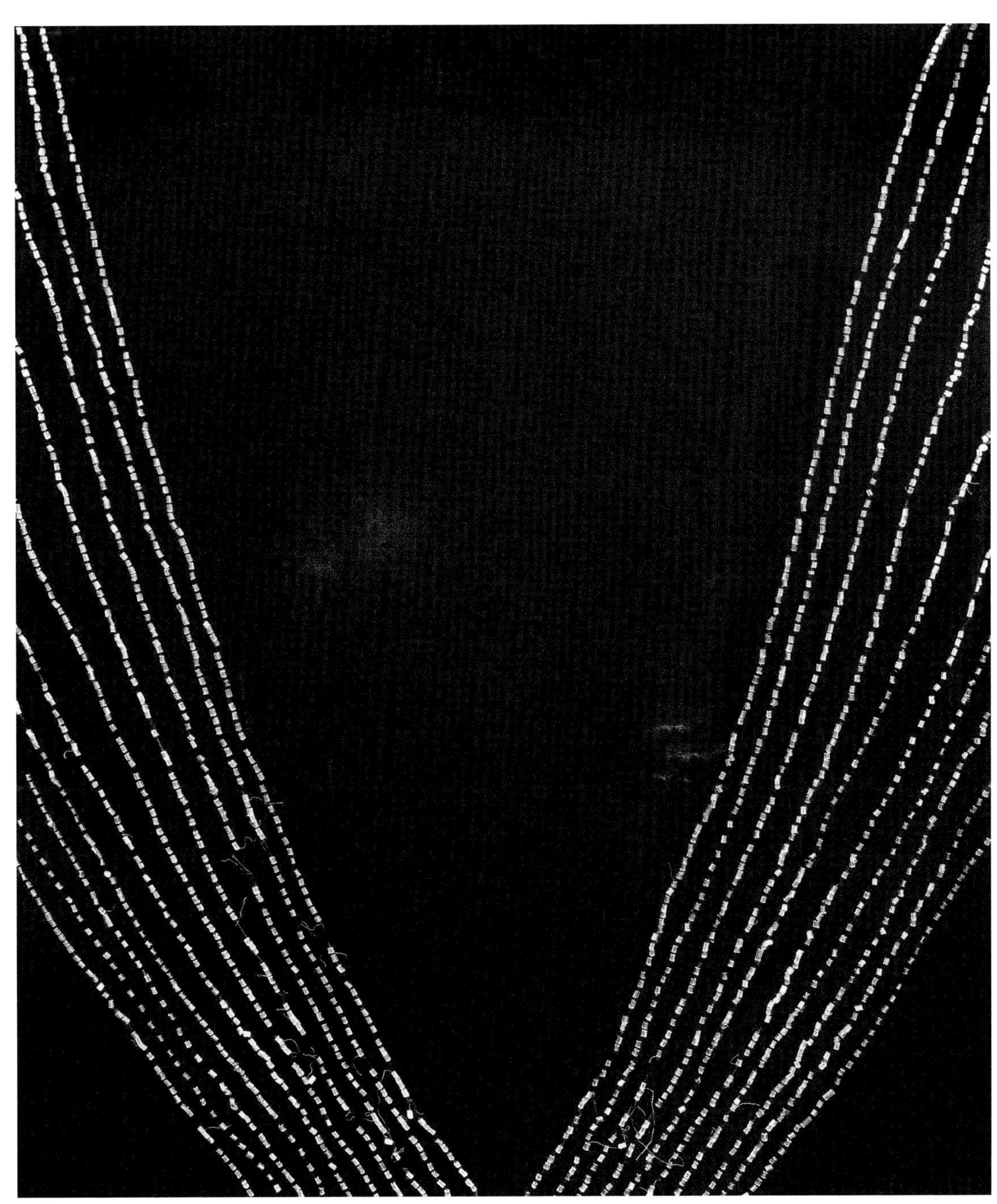

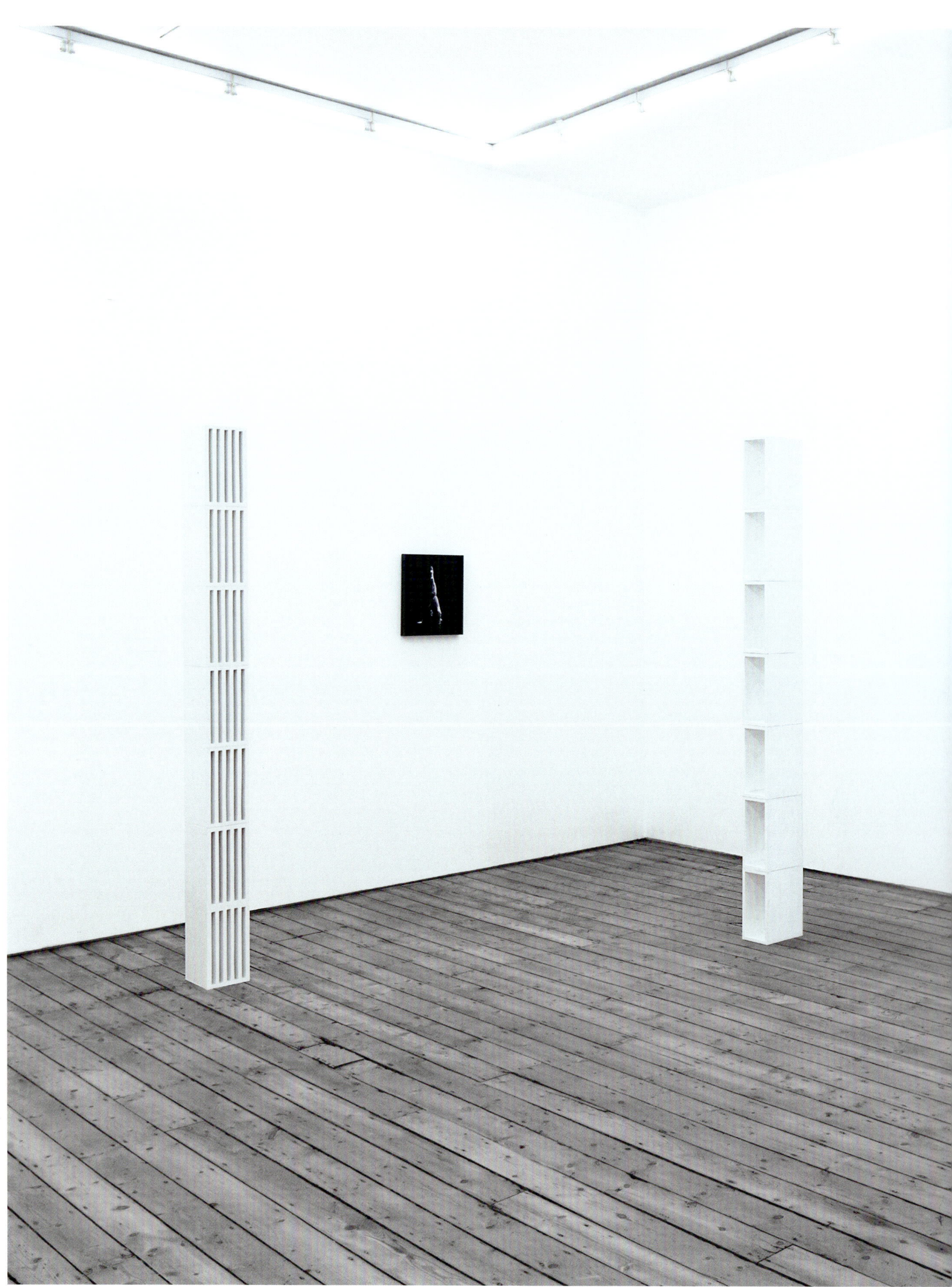

Installation view, The Approach, London, 2012

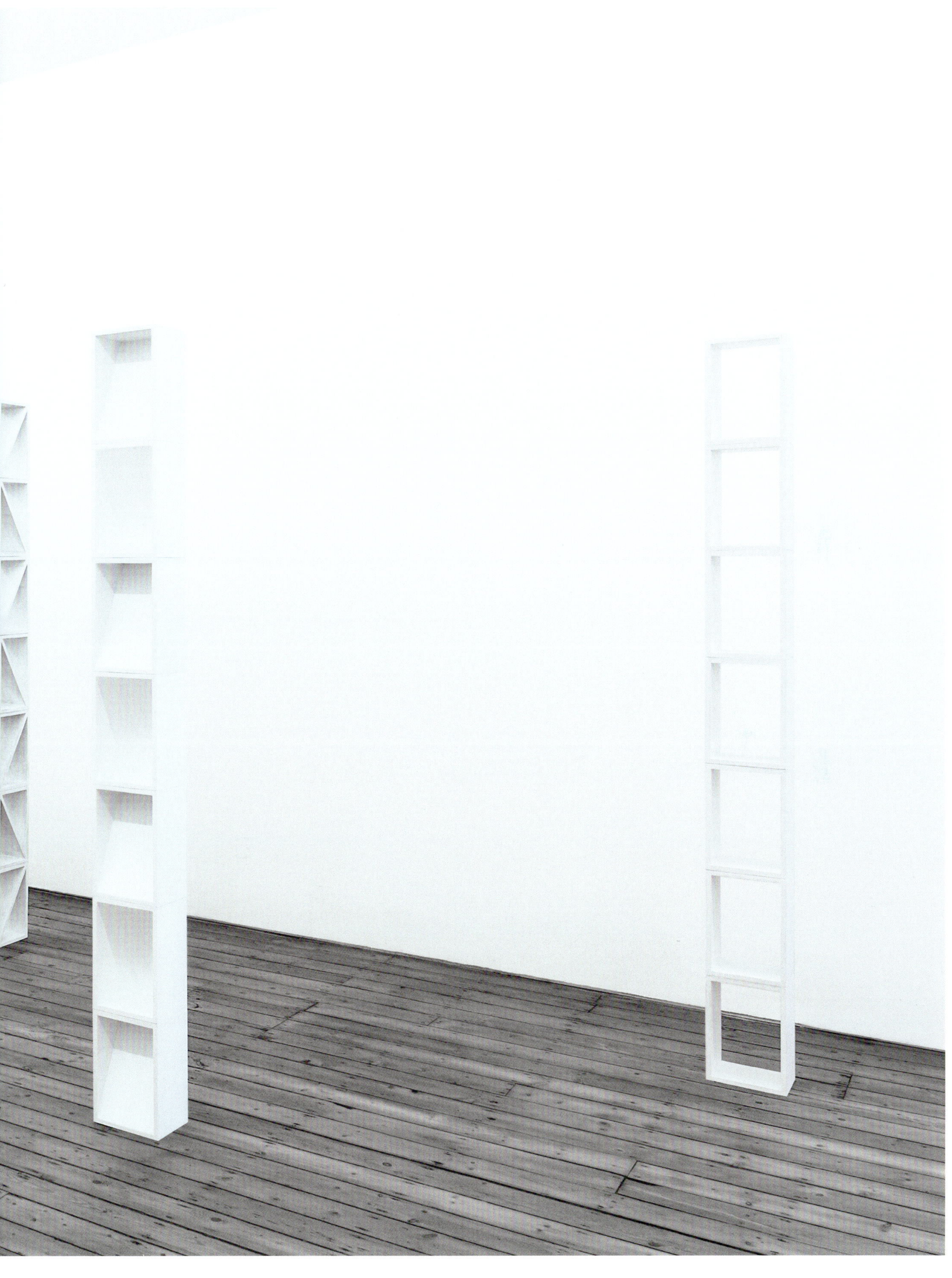

Baltimore Dancers, Nine and *Ten*, 2012

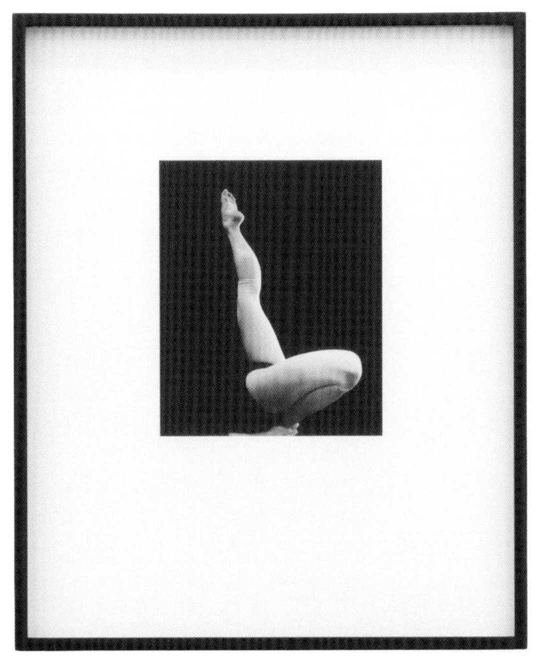

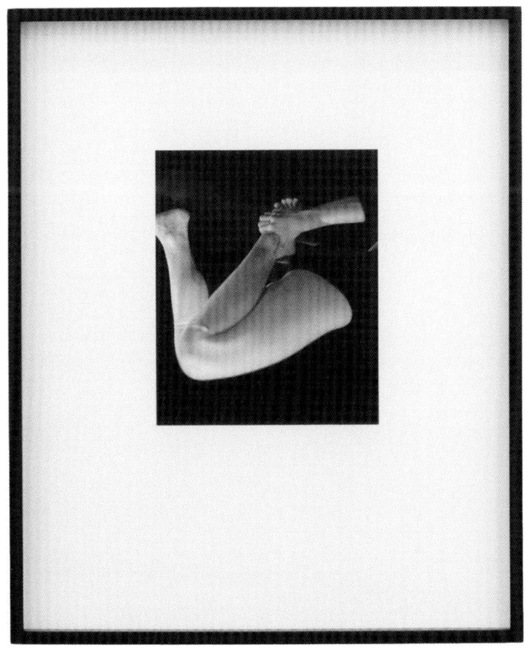

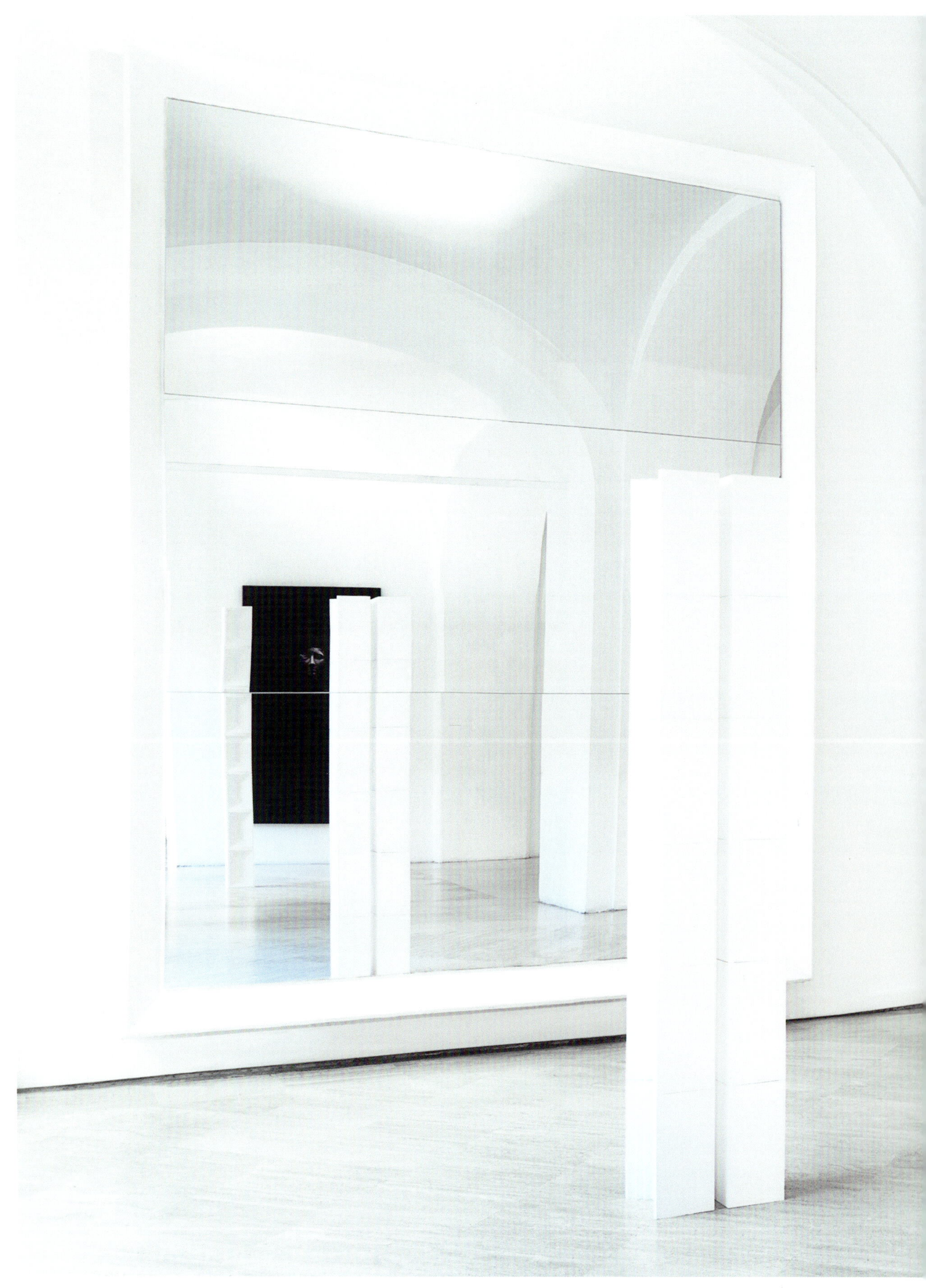

Installation view, *Sara VanDerBeek*, Fondazione Memmo, Rome, 2012

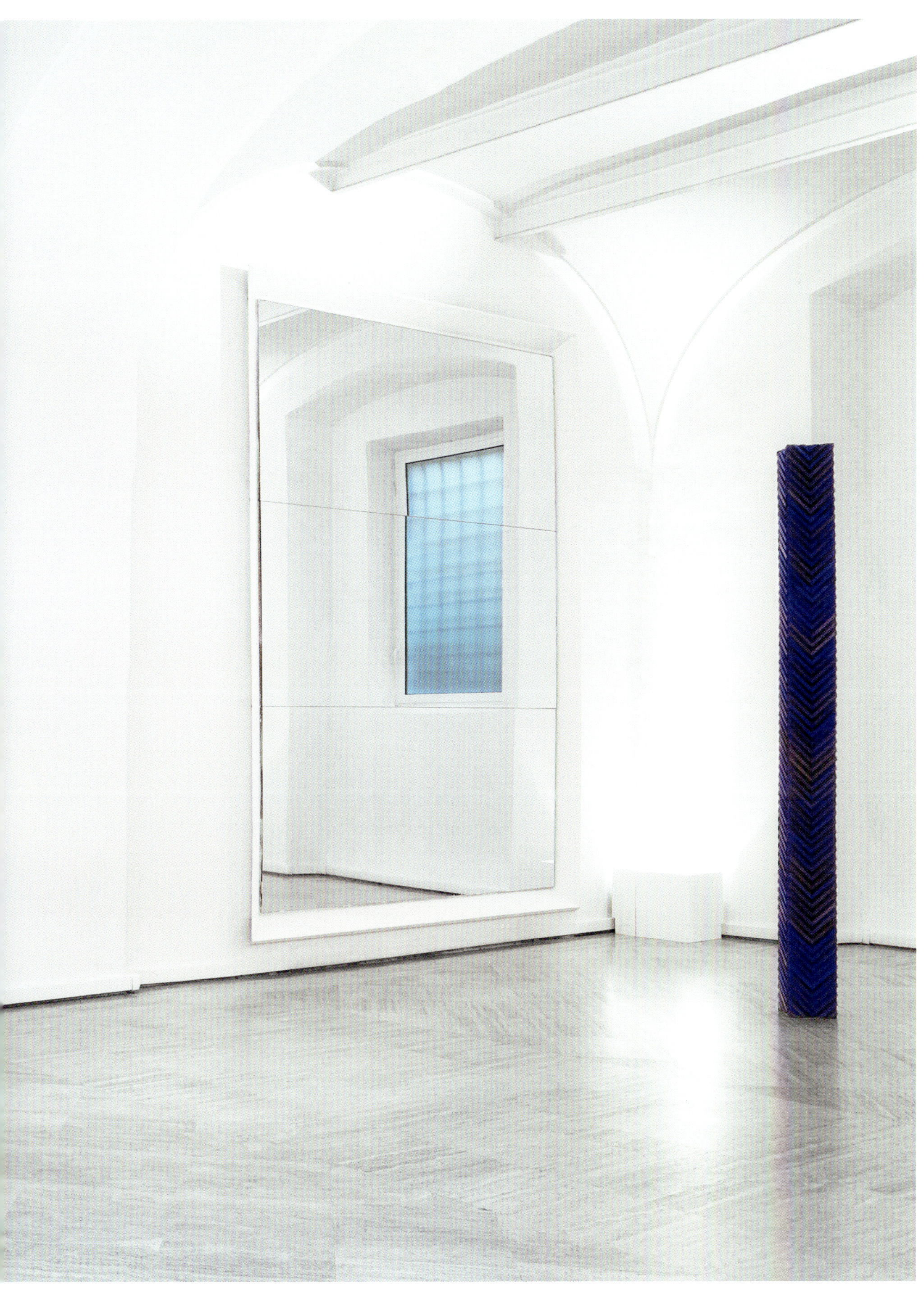

Mask, 2012

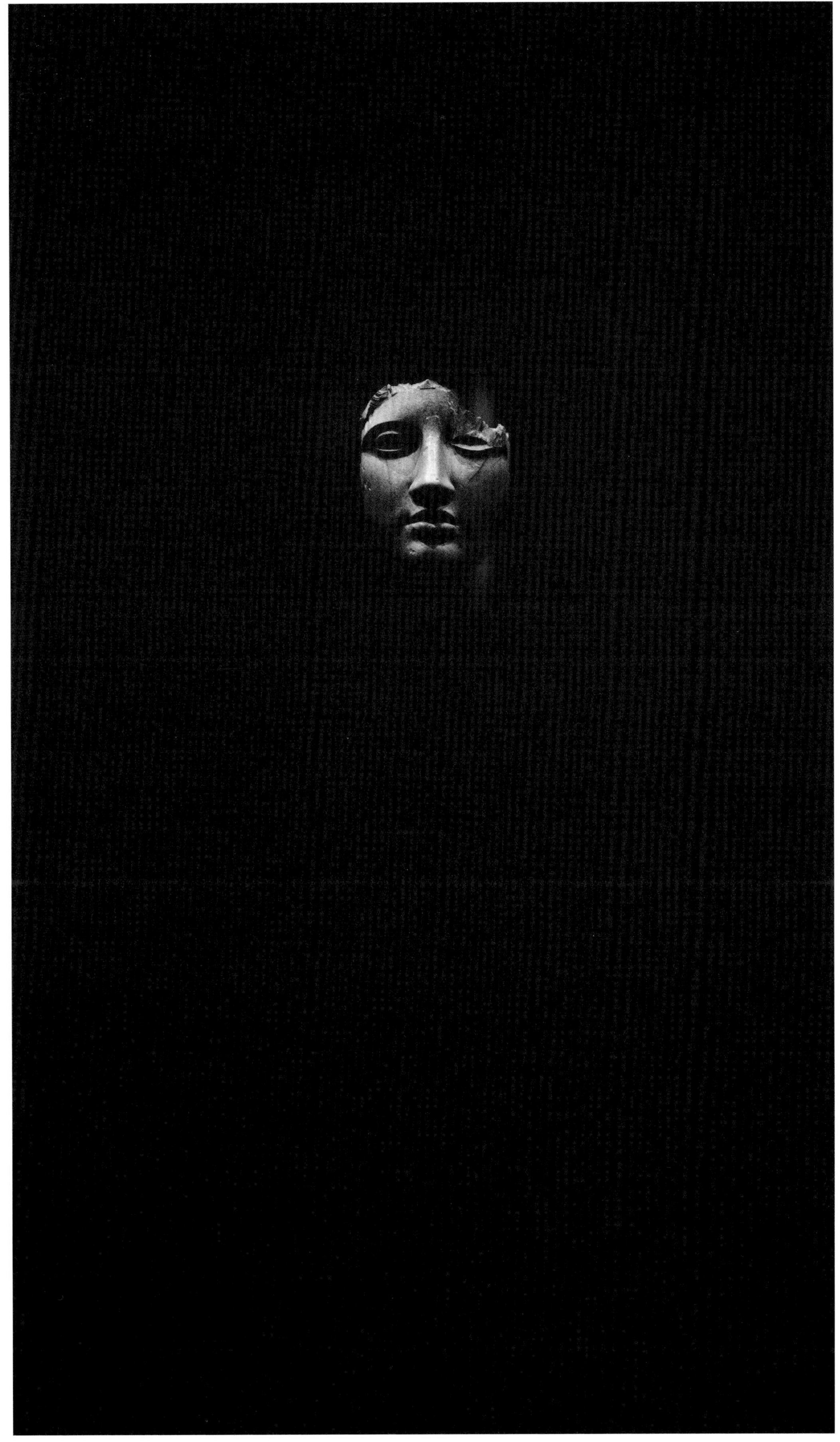

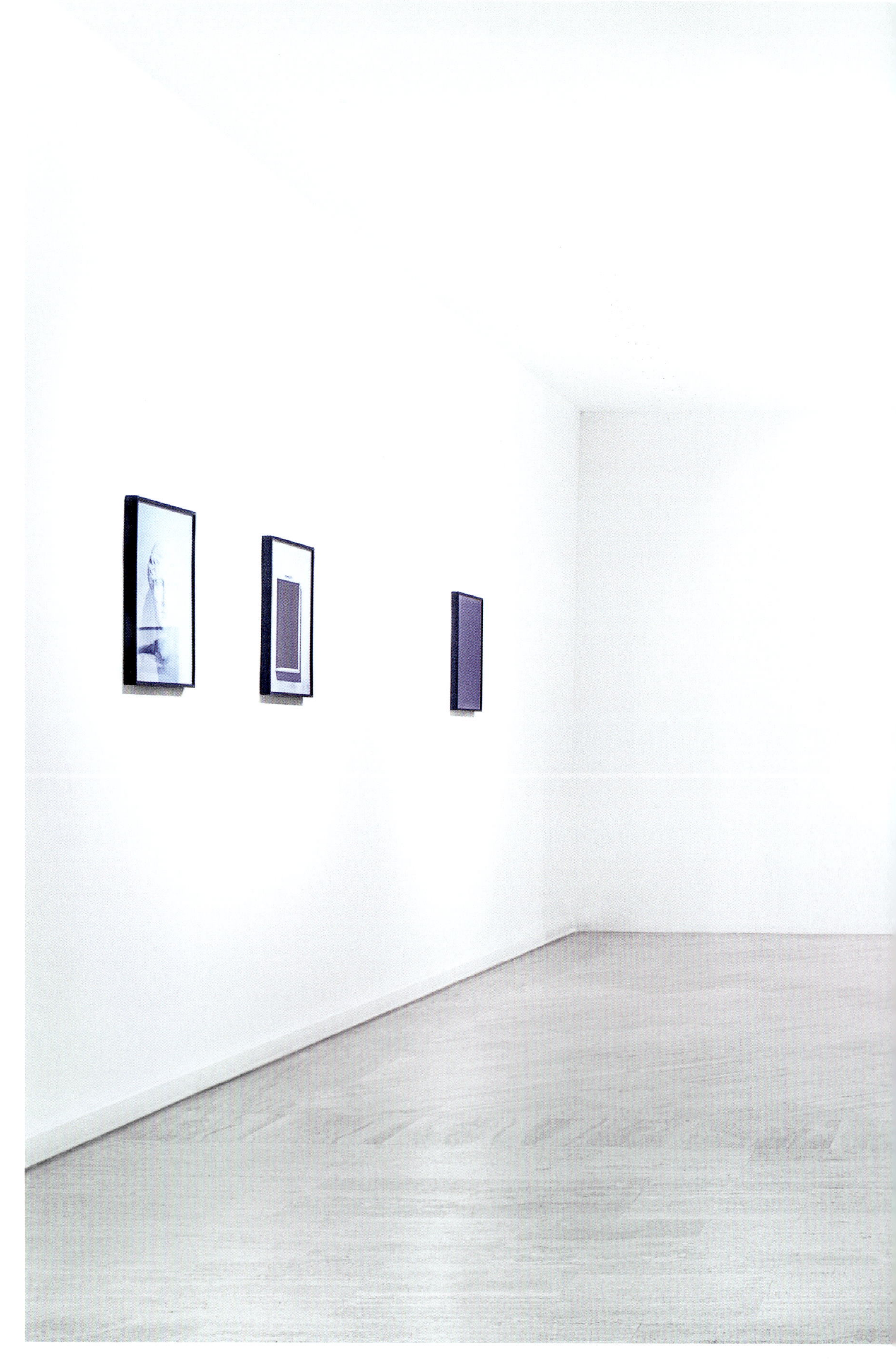

Installation view, *Sara VanDerBeek*, Fondazione Memmo, Rome, 2012

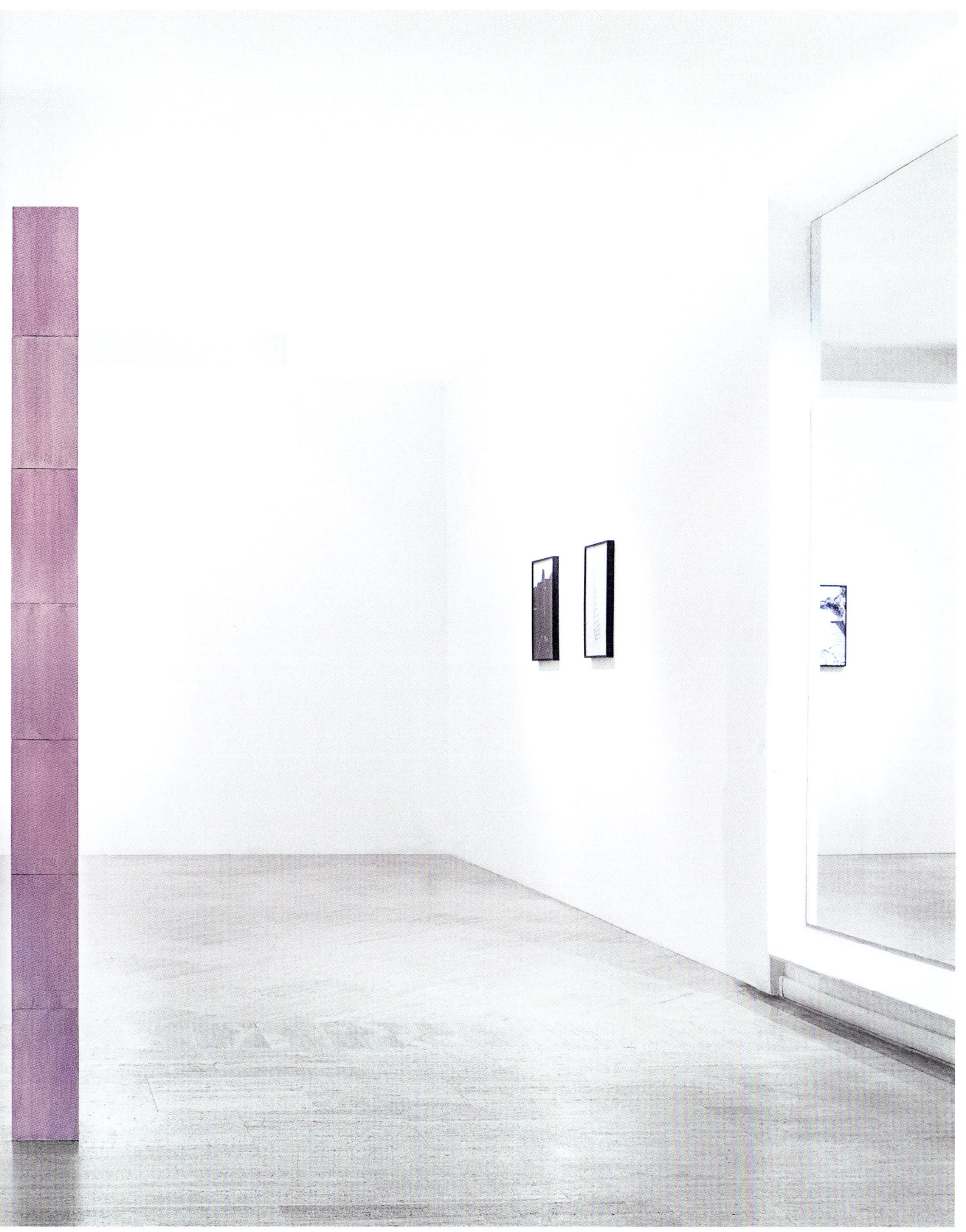

Caracalla, 2012 > Installation view, Metro Pictures, New York, 2013

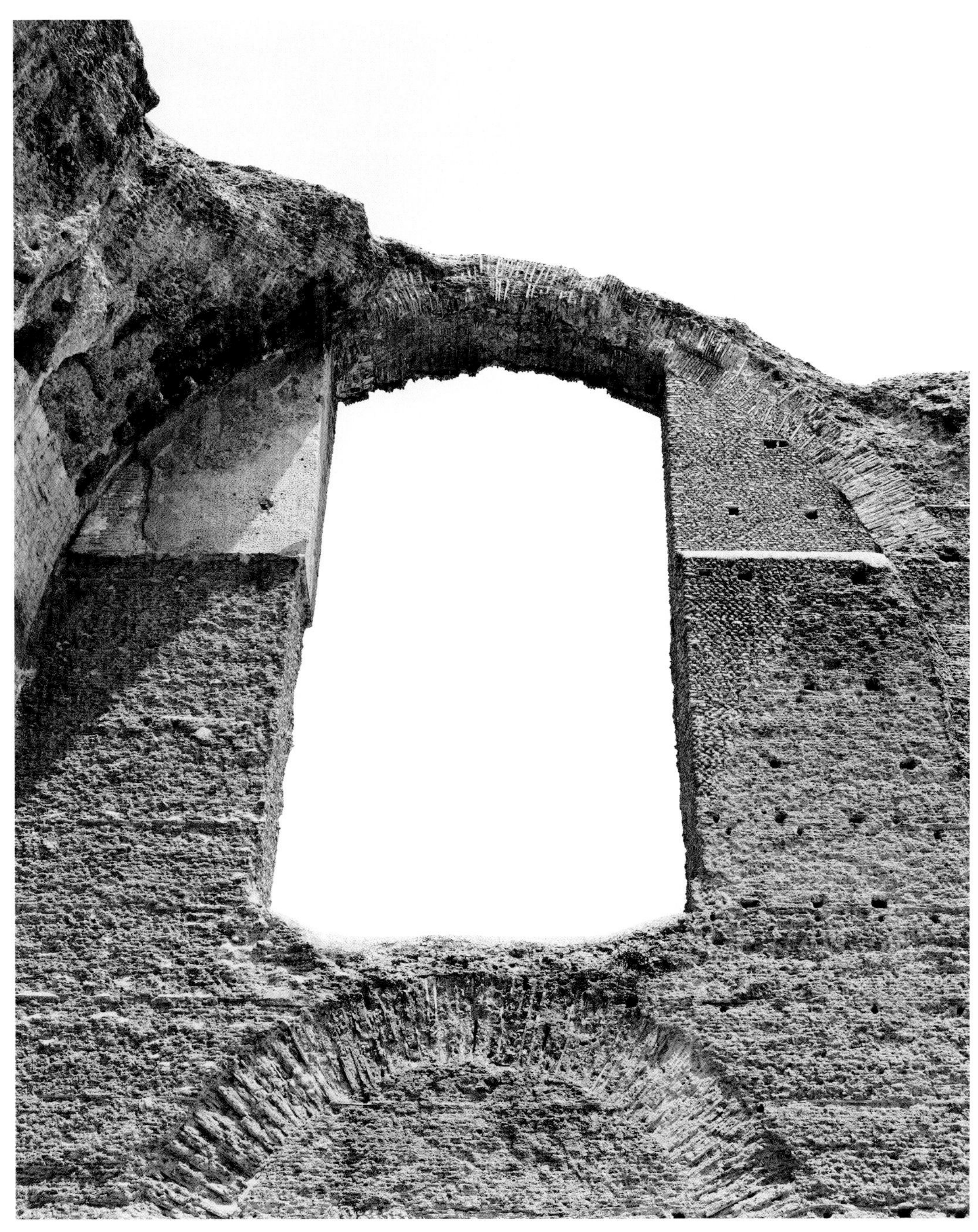

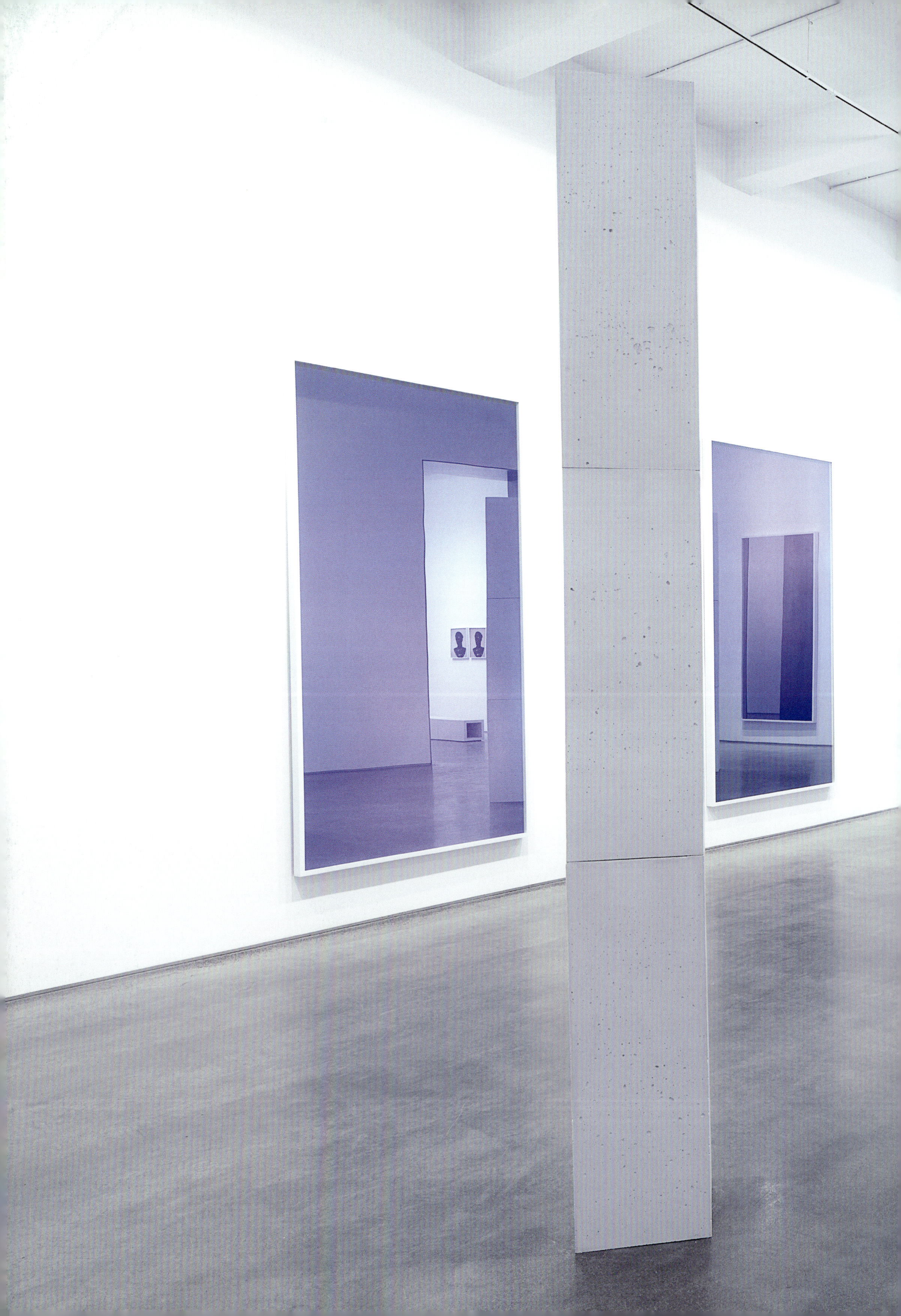

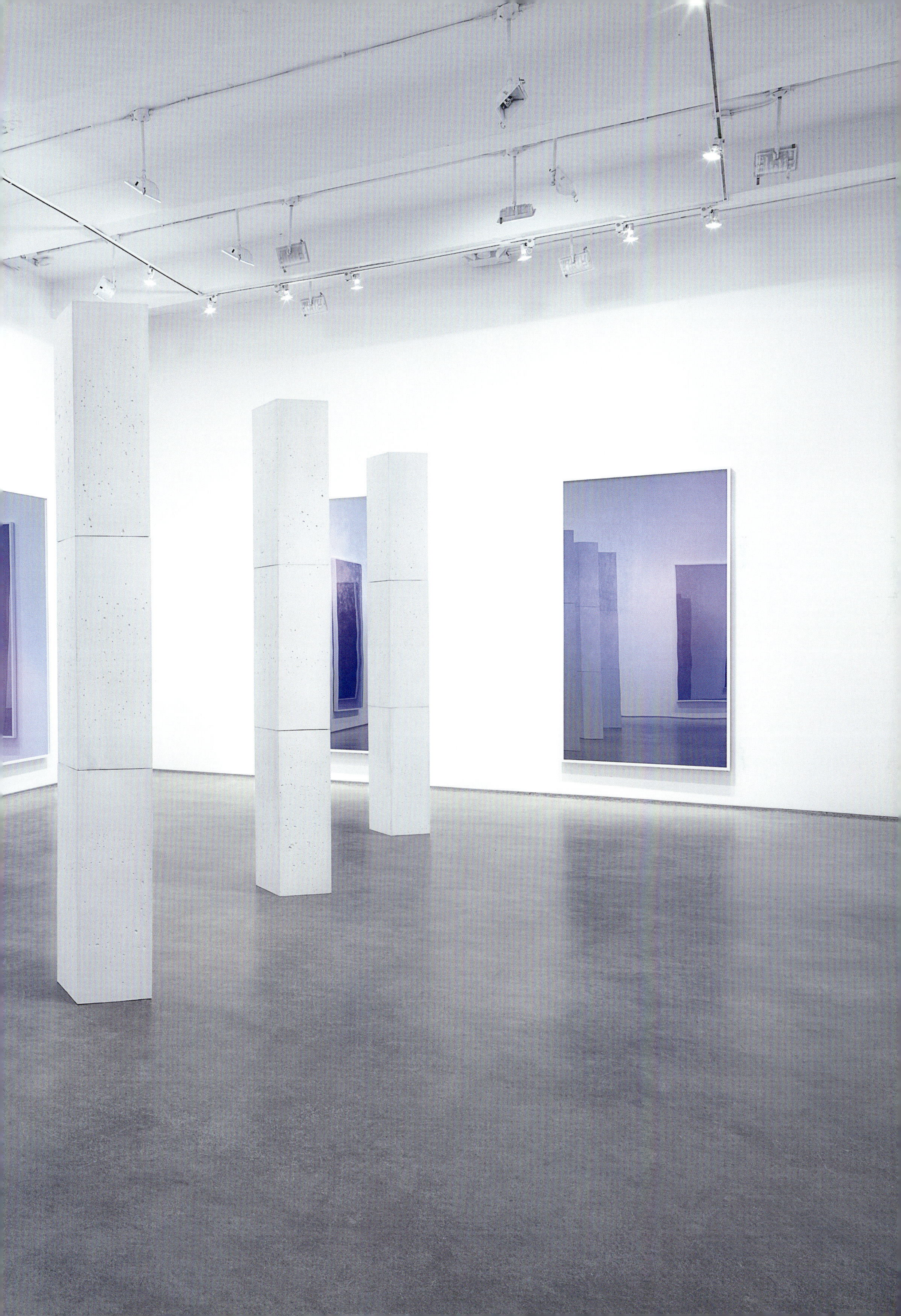

Pink Nude, Blue, 2013 > *XXVI,* 2013, and *Roman Women VIII,* 2013, installation view, Metro Pictures, New York, 2013

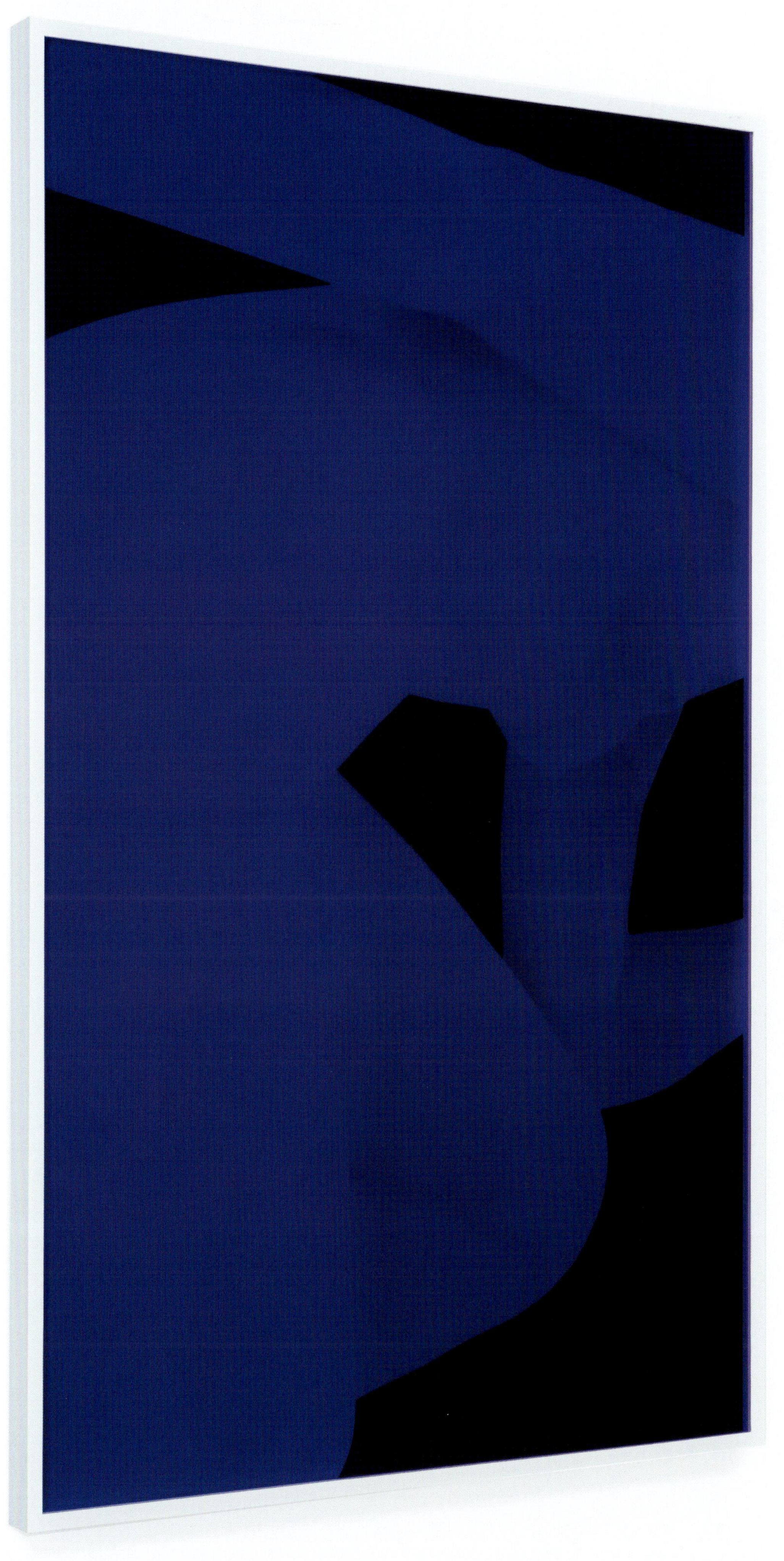

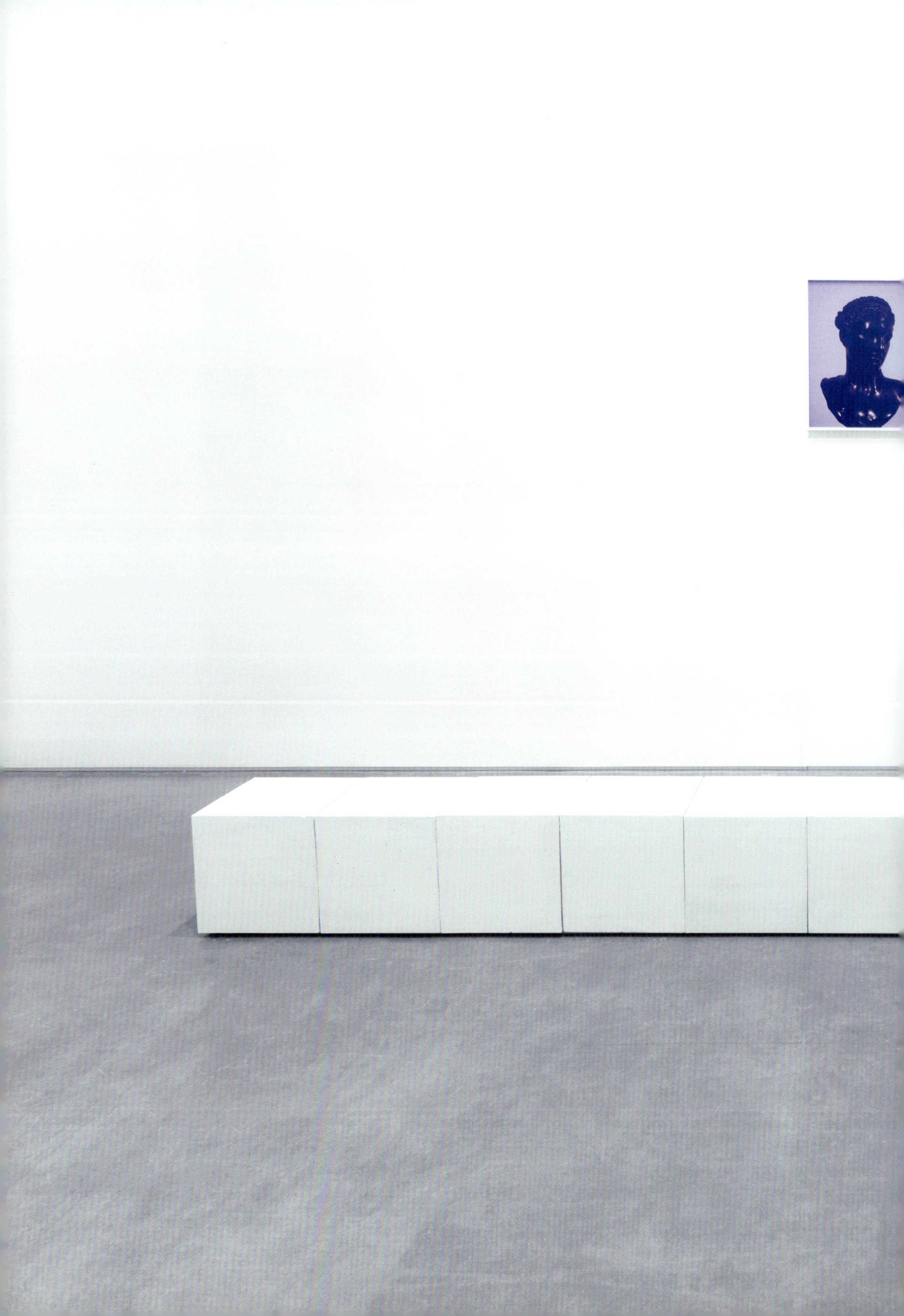

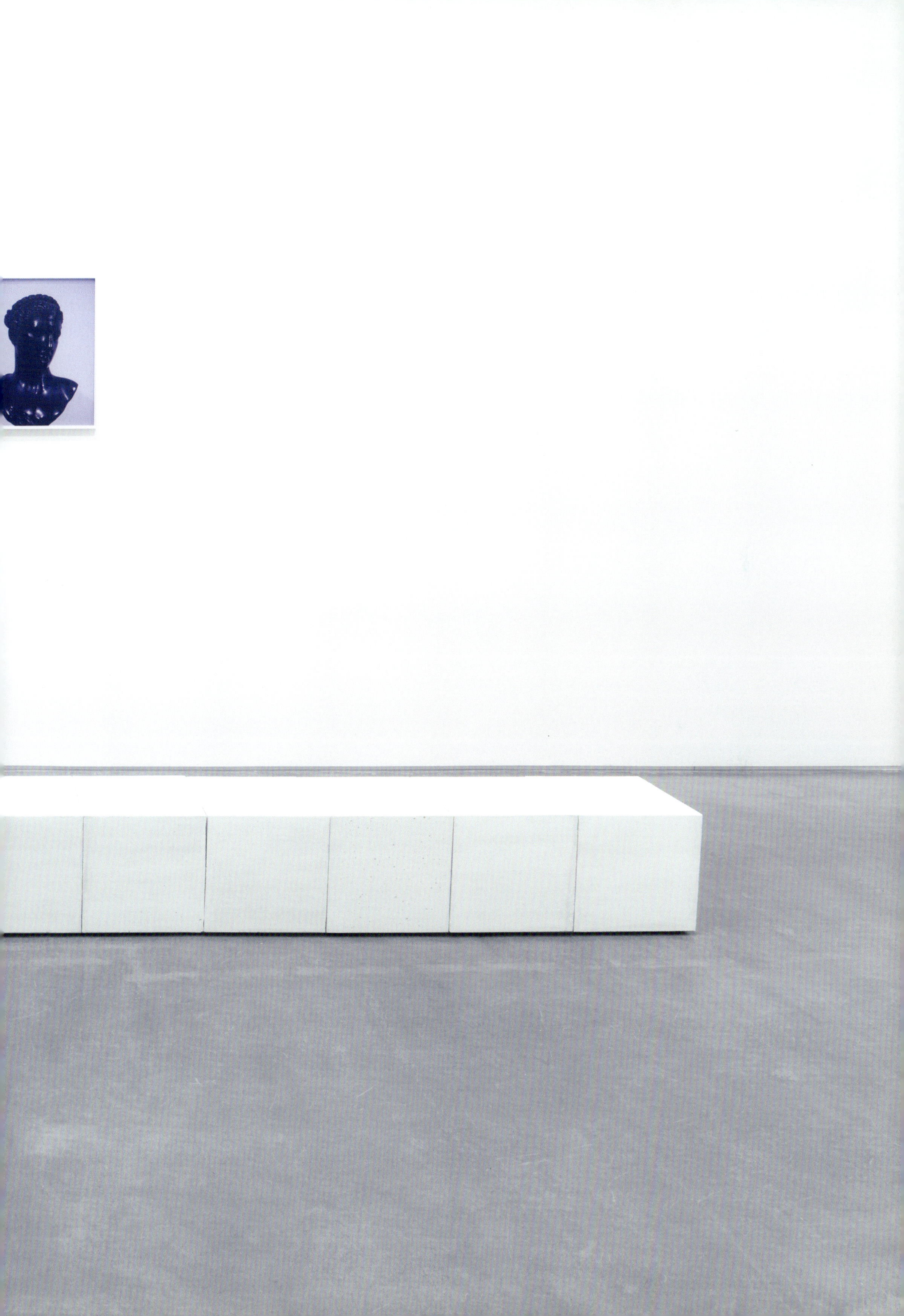

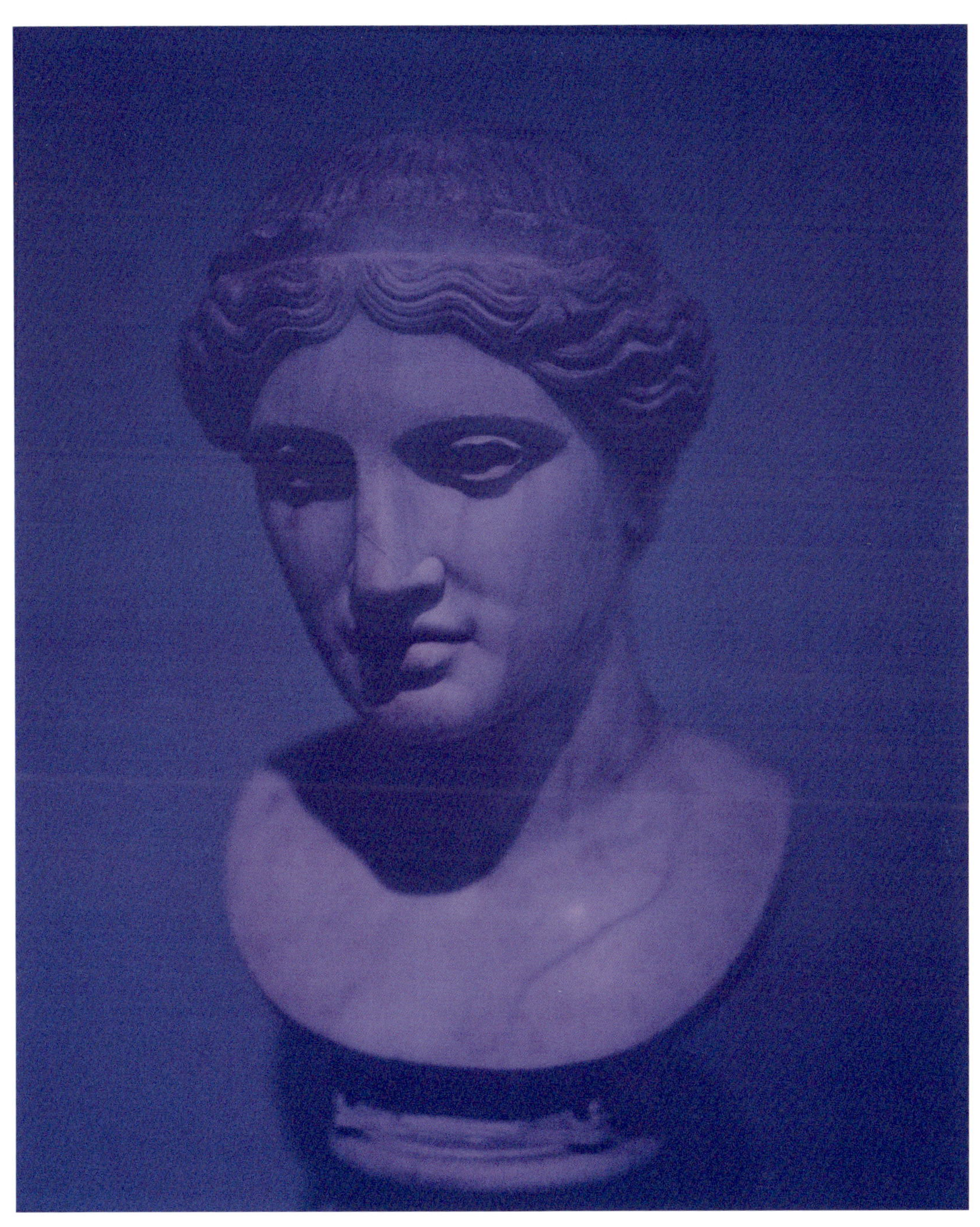

Parallel, 2013

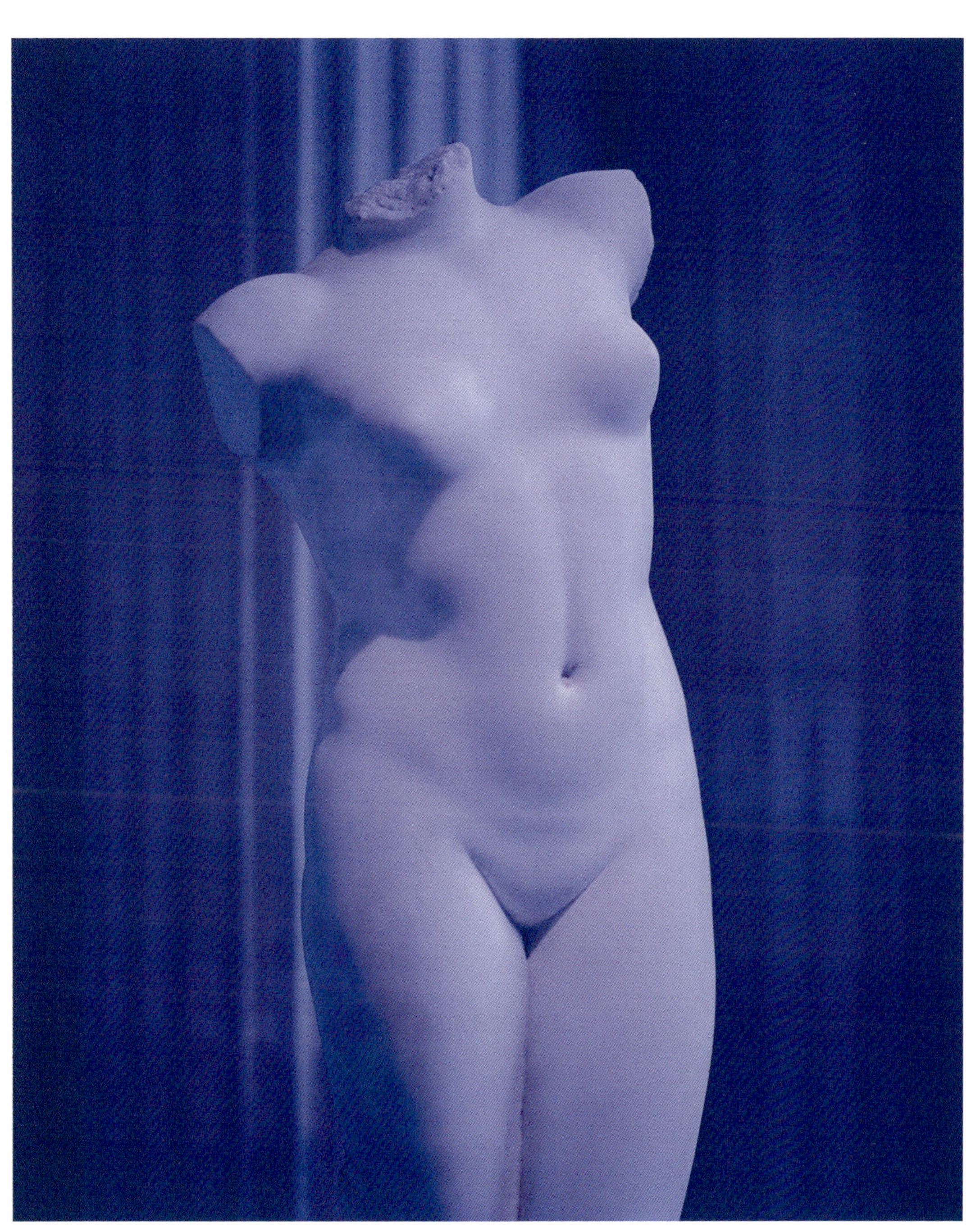

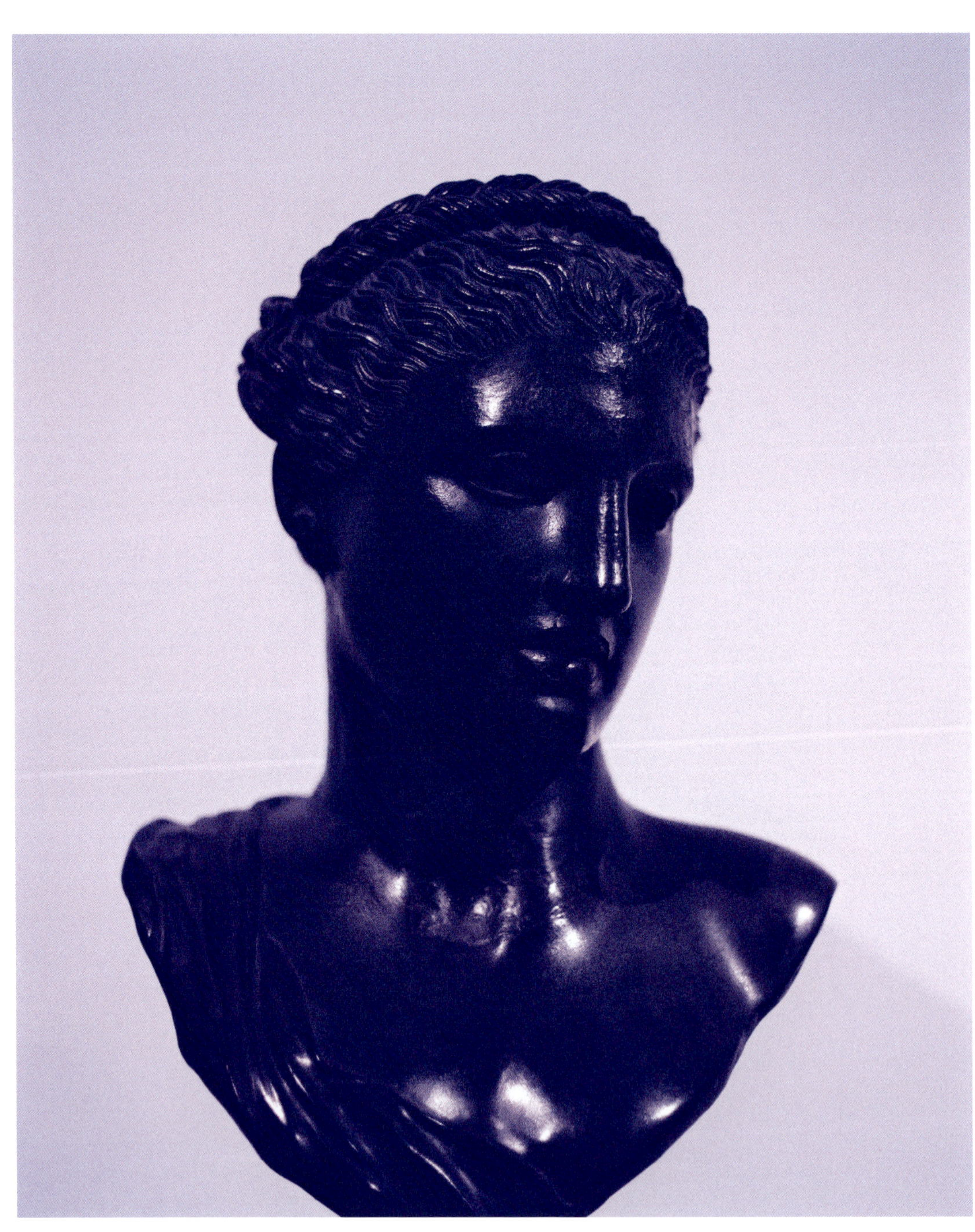

Roman Women VIII, 2013

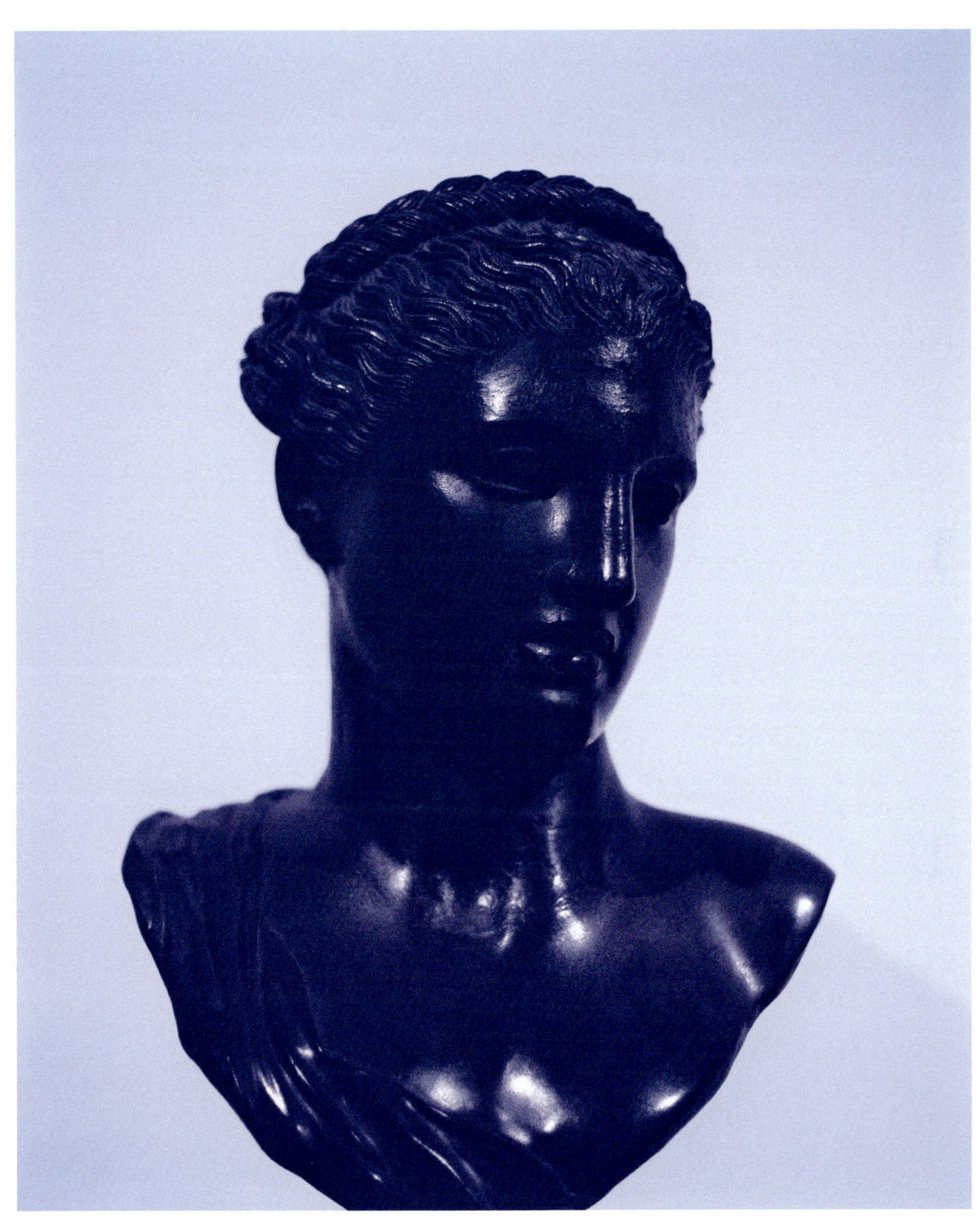

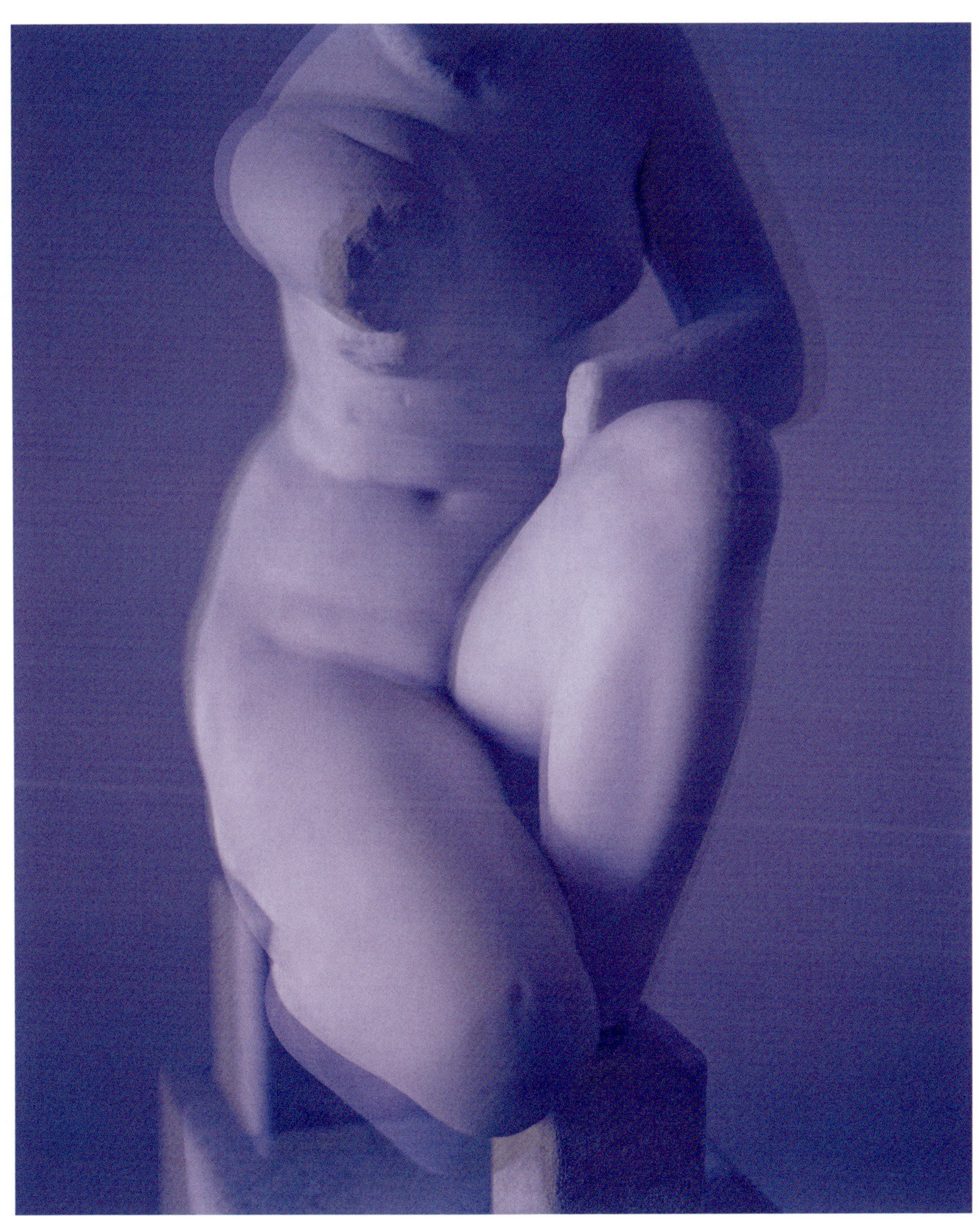

Shift, 2014

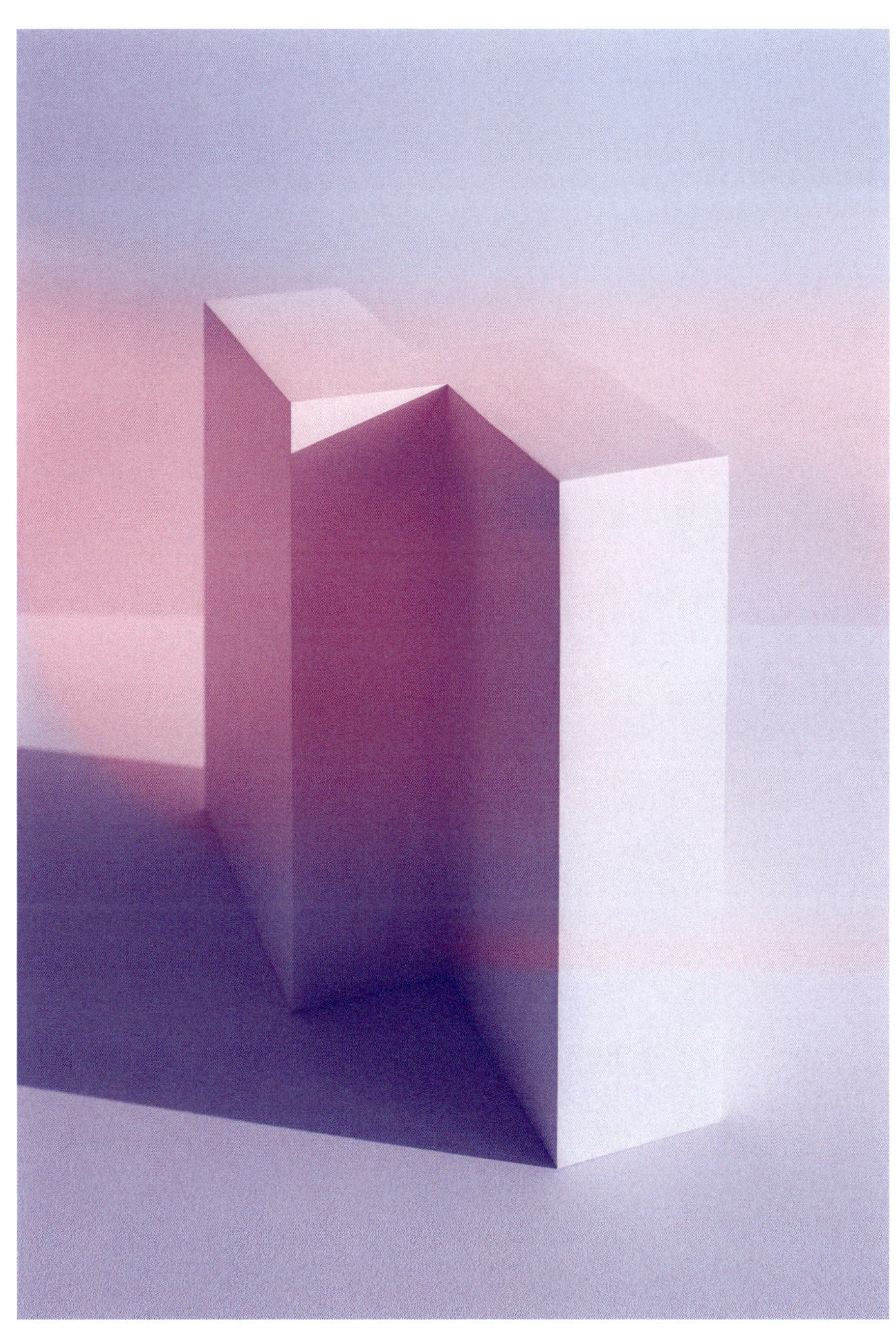

Pyramid Steps, Day, 2014

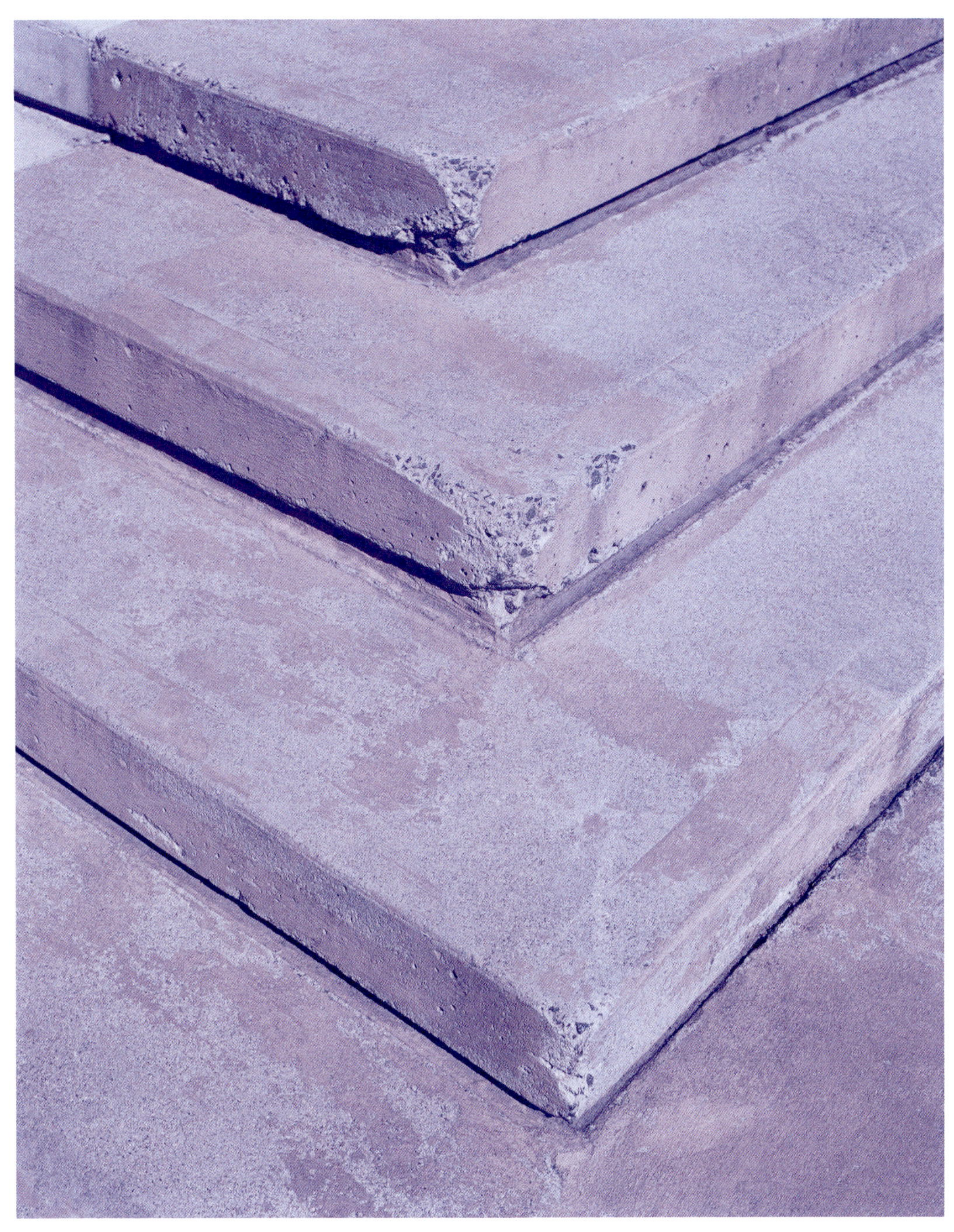

Synthetic Geometry, 2014

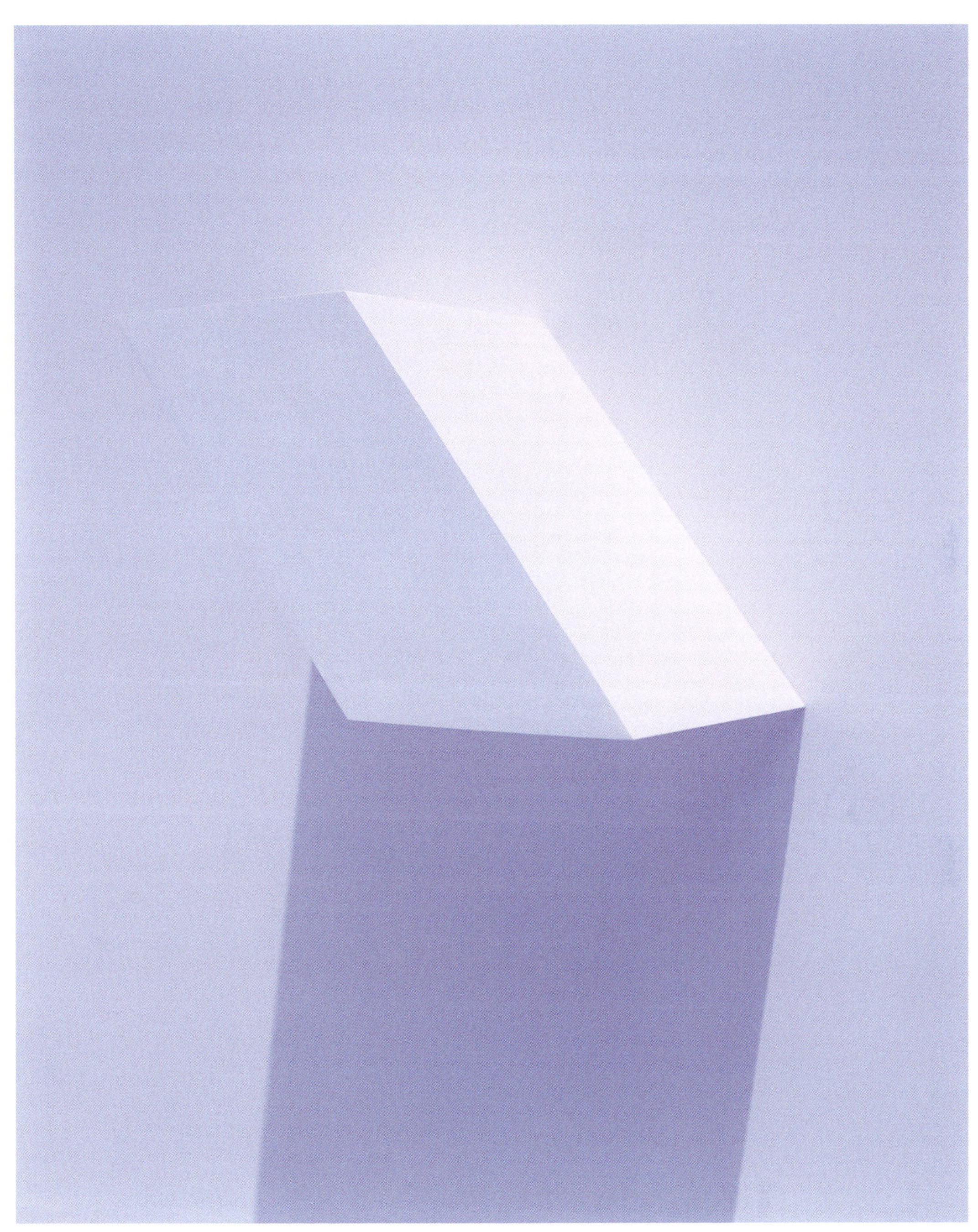

Ancient Solstice, 2014

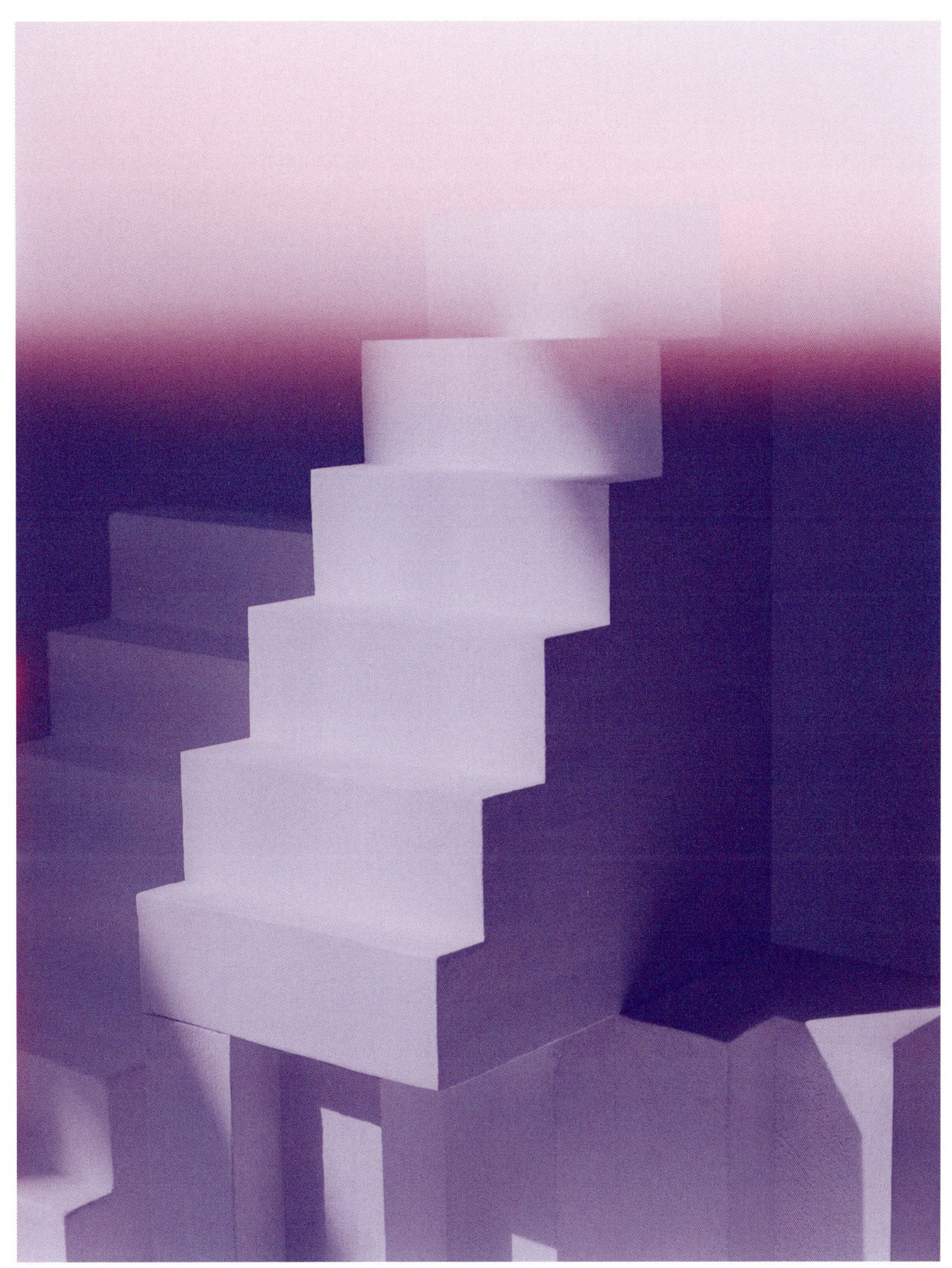

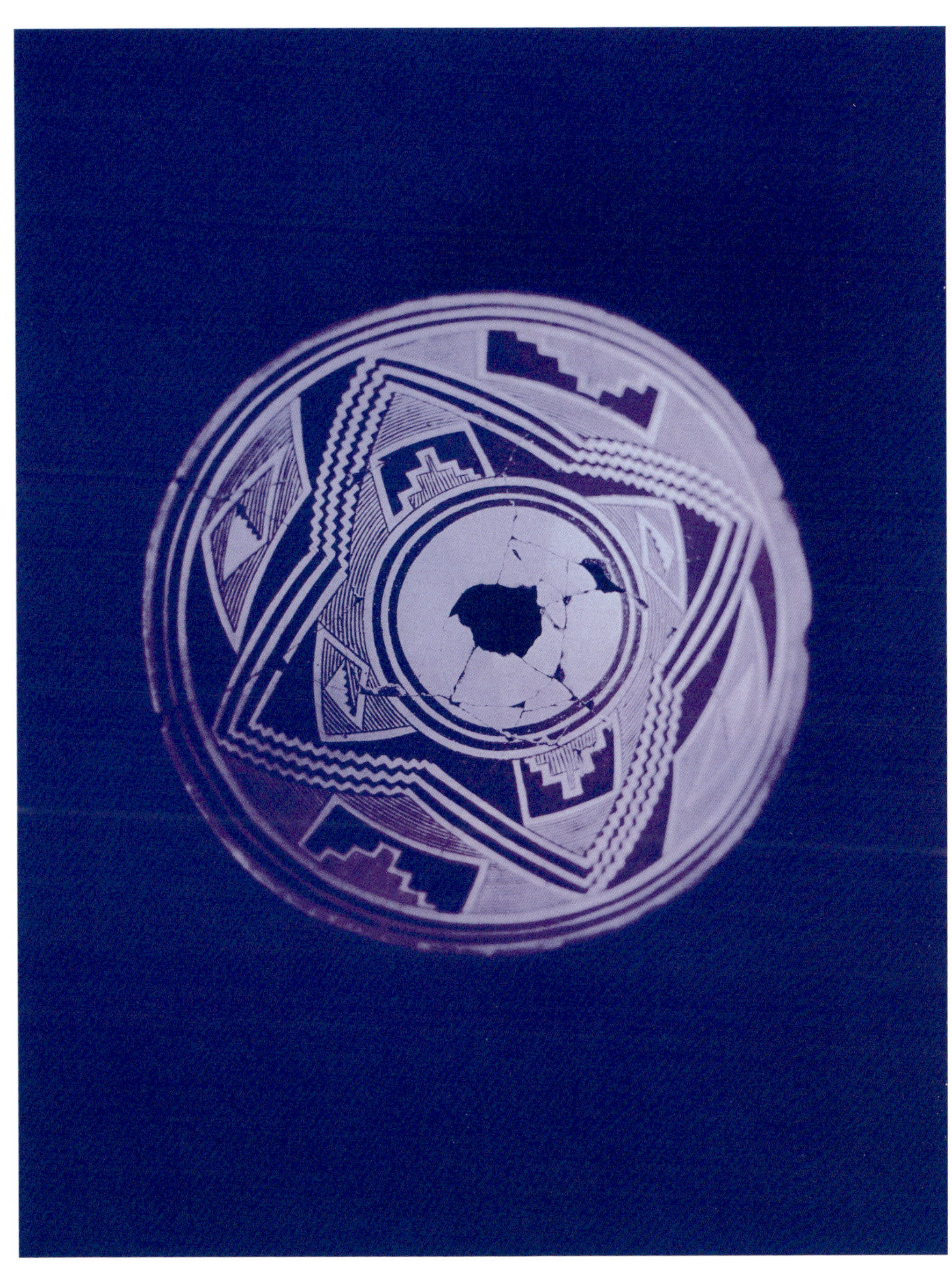

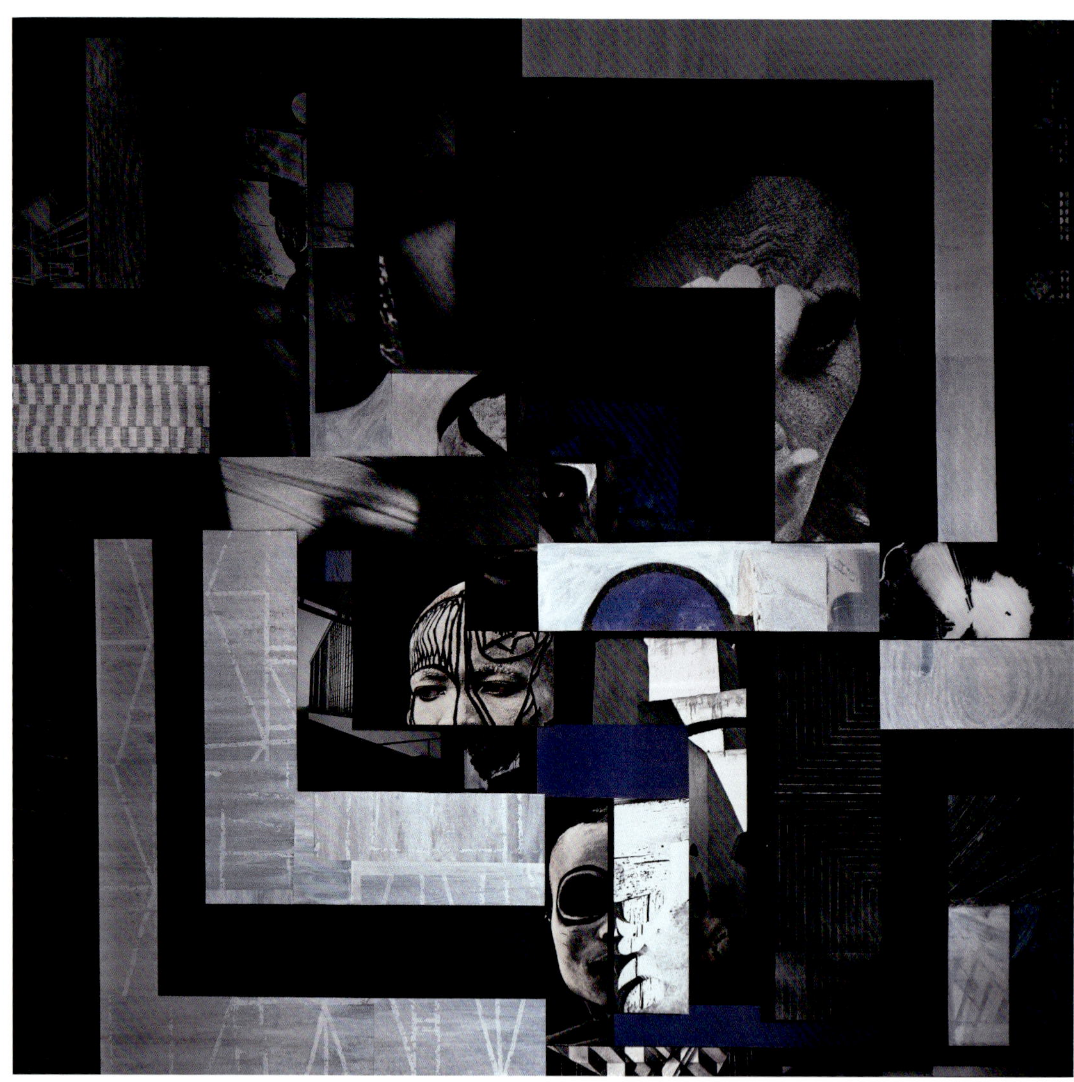

Delaunay, 2008

Sara VanDerBeek in Conversation with Roxana Marcoci: On the Conditions of Photo-Based Culture

Roxana Marcoci I'd like to start with your chromogenic color print *Delaunay* (2008), a work I know rather intimately because it is in the collection of The Museum of Modern Art. I have looked at this particular image over time and up close, and return to it now as a reference point to discuss the conceptual underpinnings of your practice. In an earlier conversation we had [December 9, 2014], you mentioned that you based *Delaunay* on a tapestry design by artist Sonia Delaunay-Terk, who was co-founder of Orphism and pioneer of color-based abstraction. Indebted to the philosophical theories of Henri Bergson, Sonia and Robert Delaunay developed the concept of *simultanism* (all things are simultaneously present to consciousness), which led to their radical experimentation with colors and designs in prismatic collages, paintings, and, in Sonia's case, also book bindings and dresses.

Sara VanDerBeek Sonia Delaunay-Terk has been and continues to be a reference point for me. Her work *Electric Prisms* from 1913, for example, is considered a reflection on modern life in the early twentieth century, yet I also see its title and the Delaunays' notion of visual simultaneity speaking to our current twenty-first-century, pixel- and screen-based culture.

RM You have, in fact, expanded the Delaunays' modern idea of simultaneity in your own practice by mining extant images from numerous sources, including art-history survey books, personal albums, archives, newspapers, and magazines. More specifically, your work *Delaunay* draws together reproductions of a Frank Stella painting, a Rayograph, African textiles, Kabuki actors, and Leni Riefenstahl's photographs of the Nuba people. Can you talk about the principle of simultaneity in your work?

SV One way I see this principle manifest in my own work is through the layering of multiple images in a single frame. Recently, in *Electric Prisms,* a work I completed in 2015, twelve framed images are each comprised of two layers. The composition remains the same in all twelve images, yet when viewed as a sequence the objects depicted take on varying spatial and temporal qualities via subtle color shifts from one image to the next. Starting on the left with the deep blue of night, the framed images progress through hot pinks and reds of dawn, arriving at the strong contrast of daylight and then shifting again toward the dusky pink and blue crepuscular mix at day's end. The succession of forms moves from concrete and tangible to ephemeral and translucent, eventually fading out by the end of the sequence.

RM What does "simultaneity" mean culturally and, more specifically, how have you translated this concept into the present?

SV The color combinations within *Electric Prisms* (2015) were developed from my recent research trips through North and South America. They also refer directly to textiles used by Delaunay-Terk and Anni Albers, who in turn both drew upon ancient pre-Columbian textiles for their own work. I was thinking about the simultaneity of contemporary culture as advanced by Sonia Delaunay-Terk, as well as the continuities and continuums throughout a lifetime, throughout a larger shared history and the ways in which this accumulation of experiences results in a dynamic whole that at times is formed like a film—a sequence of specific moments that are layered over and amongst one another.

RM How does this filmic concept of simultaneity become enacted in your work?

SV Through continuous formal experimentation, I strive to create a sense of expanded duration, what can be thought of as an accumulative movement within a static image. This has resulted in new forms of collage and ways of layering the photographic image. As I move away from using found imagery toward photographing on site as well as bringing the experimentation of the studio and my process into the exhibition space itself, I have returned to a consideration of simultaneity as a way in which not only to convey but also to ramify the precarious and fragmentary condition of lived experience.

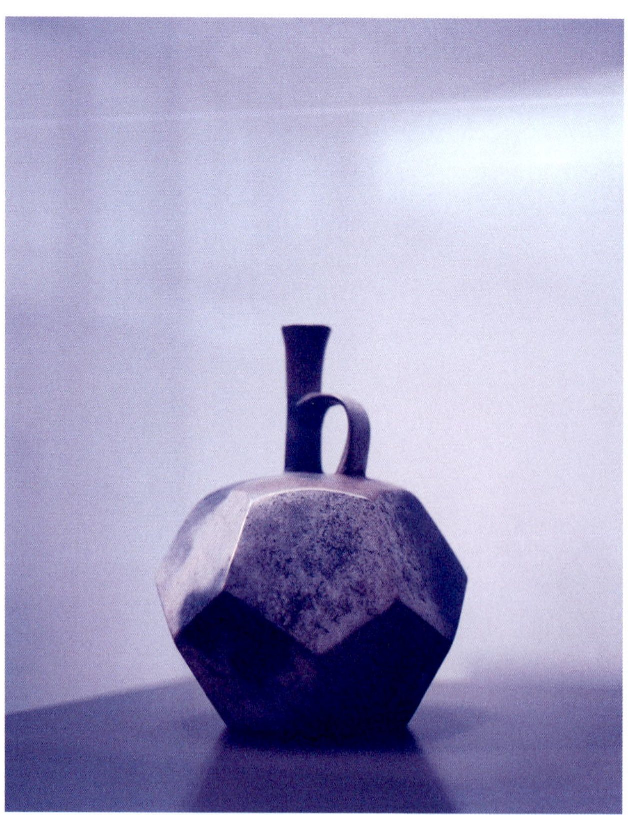

Chorrera, 2014

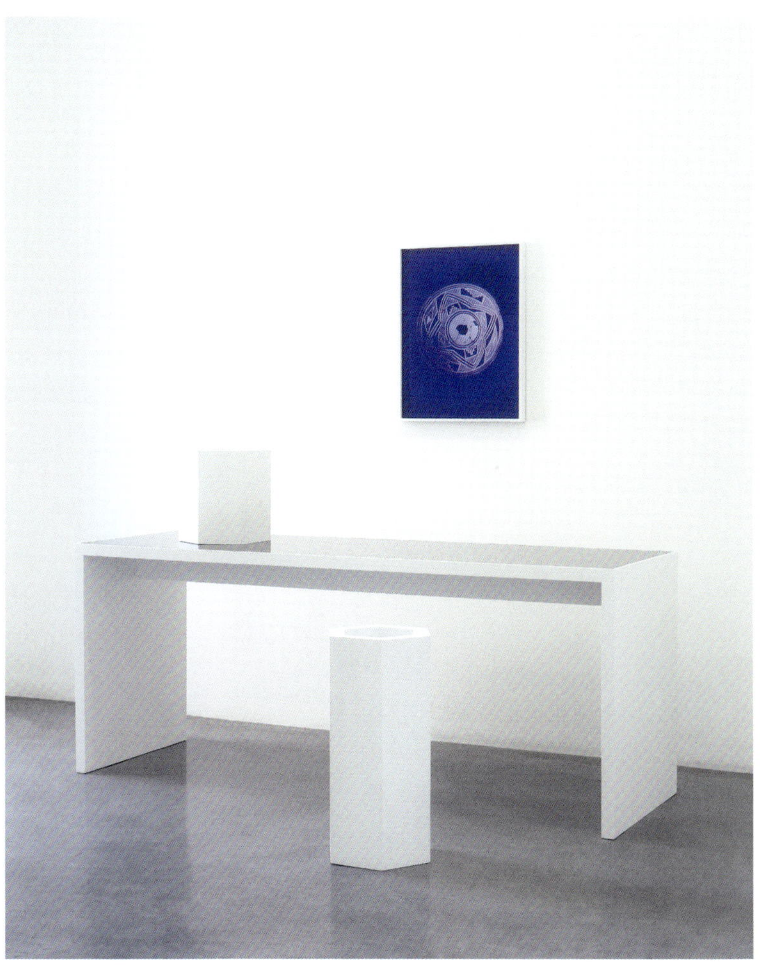

Lunar Calendar, 2014

When working on a series that came to be titled *Ancient Objects, Still Lives* in 2014, I had a unique opportunity to work with Casa del Alabado, a pre-Columbian art museum in Quito, Ecuador. I was granted access to photograph rare ceramic vessels created by the ancient Chorrera culture between 1300 BCE and 300 BCE. They effectively employed geometric forms and patterned adornment to reach a balance of formal resolution, complex stylization, and spiritual function. Additionally, the shapes of certain vessels could have easily been mistaken for modern pottery, and certain patterns were similar to those I had seen on ancient Greek amphora. These types of cross-epochal and -cultural connections are of ongoing interest to me as they complicate narratives around issues of importation, cultural influence, and formal adaptation that we typically ascribe to more contemporary iterations of globalization.

You have taken on the correspondence between South America and Europe, advancing transmodernism in the exhibition *From Bauhaus to Buenos Aires: Grete Stern and Horacio Coppola* [May 17 to October 4, 2015], while more recently exploring the crossover of artistic communities in *Transmissions: Art in Eastern Europe and Latin America, 1960–1980* [September 5, 2015, to January 3, 2016]. Of particular interest to me is the feedback loop between Bauhaus and other pedagogical experiments, such as Black Mountain College, with that of ancient indigenous cultures in both South and North America.

RM A key focus of the exhibition *From Bauhaus to Buenos Aires* at The Museum of Modern Art, New York, was on the Bauhaus laboratory and the radically photophilic moment of the nineteen-twenties and early thirties, which saw in photography a means to redefine both human perception and social worlds. That moment resulted in the formation of two contrasting yet loosely related modernist tendencies: *Neue Sachlichkeit* (New Objectivity) and *Neues Sehen* or *Neue Optik* (New Vision).

SV After seeing *Transmissions* and, in particular, Juan Downey's video installation in which he filmed and shared the footage with various indigenous individuals, how do you see the recognition of these new counter-geographies playing out after World War II?

RM This is the premise of *Transmissions,* which I co-organized with my MoMA colleagues Stuart Comer and Christian Rattemeyer. It focuses on parallels and connections among artists active in—and in reference to—Latin America and Eastern Europe in the sixties and seventies. During these decades, which flanked the widespread student protests of 1968, artists working in these distinct political contexts developed cross-cultural networks to expand and circulate their artworks and ideas. I think that artists have always tried to develop alternative circuits for intellectual exchange, and as you alluded to earlier, artists often bring art into daily praxis to reach a wider public and exert an impact on society. I want to return to this notion of a fragmentary and prismatic conceptual process that you outlined earlier. Can you talk about how this is reflected in your production methods?

SV I work both in the more controlled setting of the studio and out in the world capturing images of objects, forms, surfaces, and spaces in a more aleatory process. I prefer a medium-format SLR film camera primarily because it is flexible and I can move quickly and carefully. I use film for its strength and range and then scan the negatives, which allows me to continue refining the images in the digital printing process. I can exploit the strengths of digital and analogue processes to yield an image that embraces and explores hybridity, both formally and materially, in the actual makeup of the properties of the image.

RM This brings to mind the "montage-collision" work of cultural theorist Aby Warburg, a slightly older contemporary of the Delaunays. His iconological experiments with photographic layouts in documenting civilization led to the *Bilderatlas Mnemosyne* (Mnemosyne Atlas) in 1924, a vast pictorial atlas he left unfinished in 1929, at the time of his death.

SV Philosopher Giorgio Agamben noted that Warburg once enigmatically defined *Mnemosyne* as "a ghost story for truly adult people."[1] I like this idea of the past as something spectral and transformative. What I find even more compelling is what Agamben goes on to say: "If one considers the function that he assigned to the image as the organ of social memory and the 'engram' of a culture's spiritual tensions, one can understand what he meant: his 'atlas' was a kind of gigantic condenser that

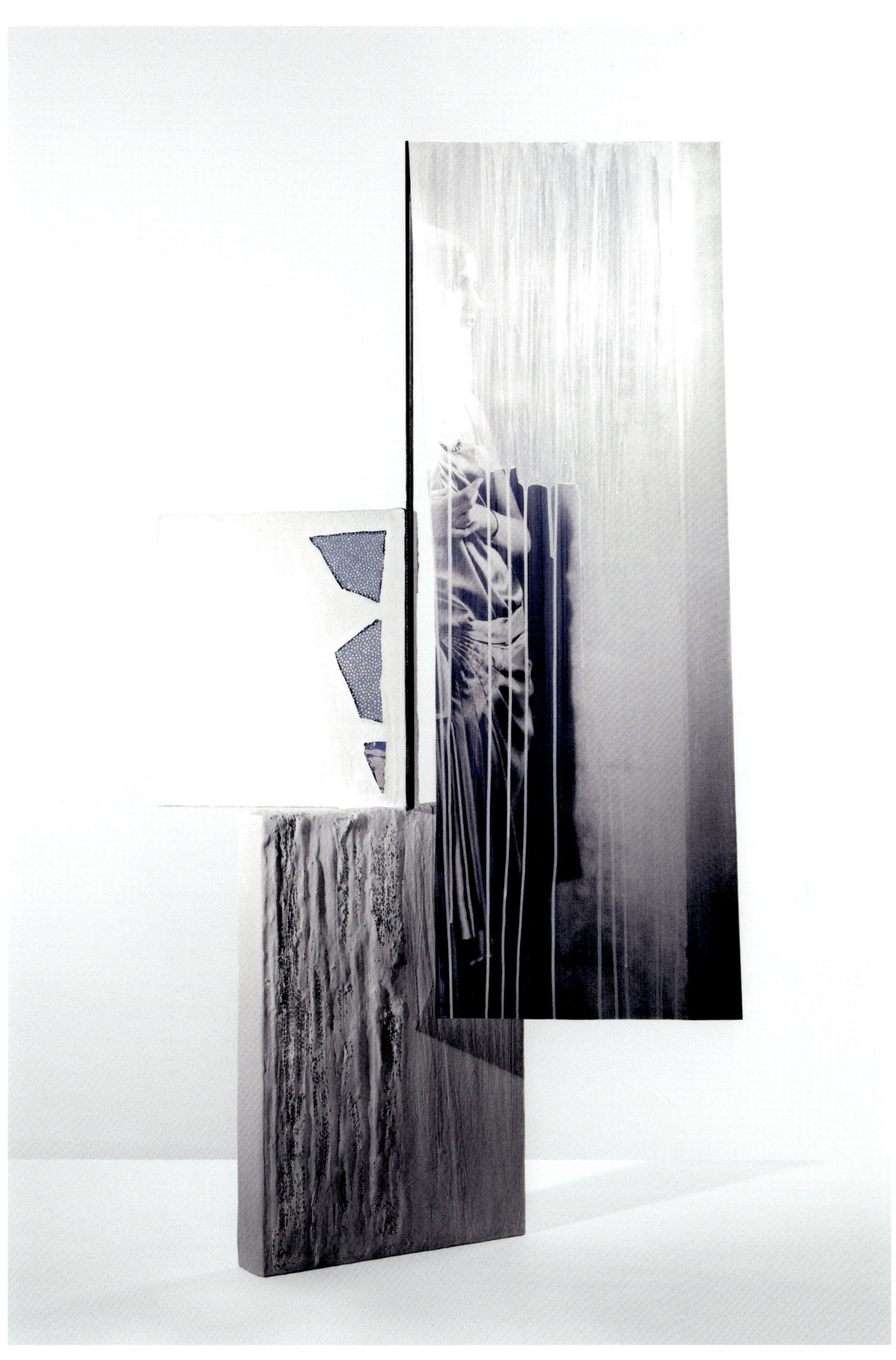

After, 2009

gathered together all the energetic currents that had animated and continued to animate Europe's memory, taking form in its 'ghosts.'"[2] Despite the historical specificity of Agamben's description, I translated this into contemporary terms, and the condenser he refers to immediately in my mind becomes the Internet.

RM There are analogue parallels. The physical architecture of the *Bilderatlas Mnemosyne* comprised seventy-nine large screens covered with black fabric. Between ten to thirty photographs were affixed to each screen. Disparate in their sources—artworks, advertisements, postage stamps, and newspaper clippings—they were grouped around shared themes, or around the formulas of emotional style that Warburg called *Pathosformel*. These images were formally related but separated by centuries of culture. Warburg's primary aim was to bring into focus recurrent motifs, "movement" or "performance," for example, based on gestural and physiognomic formulas.

SV This type of typology of recurring motifs that cut across centuries, which you just mapped out, combined with the way that Warburg physically layered his black-and-white images upon black fields of canvas, presaged the current logic around interfaces where there is no hierarchy and images are the dominant form of communication.

RM Can you expand on that idea as it relates to specific bodies of work? Your four-panel *A Composition for Detroit* (2009), which was included in the *New Photography 2009: Walead Beshty, Daniel Gordon, Leslie Hewitt, Carter Mull, Sterling Ruby, Sara VanDerBeek* [September 30, 2009, to January 11, 2010] exhibition at MoMA, comes to mind in terms of a relational montage of images and the cultural connections between them.

SV I was thinking about the variability of images and their sliding significance within our collective memory when making this and earlier works such as *Delaunay*. Pragmatically, I was also thinking about the way most of us work now—on a screen, often layered with a divergent array of windows, icons, and messages. Also both Warburg's *Bilderatlas Mnemosyne* and Edward Steichen's 1955 design for *The Family of Man* exhibition at MoMA [January 24 to May 8, 1955], which famously plied photographs into an immersive environment, were in my peripheral view.

More significantly, *A Composition for Detroit* was made after an initial visit to Detroit, at the height of the economic crisis in the United States. Designed as one work, it consists of four large-scale constructions resting in a dark blue, almost black field, captured and printed as four large photographs. The decision to make a single work that moved in time from back to front and from left to right in a broken syncopation resulted from my experience photographing factory buildings in various states of decline around that city. Images by artists who had influenced my approach to this project, such as Walker Evans, as well as photojournalists and other concerned photographers like Leonard Freed were interspersed with details from publications covering the 1968 riots that had occurred in Detroit. I used certain details from these pictures in still-life images I photographed and then reincorporated these images into the larger constructions. Re-photographing the works of others as well as my own—

this echoing—was an attempt at translating the continual impact of past events on the present state of the city and, for that matter, the country as a whole. Detroit, as well as Baltimore and Cleveland where I have subsequently worked, have become visible markers of how divisions within class and race can be starkly illustrated via the dividing lines of urban decay. The lasting impact of the Detroit riots could be felt throughout all parts of the city some forty years later. *A Composition for Detroit* was the first work that included images I had taken directly on site. It has since changed the way I work. From this initial experience of research via a direct physical engagement with a place and a community, I have increasingly captured research- and site-based images as a means of engendering studio-based work.

While I had created larger screen-like constructions prior to this work, *A Composition for Detroit* felt like a culmination of various experiments in simultaneity, collage, and constructed photography. In particular, *The Principle of Superimposition II* (2008) was a predecessor. Created at the same time as *Delaunay,* I built a screen structure modeled on a folding screen designed by architect Eileen Gray and photographed it set against a black seamless backdrop. On each section of the screen I placed a singular image, or a collage made with strips of images layered diagonally across the panel, like a filmic cross-fade made concrete. Multiple moments, cultures, and perspectives were combined to create a shifting screen of memory in which both the personal and the universal rest in equal scale with one another and moments from the past and present rise and recede in the dark theatrical space of consciousness.

RM Your idea of a "filmic cross-fade made concrete" is a compelling description, and in many ways this process you described is analogous to the shifting role that photography has played throughout history as a medium for cataloging existence.

SV Steichen and Warburg are only two examples of the ways that photography has been inextricably linked to documenting "civilization." How do you think what has been characterized as the medium's democratic nature is shaping our sense of the world and how we document culture as a whole?

RM Photography is a populist medium: it belongs as much to amateurs as to professionals. Walt Whitman said that photography provided America with a new, democratic art form. When used as a tool for self-representation, it has agency. But, in speaking of Warburg and Steichen, I think that they had different intentions and so was the reception of their ideas. It's true that both devised specific layouts that invited a new way of reading photographs. Their layouts were structured like visual essays, a hybrid genre of critically self-reflexive commentary and images. Warburg and Steichen were both keen in supplanting the slow-paced linearity of art-historical text with the fast-paced jump cut of visual montage. Your work, whether *A Composition for Detroit* or *Delaunay,* does this by offering similar jumps, cuts, and repetitions. Constituted as potential atlases of pictures within pictures, these works suggest that there is no closure in the interpretation of the history of art. Your associative approach to image-making seems to ask, "Is photography an object, an image, or a way of looking?"

SV Your reading of those works feels apt. Whitman—his particular meter often jumping from intimate exacting moments to more nebulous grand pictures of existence in a single poem—fascinates me. I often think about how my approach to images could emulate a practice such as his. I agree that this line of inquiry you set up—Is photography an object, an image, or a way of looking?—remains pressing within contemporary photography. How do you see the critical reception of Steichen's *The Family of Man* factoring into more recent photography discourse?

RM Made after World War II, *The Family of Man* enjoyed huge popular success, attracting some nine million viewers. It traveled around the nation and, thanks to the United States Information Agency, also internationally to thirty-seven countries. Yet, a number of critics from Roland Barthes to John Berger denounced the show as American mythology and an act of cultural colonialism. It is only recently that theoreticians such as Ariella Azoulay have been reevaluating the exhibition's universalizing potential through the lens of democracy and human rights. In 2011, *The Family of Man* became the subject of a conference in Arles, its contents published by the LUMA Foundation, the Center for Curatorial Studies at Bard College, and Sternberg Press. The book, titled *The Human Snapshot,* is a collection of essays that foregrounds the idea of a "citizenry of photography."

SV And how would you frame Warburg in relation to this type of reevaluation?

RM Warburg, as mentioned, was preoccupied with the role of photography in documenting civilization. Yet, his encyclopedic project was not conceived in response to contemporary history. Nor was Warburg attempting to build, as Steichen did, a linear presentation of history, or rather narration, through images—from lovers, to childbirth, to household and careers, then to death, and finally, full cycle, back to children in the end. Instead, his project was intended to activate the viewer's memory of past art history, or what he called "the afterlife of antiquity." Warburg called the *Bilderatlas Mnemosyne* an "iconography of intervals," since it was based on historical anachronisms and discontinuities. Warburg's nonlinear, relational montage of images was intended to formulate an art history without artistic progress from one image to the other. He was one of the first to organize the presentation of large groups of photographs by editing them into flexible arrangements or montage-like sequences. It's a sensibility your work shares: activating the images' latent effects through resonating juxtapositions, and orchestrating the construction of a new temporality paced by looking at an assembled sculptural installation made of a heterogeneous mix of images.

SV "Activating latent effects," as you elegantly described, was central to my exhibition *To Think of Time* at the Whitney Museum of American Art [September 17 to December 5, 2010], where I created three hangings of photographs based on three of Whitman's poems. Central to this exhibition was *The Sleepers,* in which still lifes of hand-cast and sometimes painted sculptures that I made in the studio were mixed in with close-up views of the scarred surfaces of nine different foundations I photographed in the Lower Ninth Ward in New Orleans that same year. Although each piece was an autonomous image, this series, perhaps even more than the layered constructions we have discussed, presented the sequencing of images in direct relation to their spatial locale in both a poetic and filmic manner. As a montage, the three hangings appeared much more linear than pieces I had made previously if you "read" the images from left to right around the room. When I took a group of high school students that I was working with at the time through the show, I learned that most people weren't starting at the first poem. They entered the room at various angles and, in a way, made up their own poem that often ran opposite to the prescribed path I had imagined for the viewer. Over the course of the exhibition, I began to consider it more of an evolving and fractured montage that changed upon each person's individual viewing experience. *Foundation, Deslonde Street* (2013) from this series is particularly important to me. Its surface conveys a whole course of human construction moving from the remnants of pictographs or fragmented floors at archaeological sites to that of contemporary buildings and homes in which the outlines of standardized materials and measures are apparent. All that remained were the traces and outlines embedded in the concrete, marking a traumatic past and also literally providing the foundation for yet unrealized activity.

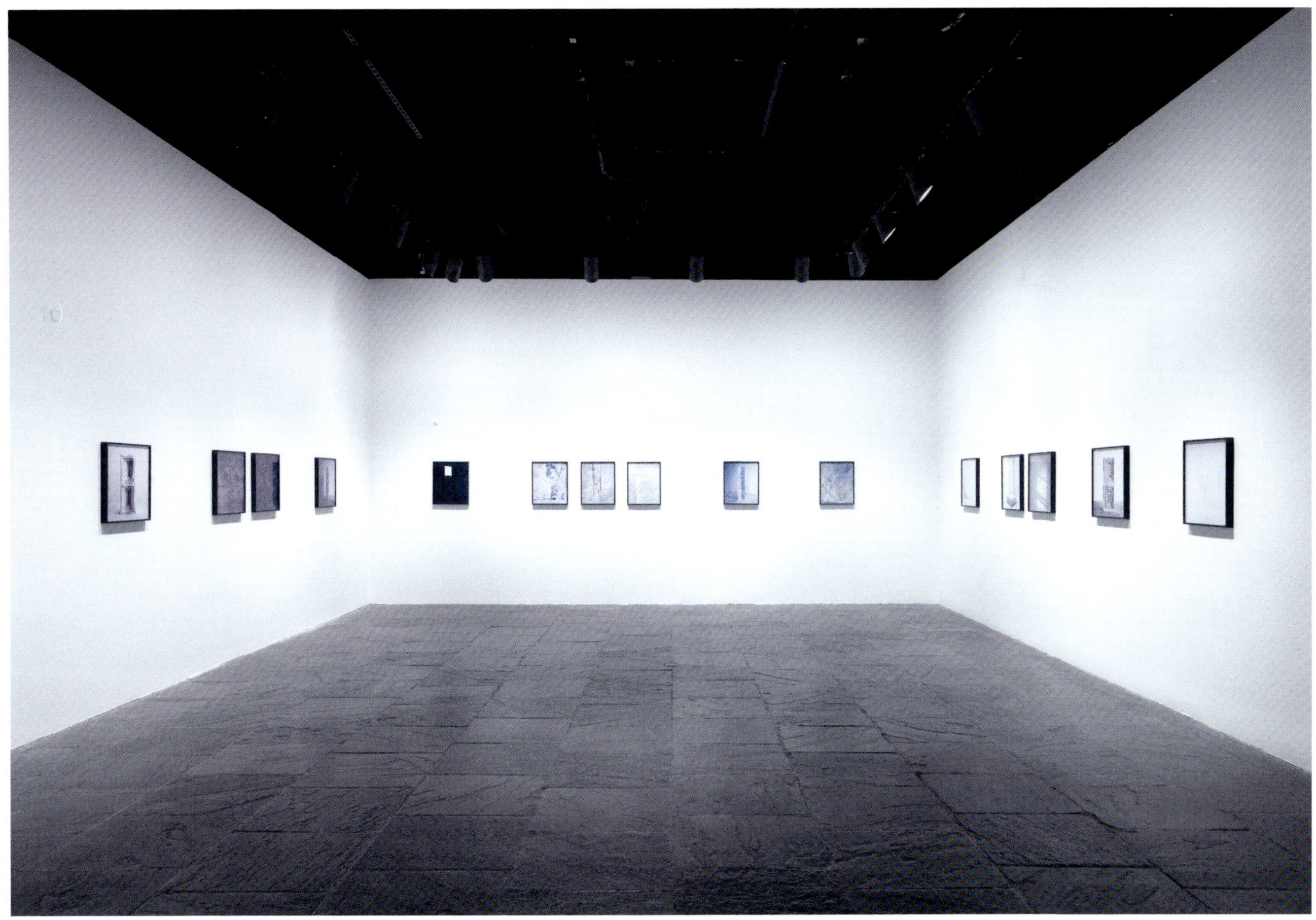

Installation view, *To Think of Time,* Whitney Museum of American Art, New York, 2010

The physicality of photographic montage was foregrounded in your essay for the catalogue that accompanied your MoMA exhibition *The Original Copy: Photography of Sculpture, 1839 to Today* [August 1 to November 1, 2010]. You discuss montage as "an organizational system based on a fragmentary, composite syntax of pictures culled from newspapers and magazines."[3] Montage—its use, application, and our understanding of it today in the early part of the twenty-first century—seems to have shifted along with the technological changes that are impacting the larger media landscape.

RM Hannah Höch, like other artists working with photomontage early on, including George Grosz, John Heartfield, Raoul Hausmann, and Gustav Klutsis, realized the activist power of this new medium. Höch, for one, used photomontage to examine mass-media representations of women in post–World War I Germany. Her politics engaged race and ethnography, and a prevailing theme in her work was the tension between the sexually liberated *Neue Frau* (New Woman), whose androgynous look reflected the period's deconstruction of rigid masculine and feminine identities, and the image of idealized femininity.

The role of photomontage in shaping mass consciousness only intensified after World War II and peaked during the period of the Vietnam War. Höch's critique of the clichés of mass-media representation proved to have had a lasting influence on women artists, specifically on the generation emerging in the nineteen-seventies and early eighties.

SV That moment of the seventies and early eighties remains vital yet often overlooked. Whose work in particular do you think takes up the earlier politics of photomontage?

RM I am thinking of Martha Rosler's photomontage series *House Beautiful: Bringing the War Home* (1967–72) as part of her antiwar and feminist activism, in which the artist spliced images of Vietnamese citizens maimed in the war, from photographs published in *Life* magazine, into images of the homes of affluent Americans, from the pages of *House Beautiful,* thus making viewers reevaluate what she called the "here" and "there" of the world situation. I am not sure if photomontage—whether digital or analogue—has the same political inflection today. In the age of the Internet, it has certainly allowed for a conceptual shift in the understanding of what a picture can be. Reality now widely consists of images. This means that one cannot even begin to understand reality without understanding forms of visual montage.

SV Martha Rosler's work is undeniably powerful. For the reasons you just enumerated, I included her 1982 video *Martha Rosler Reads Vogue* in a show I organized at Guild & Greyshkul in 2008. It was called *The Human Face Is a Monument* and was developed around artists—primarily female—working with the figure. Central to the exhibition was a work by Sarah Charlesworth titled *Figure Drawings* (1988/2008). I helped Sarah to produce this work for the exhibition after a number of conversations with her about her participation in this context. She had the idea originally in 1988 and, in what I thought was a really brave move, returned to the idea and realized it for the show. This experience is reflective of the long-standing relationship I had with Sarah personally—through our intimate discussions about art, our practices, and our lives, as well as the lessons I gleaned from her work that continue to be a reference point. Sarah's particular approach to found imagery and her subtle and effective use of collage in works like those from her *Objects of Desire* series from 1983–88, for example, demand close and careful looking. When you move in on a visual detail, like the hard cut edge of the alluring blonde hair pictured in *Blonde* (1983–84), you are then immediately hit with its violence. And simultaneously, a void and aching is conveyed by that cut. Sarah's work turns on the precarious ways that presence and absence struggle to find a sense of balance—albeit one that remains tensional. It's an affective balance that I find can appear provocative as well as haunting and something I strive for in my own work. Both of these women and also Barbara Kasten have been incredibly influential on my thinking and my approach to image-making.

RM I'd be curious to hear you speak of the ways you enlist earlier photo-cinematic techniques. It seems to me that László Moholy-Nagy's and Man Ray's experiments with multiple negatives and photographic montages inform your practice. Their experimentation with photographs provoked a reimagining of the visual experience of objects. You use photography to call into question the notion of traditional sculpture by assembling objects and images as subjects for pictures that amplify a sense of photogenic porosity. Is photography a tool to construe the sculptural? And, what about the space of sculpture and choreography in your work?

SV It would be disingenuous for any artist working with the abstract qualities of photography in the current moment to not feel indebted to the early experiments of Moholy-Nagy and Man Ray, myself included. While they definitely inform my practice, it's important to think about how those processes and images from the early part of the twentieth century have been mediated by other artists. I recently read in Matthew Witkovsky's 2011 essay "The Unfixed Photography" that Bruce Nauman, having seen a retrospective of Man Ray's work in Los Angeles in 1966, equally admired the diversity of his practice. What I found significant was this abutting of two formative eras that have great resonance now for myself and others and the implied sense of accumulation and feedback in that moment of recognition on behalf of Nauman. Yet there was also a sense of passage and a movement from one way of working to another.

Inherent within this and our discussion of montage is a question of physicality and materiality. We are moving from the physical gestures involved in a nineteenth- and twentieth-century-based notion of image-making, such as the actions of capturing an image on a negative or collaging images via multiple negatives, or other earlier photographic processes such as silkscreens, photo static/lithographic prints, et cetera, to that of the present moment. We seem to be somewhere between the tangible object and the ephemeral accumulation of information, and with this, the notion of the physical image or the image as a resulting artifact of a physical process (performative or otherwise) takes on new meaning.

RM That's an interesting point. It relates to ideas teased out in one of the most recent exhibitions I co-curated at MoMA, *Ocean of Images: New Photography 2015* [November 7, 2015, to March 20, 2016], which, as its title points out, refers to the Internet as a vortex of images, a site of piracy, but also to what Jeff Wall called in a text from 1989 "liquid intelligence."[4] Photography as liquid, in flux, performative, not fixed. Some of the most promising experiments today engage photography as an unfixed field where digital and analogue, virtual and real, online and offline cross over. There are various ways of experiencing the world: through images that are born digitally, made with scanners or lenses in the studio or the outside world, presented as still or moving pictures, remixed online, or morphed into three-dimensional objects.

SV Your point underscores what I think of as a shifting sense of the physical, which at times acts as a stand-in for the actual amongst the mediation inherent within photographic capture. The photographic then in turn takes on aspects of the virtual, of the imagination, and of the subconscious, and with that I am intrigued by what are the many questions and problems that the mixing of photography and sculpture poses. Working with and against notions of documentation both inside and outside of my studio, I have been increasingly interested in pushing the printing and presentation of my final images into a nexus of two- and three-dimensional approaches. These works can then operate as a portal between an unfinished past and a reopened future.

RM Sometimes you capture sculptures, sometimes you construct them, and sometimes you examine the space between sculpture and photography. In all cases, and operating within a future anterior tense, you want to make palpable the tension between object and image. Can you speak of the process through which you choreograph an image?

SV The term choreography precisely addresses the sense of movement that occurs when an image is transformed. It is not just the arrangement of forms within a compo-

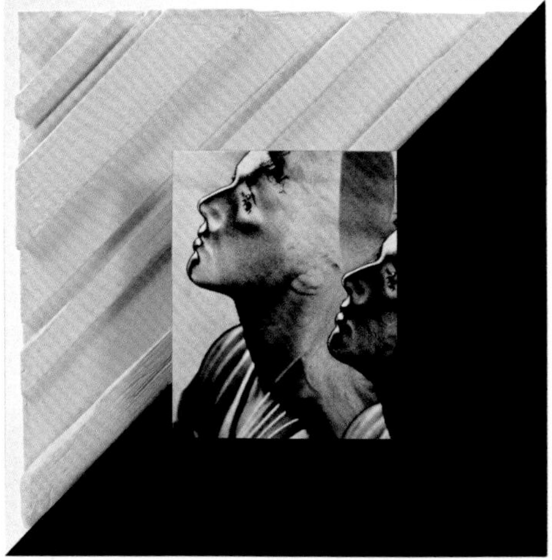

Four Photographers, 2008 (detail)

Four Photographers, 2008

sition or the placing of objects and images within a room that is choreographed, but the whole process has become about balance—the balance of the actual and the imagined.

Dance as a practice as well as dancers—as figures and forms—foreground this issue of balance within my own images. It is also an acknowledgment of the important historical relationship that dance has to considerations of minimalism, performance, and exhibition design. One reason is that dance, more than theater's narrative forms, offers a set of vocabularies to articulate what I think of as a spatial organization of interaction. This is a reference to the structure and rigor of dance mixed with the chance aspects of collaboration, the sense of gravity inherent in the body, and the importance of rhythm and timing as these elements coalesce to create the final work. I am also drawn to dance for the way the body becomes something other—more sculptural yet mobile.

RM We have spoken a few times in the past about Constantin Brancusi, who often choreographed his sculptures for the camera. Since the early nineteen-twenties, his studio space was articulated around hybrid configurations that he called *groupes mobiles* (mobile groups), each comprising several pieces of sculpture, bases, and pedestals grouped in proximity.

Pushing photography against its grain, Brancusi developed an aesthetic antithetical to the usual photographic standards. According to Man Ray, he often made out-of-focus, over- or underexposed, scratched and spotty prints, insisting that this is the way his work should be reproduced. In search of transparency, kineticism, and infinity, Brancusi used photography and polishing techniques to dematerialize the

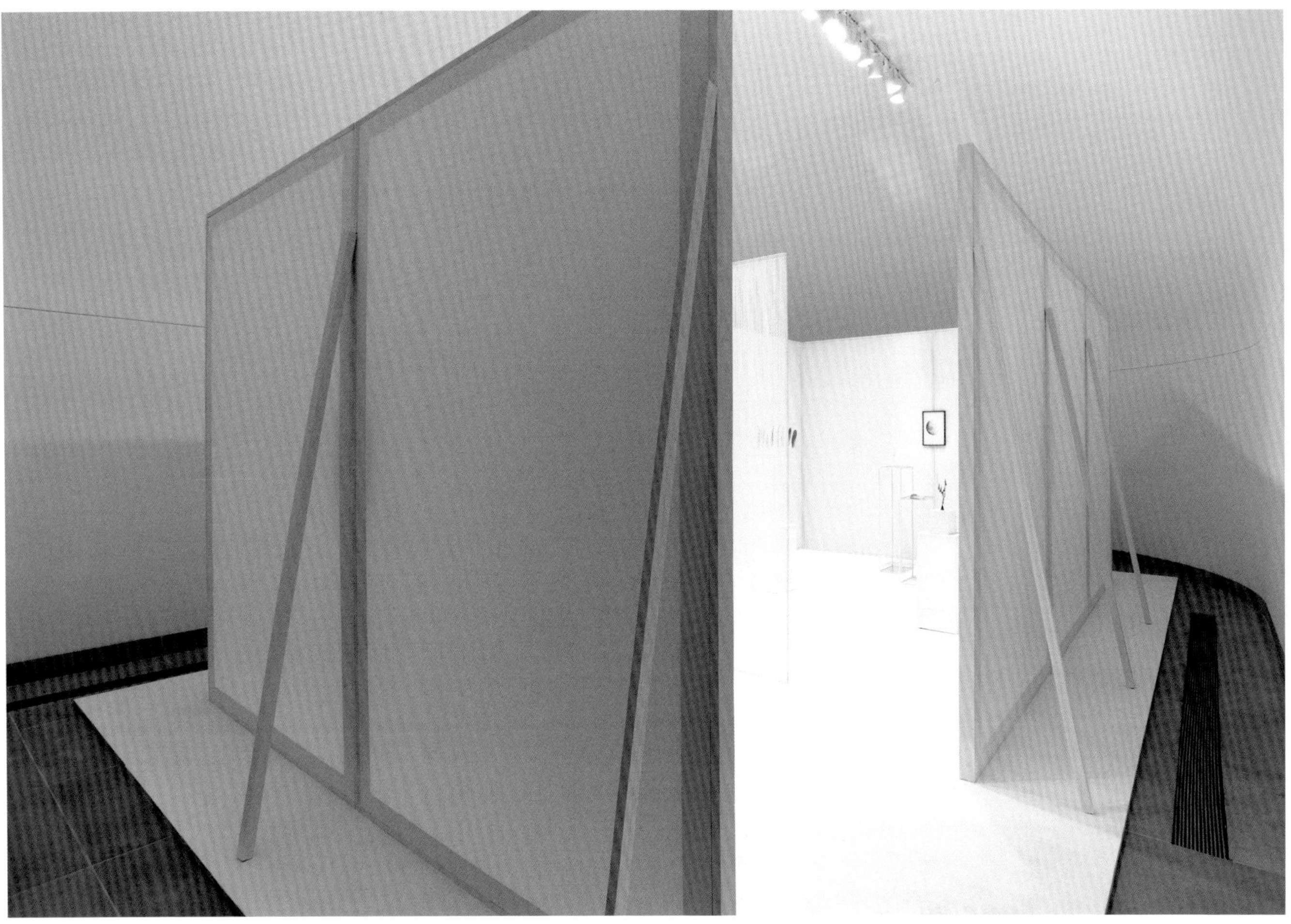

Installation view, *Hammer Projects*, Hammer Museum, Los Angeles, 2011

static, monolithic materiality of traditional sculpture. There are several important strategies in his work. One is the way he amplified the reflection of light when photographing his polished bronzes. Known as *photos radieuses* (radiant photos), these pictures are characterized by flashes of light that explode the sculptural gestalt.

SV The radiant photos are remarkable, and Brancusi's use of light to both record and disrupt or, as you put it so powerfully, "explode" the sculptural gestalt is very significant. In certain ways, it is making the tangible intangible and vice versa, so that the image is continually oscillating—shape-shifting, forming, and re-forming itself as we observe it.

RM This is an important aspect for the contemporary generation. Think of an artist like Liz Deschenes and the metallurgic surfaces of her photograms. Liz's photograms taken by moonlight or daylight are reminiscent of direct-positive daguerreotypes. Or, Lisa Oppenheim whose solarized photographs of fires are reminiscent of Alfred Stieglitz's *Equivalents,* pictures of clouds taken in the twenties and thirties. Similarly, your *Metal Mirror (Magia Naturalis)* series from 2013, framed in mirrored glass, creatively engages with abstraction and representation.

SV The phenomenological aspects involved when viewing both Liz's and Lisa's works are particularly strong. Having recently viewed a collection of William Henry Fox Talbot salt prints, in which the images rise and recede with a similar illegibility to the *photos radieuses,* suggests that abstraction and transformation have always been at the root of photography even when the motivation, such as Fox Talbot's, was to document the world in detail. Considering a synergistic practice such as Brancusi's, or for that matter Liz's, can you talk about how you think this idea of the metamorphic, or of staging, has informed contemporary installation practices?

RM Clearly Brancusi envisioned his studio as a site-specific installation. The artist Scott Burton, in his essay "My Brancusi" (1989), called Brancusi's studio a "Duchampian set."[5] This is a perceptive analogy, justifying Brancusi's special interest in Duchamp's *Boîte-en-valise (de ou par Marcel Duchamp ou Rrose Sélavy)* (1936–41), a miniature proxy for the artist's studio, containing reproductions of many of Duchamp's works and one original. Brancusi's pictures of his studio cast light on how his works should be understood. Assembling and reassembling his sculptures for the camera, he transformed each unique work into multiples. This is another aspect of specific interest to contemporary artists. I am here thinking of Jason Rhoades's *My Brother/ Brancuzi* [*sic*], an installation presented at the Whitney Museum in 1995.

SV Though both Jason Rhoades and Scott Burton used specific materials to punctuate the space for the viewer, I would say that my own strategies for exhibitions and set perspectives are more aligned with the ways that Liz works. She engages with the poetics of a space as exemplified by her recent exhibitions at the Walker Art Center [November 22, 2015, to October 18, 2015] and Mass MoCA [May 23, 2015, to April 24, 2016], both of which I had the privilege to see and experience. But I don't feel you can disregard the glut of stuff that surrounds us even in the virtual corners of our world. Even though I veer away from it in my own work, I like the intentional sloppiness that makes Jason Rhoades's emotive accumulations of goods feel even more resonant today.

RM In one interview with Anne Ellegood about your 2011 exhibition at the Hammer Museum, you referred to the exhibition space as a camera.[6] How does this inform the ways in which you present and position your work?

SV I consider closely the larger context surrounding a particular exhibition space. Sometimes in a more literal translation I use doorways to frame a sculpture. At the Hammer, and many times since, I have used white washes of paint to collapse or merge a three-dimensional object into or within its environment. The Hammer project was the first instance where I decided to show three-dimensional objects. I wanted to retain certain transformative qualities that were inherent within the still-life images I had created in the past.

RM The installation at the Hammer was a room within a room, akin to a theatrical set.

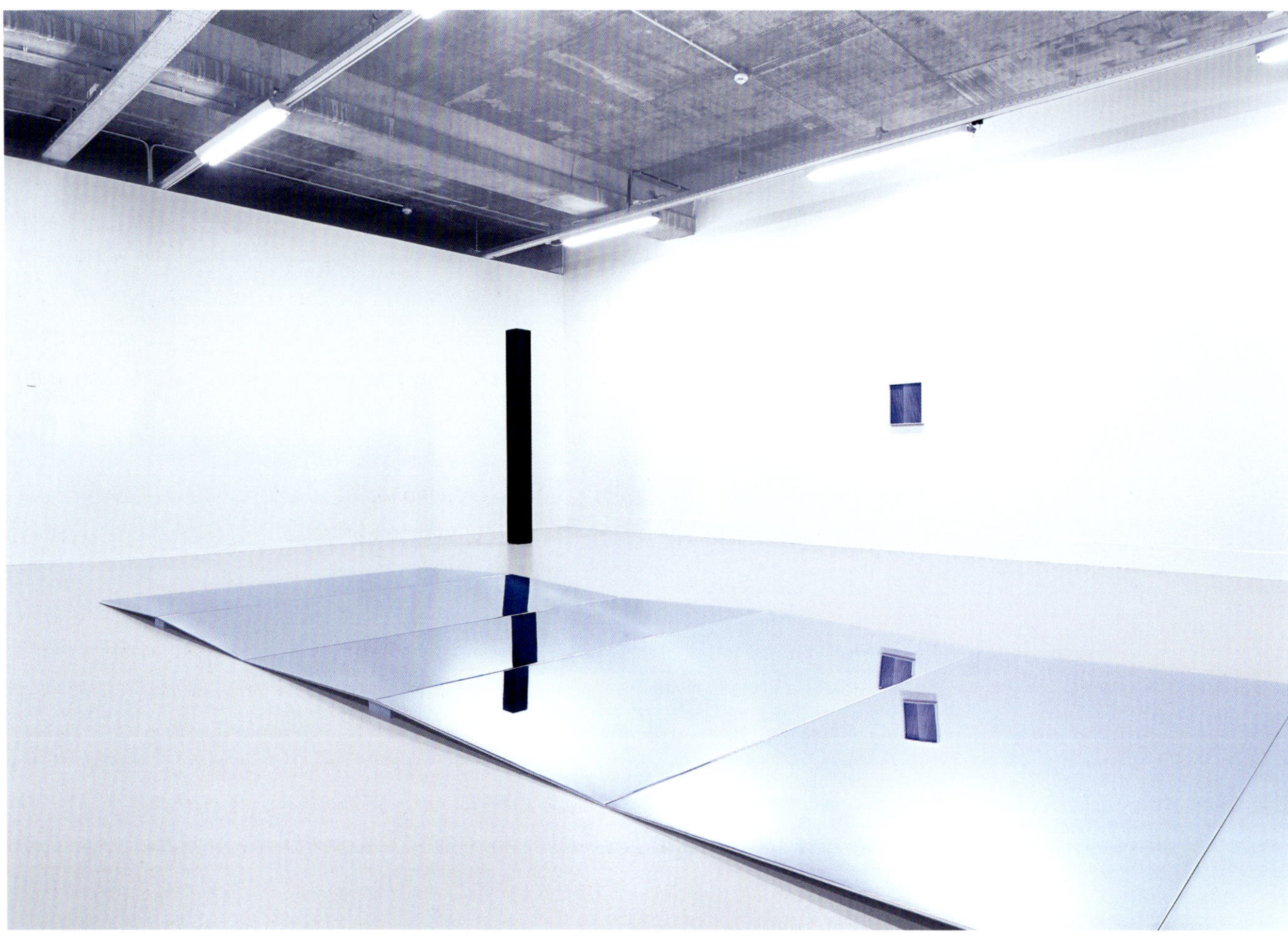

Installation view, *Sensory Spaces 6*, Museum Boijmans Van Beuningen, Rotterdam, 2015

SV While the space at the Hammer was clearly delineated by the set construction, the walls were translucent, the floor bounced light, and the site remained visually permeable.

RM Within that setting everything was precisely staged: the picture *Western Costume, Aurora* (2011), taken at the Western Costume in Burbank, California, was presented next to sculptural works, such as *Four Directions* (2011), informed by totemic forms as well as modernist designs by Frank Lloyd Wright and Jean-Michel Frank. It seems that the exhibition design was particularly poignant in that instance.

SV It was crucial in that context and does continue to inform how I address the installation of an exhibition from the onset of a project. I develop the images and the sculptures in tandem and in response to one another in the hopes of creating a total and resolved relationship. That being said, I am still experimenting. I learn a great deal with every show and very much abide by John Dewey's tenet of learning through doing. Regardless, the vulnerability of figuring things out in real time can sometimes be challenging. The Hammer project was akin to opening my intimate studio practice to the public. And while I clearly strive for a type of formal convergence between the two, the disconnect between the images and the sculptures can also create a compelling in-between space for the viewer, of which I spoke earlier.

RM In your 2013 exhibition at Metro Pictures [May 2 to June 8, 2013], you paired images of antiquities photographed at various museums and archeological sites in several European cities with abstract cast concrete sculptures. Certain pictures were framed behind blue-tinted Plexiglas, which invite analogies to early cyanotype techniques, while others were colored during the printing process such as *Roman Woman I* (2013). In each case, you were expanding the images into three-dimensional objects. How do you see the relationship between images and objects in this particular arrangement?

SV When photographing these ancient figures in person I was struck by the remaining elements of paint on their faces and bodies that I had never noticed as clearly in reproduction. This spoke of their earlier state as polychromatic forms, as both image and object. As painted figures that were disseminated into the larger empire, they communicated ideals that have continued to inform our sense of beauty, proportion, and the female form to this day. In most of the museums where I was photographing, the figures were lit with focused display lights. These spaces often also had windows, the light from which caused the resulting images to have a contrasting mixture of color. While working with the images in my studio, I realized that by isolating and removing the yellow from the ambient light captured at these sites, I could colorize the figures and push them during the printing process to reach strong pink and purple tones reminiscent of their earlier polychromatic existence.

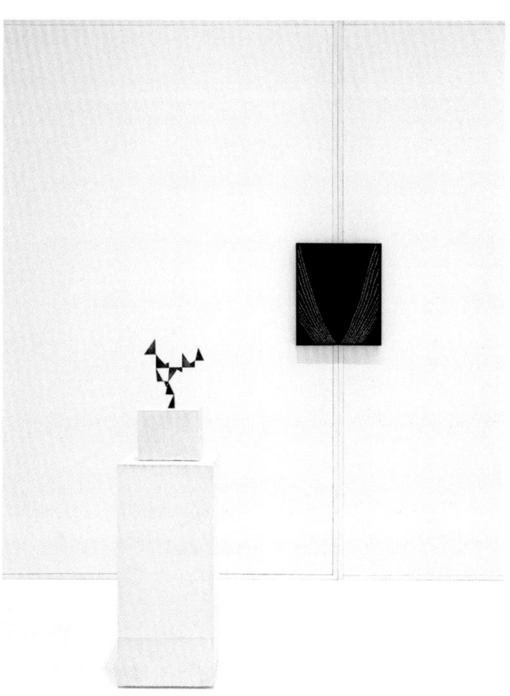

Western Costume, Aurora, 2011, installation view, *Hammer Projects*, Hammer Museum, 2011

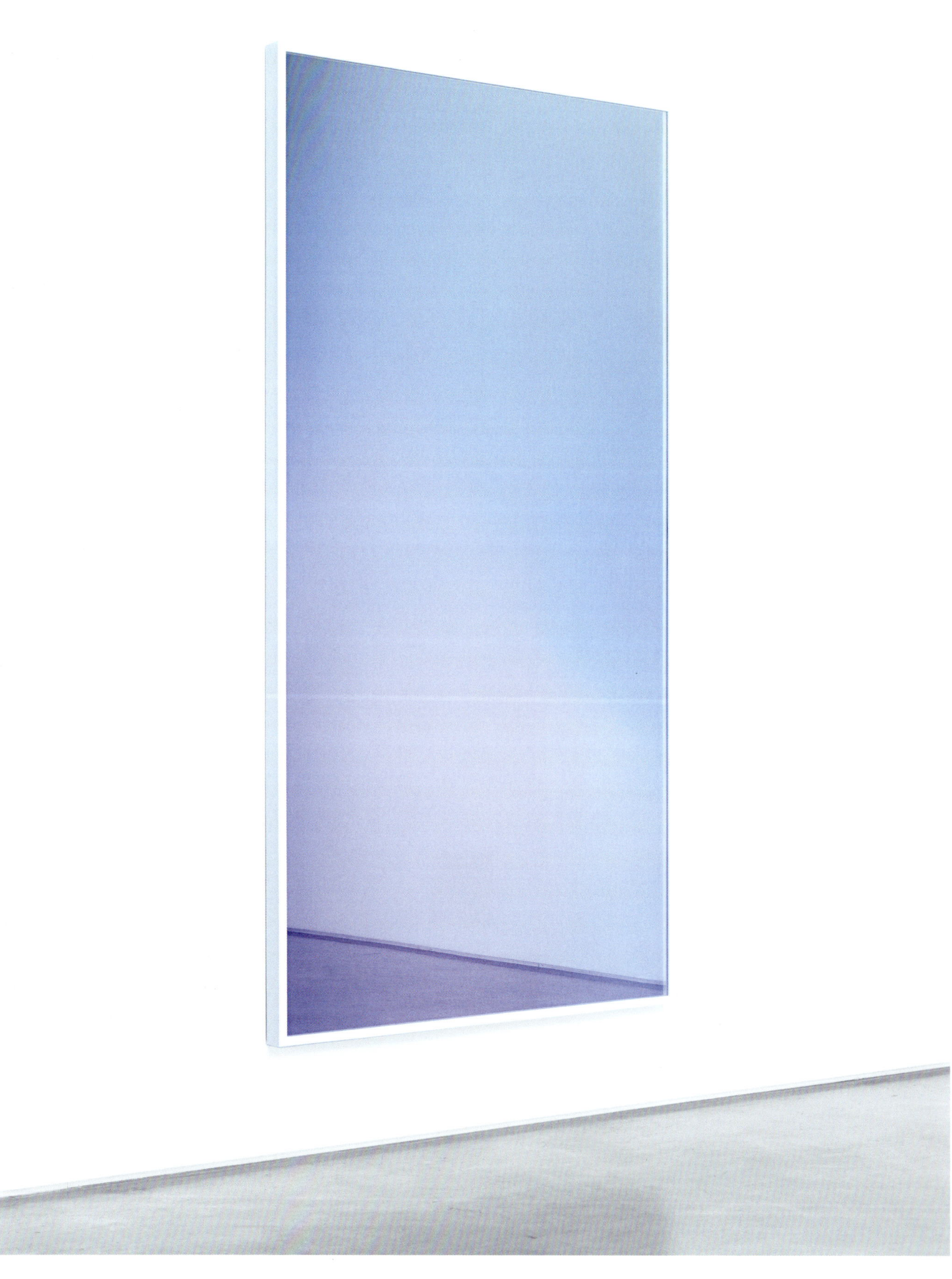

Metal Mirror VII (Magia Naturalis), 2013

In addition, the scale of the figures was usually different from what I had imagined them to be, and so I thought a great deal about scale and the body as both an abstract idea and as a physical measure of perception in this project as well. Central to the show were the eight mirrored works entitled *Metal Mirror (Magia Naturalis)* featuring details of an oxidized metal wall that had turned to a vibrant mix of iridescent pinks and purples. I had shot the images at dusk to further emphasize this transformational color field. The arrangement of the mirrored works, surrounding a central line of four modular concrete cast columns, referred to the historic palazzos in which I had photographed the figures and, more importantly, to a very specific moment I had experienced during my time in Rome. In their physicality, and shifting spectrum of light and dark, the *Metal Mirror (Magia Naturalis)* were installed to convey the weight of a setting sky against a group of ancient columns I had encountered at Ostia Antica. It was an experience in which the site, its texture, the forms amongst it, the light and time of day, seemed to coalesce into this dynamic combination of both the ancient and the modern in one succinct and powerful space. This installation was perhaps the closest I got to creating and staging a take on the "afterlife of antiquity."

Mirrors and mirroring effects are integral to photography. They appear in my work sometimes as props and in other ways as surfaces or mutable spaces, such as with these works from 2013, where the semitransparent mirrors were intended to capture, refract, and reflect subject and space, while also allowing the rust images to appear and disappear amongst the reflections. Currently, I am exploring this idea of mirroring via the transparent layering of color and form in a new series of still-life images in which new compositions are created using physical and photographic repetition.

Something I have been considering recently when moving between two- and three-dimensional work is how our sense of scale, as well as notions of the two mediums, have changed. With that my sense of the movement between the sculptural and the photographic has changed. When an image can be rendered (via a sequence of building, processing, and exporting information) and an object can be printed—collective notions and definitions of these mediums have then also been dissolved.

RM Can you elaborate on how these ideas play out in your technical process?

SV I still shoot on negative film, but by scanning my negatives and printing via a digital chromogenic process I exploit the strengths of both traditional and digital means of production. Much of the work I do digitally emulates the darkroom experiments of earlier movements such as multiple exposure and inverting images, or more contemporary color processes of dialing in and out colors as well as flashing film. Yet with some of my recent images of geometric forms, animation, filmic techniques, and digital rendering programs have become influential factors. Equally, I am thinking about the fluidity with which we move between the virtual and physical world in such that our understanding of the actual and the constructed have merged.

For example, I have been making color via adjustments in Photoshop, manipulating the way in which that program reads information by adjusting color on a pixel-by-pixel basis. I should also mention here that I am not alone when I am doing this. My printing process includes a number of important collaborations and conversations with two individuals in particular, Julie Pochron and Joshua Kolbo of Pochron Studios based in New York. The inherently collaborative nature of photographic printing is often not discussed, yet it plays a significant role in the final production of a work.

RM Can you expand on this notion of collaboration as it pertains to digital production?

SV With digital printing the assumption is that aesthetic decisions are automated and mechanized, leaving little room for the subtleties of translation and/or chance. My overall process runs quite counter to that presumption. While the digital offers a high degree of control, down to the pixel, I frequently push the process. I ask Julie to go beyond conventional printing techniques and print something for me that enters into a mysterious alchemical realm where we both cannot say exactly how the final color was achieved. For my most recent series of images, *Concrete Forms,* I gave her a selection of source material that ranged from images of pre-Columbian artifacts, modernist textiles, and that of a concrete wall I shot in Ventura, California, on a recent research trip. From these samples, we derived a sequence of color shifts that were as much about enmeshing various experiences within the compositions as they were about distinct color choices.

To turn this question back to you, Roxana, how do you navigate this shifting situation as an exhibition-maker? And how do you see these questions of transformation and migration across media manifesting themselves most urgently?

RM To take one example, in organizing *The Original Copy: Photography of Sculpture, 1839 to Today,* I focused on a specific class of visual images—images of sculpture—to consider how the one medium has been implicated in the creative reproduction and analysis of the other. Through crop, focus, angle of view, degree of close-up, and lighting, as well as through ex post facto techniques of darkroom manipulation, collage, montage, assemblage, and seriality, artists using the camera, I argued, have not only interpreted artworks but also created stunning reinventions of them.

Through its 177-year history, practitioners of photography have come from other fields—from science (Fox Talbot); from theater, or more specifically the diorama, a theatrical device that anticipated the motion picture (Daguerre); from painting (Fenton, Nègre, and many others); and from sculpture (Brancusi). Today the work of R. H. Quaytman, Rachel Harrison, Wade Guyton, Jimmy Robert, and Tris Vonna-Michell, among others, reminds us that photography remains open, unfixed, in flux, porous, and able to contaminate other practices, which brings up the question of performativity. What do you see to be the relationship between dance and photography? How does one inform the other?

SV The space in which I set things up for the camera is a performative space. The darkness in my camera surrounds the image like a proscenium. I am staging still lifes and working with light and color at the moment of capture and throughout the printing process in ways that borrow from scenography or cinematography. The stylization of

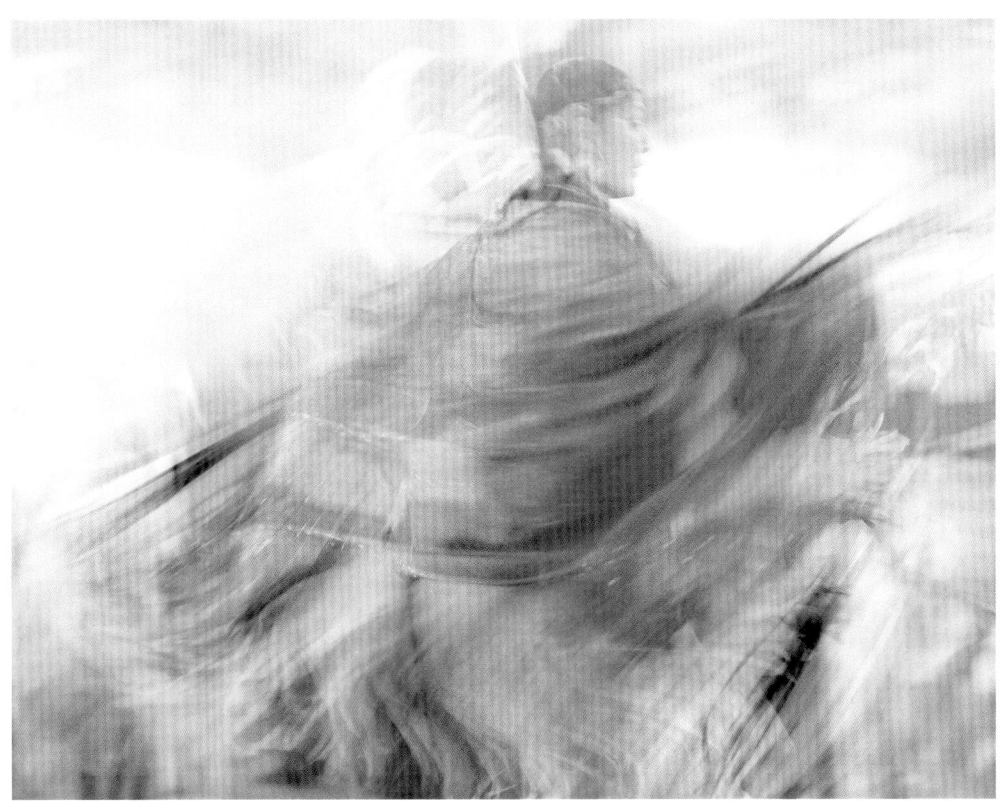

Sonya Flores, Fancy Shawl Dance, 2011

the image or the sculpture contributes to the overall narrative. Certain choices seek to implicate the arching ways in which artifacts have been displayed as part of a museological and thus historical impulse. I often think of how these techniques of display contribute to the mythologizing of historical progress and how, what, and who is and isn't included in the official tableaux. I am drawn to the markers of theatricality within this complex process. But this makes it seem like I cast a gimlet eye on the artifice of performance, and that is not the case at all. In many ways, my project at the Hammer was an attempt to slow down and even freeze certain live moments in order to exaggerate the weird duality of experience and performance.

RM Your photographs of "performance" are notably images of dancers; you've taken a series of photographs of Los Angeles-based dancer Sonya Flores and also photographed modern dancers for the series *Baltimore Dancers,* for instance. More specifically, you have discussed how your interest in Native American dance and regalia relates to a broader concern with performance.[7] How did this become manifest in the Hammer project?

SV I met Sonya Flores, a professional Native American dancer and instructor at a public powwow in Los Angeles. I approached her after watching her perform the fancy shawl dance. The term "perform" is fraught in this context as I have learned from Sonya and others. There is a spiritual aspect to certain dances, and though shared publicly they remain sacred. I was struck by the way the ribbons of the shawl enveloped Sonya's body and her figure intentionally became a moving mix of lines, shapes, and energy. I worked with her on several aspects of the project that was eventually installed at the Hammer Museum. I cast her face and used it in one of the sculptures. I filmed her at several locations and had her enact the fancy shawl dance in the room I had built in the Hammer gallery before the images and objects were installed. The room was arranged as a set, and the photographs and various abstract artifacts had the ineffable quality of awaiting the performance or perhaps a space in which a performance had just transpired.

In considering performativity, what do you think of the mediation of live performances such as those streamed online from an institution such as MoMA? How do they impact our understanding of human scale and what constitutes the "live"? How do these streamed events shape questions of accessibility and audience engagement? Or, in the case of the Google museum, how do they open exhibitions to a larger public that is both there and not there?

RM Everyone, it seems, needs an online presence, needs constant exposure. Visual culture theorist Jonathan Crary speaks of this in rather bleak terms in his book *24/7: Late Capitalism and the Ends of Sleep* (2014), noting that our society is always engaged, interfacing, interacting, communicating, responding, or processing within some telematic milieu. He calls this the connectionist paradigm. Yet communication is not the transmission of images but an ethos of sharing. While spectacle, Crary argues, is the expropriation of that possibility: the production of one-way communication.

Regarding the live streaming of performances, earlier this year I invited to one of MoMA's forums on contemporary photography Barbara Clausen, who teaches performance theory and history at the University of Québec, to discuss the relationship between the immediacy of performance versus its representation via photographic or filmic representation. She argued that what we perceive as "live" performance is always subject to mediatization since each performance is already built on the relationship between mediated and so-called authentic identities. Speaking of performance and your interest in dance, you have described "a connection between found movement and found materials."[8] Can you expand on this?

SV This is a reference to the influential way that Yvonne Rainer's early choreography emphasized the quotidian over the virtuosic, people walking down the street, for example, in groundbreaking works such as *Trio A* (1966). I drew on Rainer's vocabulary of everyday movement over the dramatic for my exhibition at the Baltimore Museum of Art [April 12 to September 20, 2015].

RM In *Steps* (2015) installed as part of that exhibition, you used horizontal marble planks that were the relative size—same height and width—of the steps leading up to the Baltimore Museum of Art's Neoclassical building.

SV In conceiving the Baltimore Museum of Art show, I kept returning to the marble steps. They are not specific to the BMA but are ubiquitous throughout Baltimore's historic districts. I isolated them as a sculptural form within the museum to underscore their liminal qualities—the ways that these steps often function as a space of

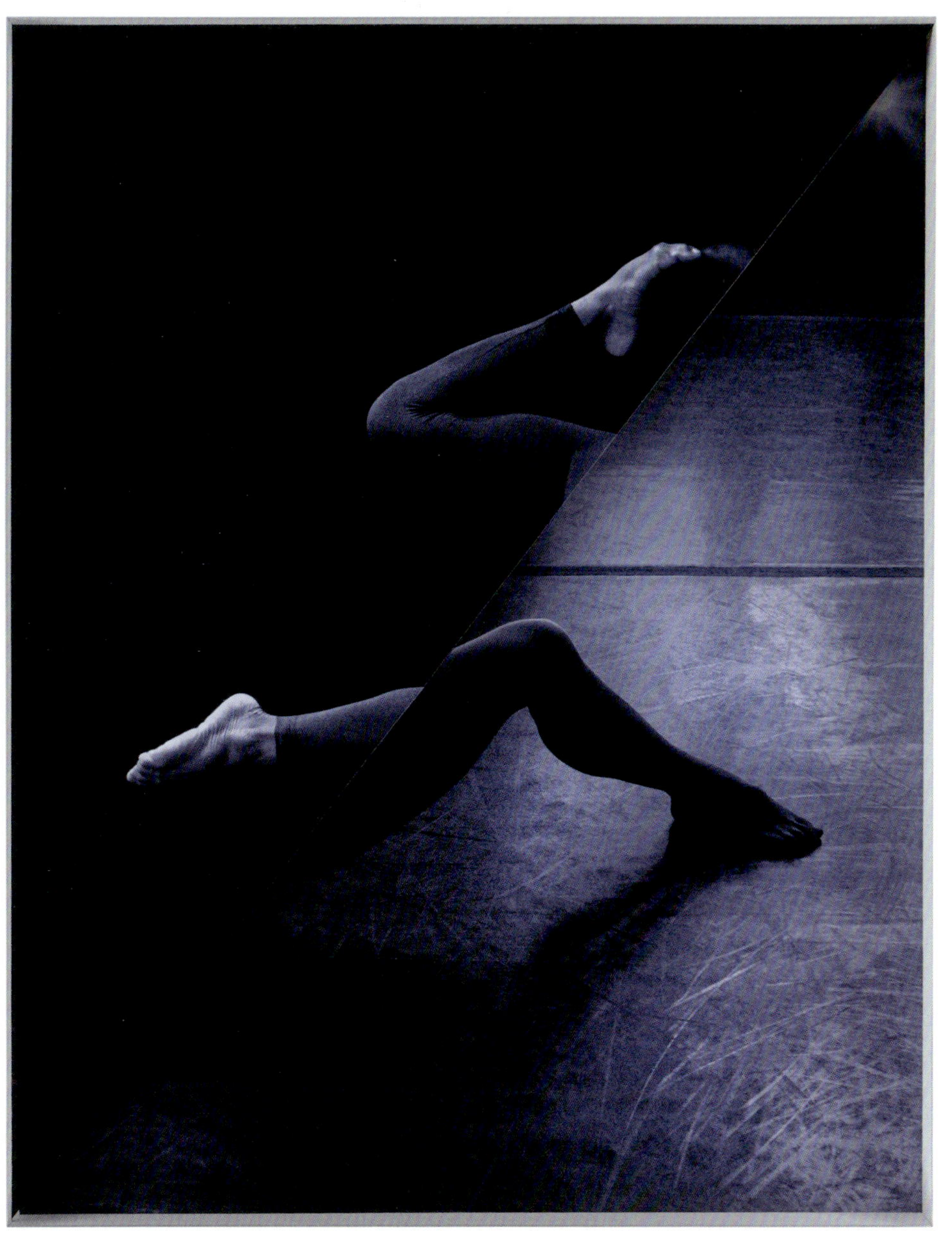

Orpheus, 2015

transference and transformation. Because these white marble steps are visible in almost every neighborhood of Baltimore—they appear on both stately grand buildings and on many of the city's row houses—they are one of the few recognizable and shared forms that transcend the city's civic and residential borders. And, more significantly, I see them as one of the few connectors across a racially and economically divided city. I laid six four-foot lengths of marble with the same proportions and scale of a normal riser end-on-end in the center of the gallery. This changed the up and down movement ascribed to their function to one that was linear like traversing across a plane as you would when you walk through the city. Their original utilitarian purpose remained, which I equated with Yvonne Rainer's isolation of specific gestures. I treated the length of the marble steps with a thin glaze of translucent white paint so that they were also like a memory object, a representation of the accretion of time and a conflation of experiences more than a literal translation of a step.

RM Your photographs of modern dancers have inspired the aesthetic decisions of your recent sculptures and assemblages, which are minimal and abstracted. This experiential dimension of your work made me think of Simone Forti's *Dance Constructions* (1960–61) or the way Scott Burton would incorporate furniture in his performances in the seventies, as he did, for instance, in his *Pastoral Chair Tableau* (1975), in which he staged modern chairs in front of a blue curtain. Can you speak more of your recent exhibition in Baltimore and the ways in which you connect human movements to the hard-edged sculptural work you are making now?

SV I saw Forti perform this last spring, and it was a strange, mesmerizing, and brave performance that, like her work overall, continues to deliberately oppose established modernist dance patterns of development and climax. Anne Truitt's columnar works and her distillation of form and color were also a point of reference in this exhibition, which took place next to a gallery that featured her work from the Baltimore Museum of Art's deep holdings. The triangular shapes used in *Modern Symbols* (2015) directly refer to Rudolf Laban's innovative notation system in which triangles convey the direction of movement within a dance. But the larger context of the city itself cannot be overstated. I was returning to my home, but that home was no longer there. The city was in a traumatized state and that sense of the hard edges of loss is in this work, too.

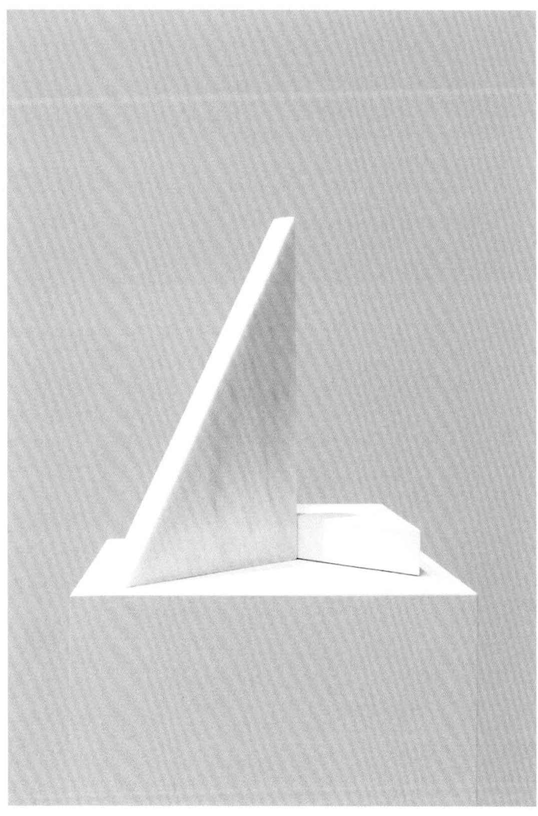

Modern Symbols, 2015 (detail)

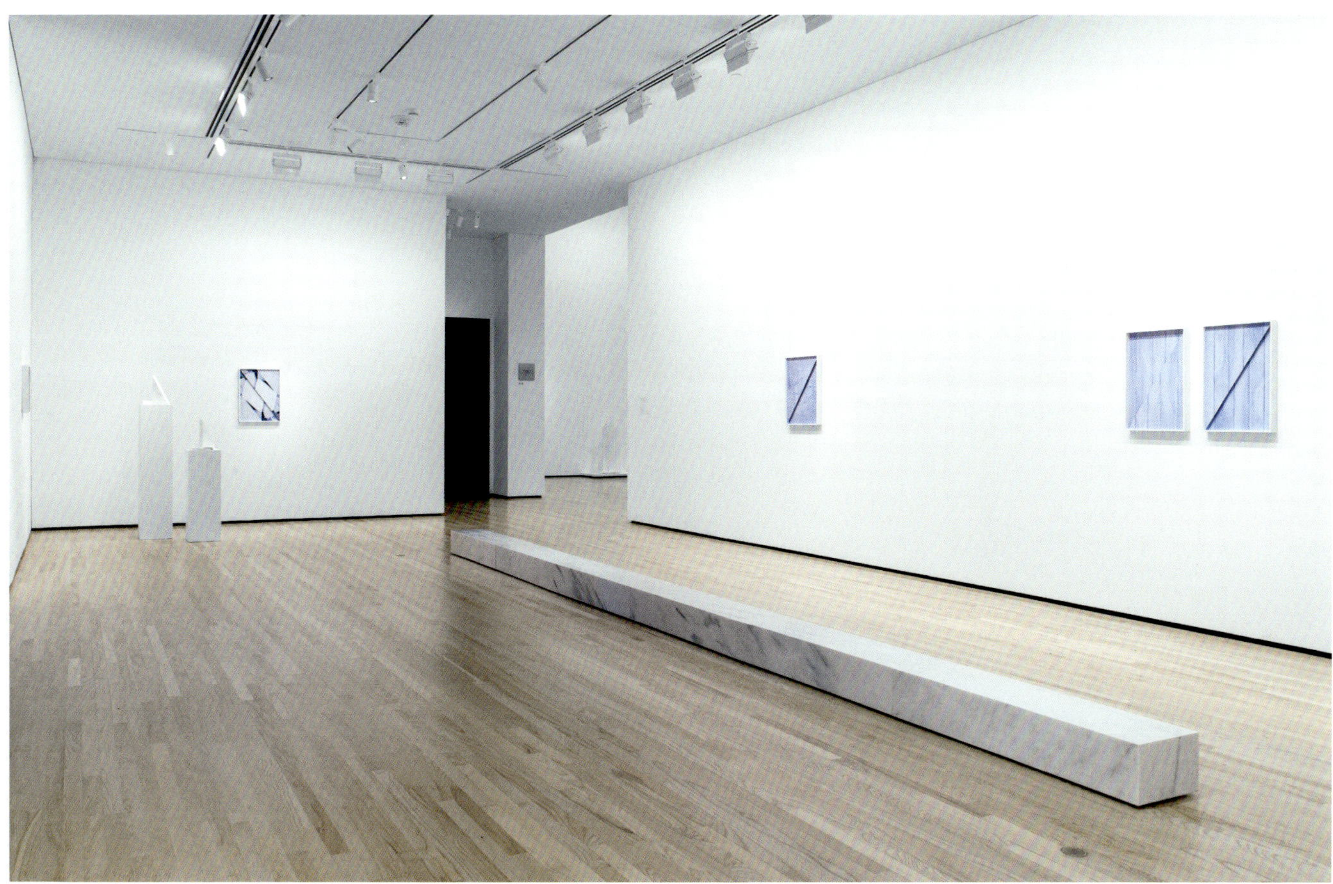

Front Room: Sara VanDerBeek, Baltimore Museum of Art, Baltimore, 2015

RM You have taken photographs in Baltimore, New Orleans, Rome, Detroit, and Rotterdam, among many other places. Does your sculpture relate to an interest in architectural and urban history? And how is this related in turn to the politics of a social landscape?

SV Like so many other artists and writers, I think of the contemporary urban environment as an expanded field of perception that is fragmented yet expansive in nature. It is a realm of simultaneity rendered in its most physical and psychological terms. Cities remain connection points, and therefore they are by definition sites of inclusion and exclusion. The death of Freddie Gray and the unrest that followed in Baltimore, as well as countless other unnecessary deaths in and around American cities, have drawn attention to the chasms in equality and rights that remain to be recognized, let alone resolved. Both convergent and discordant, cities by their very scale and density mirror and amplify our fractured existence. With my interest in the historical layering of cities, built up and eroded over time due to natural cycles as well as economic ones, I often photograph in abandoned or overlooked areas within city centers. Therefore, an important component of many of my projects has been to engage with groups—primarily students—to try and see how their own capture, cropping, and editing of images generates different forms of meaning.

Most recently, in conjunction with my exhibition at the Baltimore Museum of Art, I led a week-long workshop for high school seniors at the Baltimore School for the

Arts that concluded with a public exhibition reflecting their individual sense of the city's complex struggle during this difficult time. My experience at the Baltimore School of the Arts, first as a student myself and also coming back to do this workshop in 2015, combined with my educational experience at Cooper Union, has made me aware of the lack of resources given to the vital enterprise of public education and civic engagement at the present time. The sad irony is that while public art education is often the first cut made to a budget, my own experience in the classroom has shown how the act of careful observation and critical engagement with our own communities cultivates empathy.

RM The pedagogical aspect of your artistic practice and engagement with student communities is critical to understanding the relationship between aesthetics, experience, and political agency. Much of the language you use to describe your work conjures a sense of urgency, as in a consideration of the politics of power, but it also relates to temporality: to documenting movement or change, to the passage of time, to an oscillation between the antique and the modern, to an interest in memory. We touched on the concept of simultaneity at the beginning of our conversation, but can you tell me more about the idea of duration in your work?

SV My work rests somewhere between the metamorphic and the photographic. Color, contrast, and composition translate my experiences of the physical world into an amalgam of the actual and imagined. The works are also intended to be both fixed

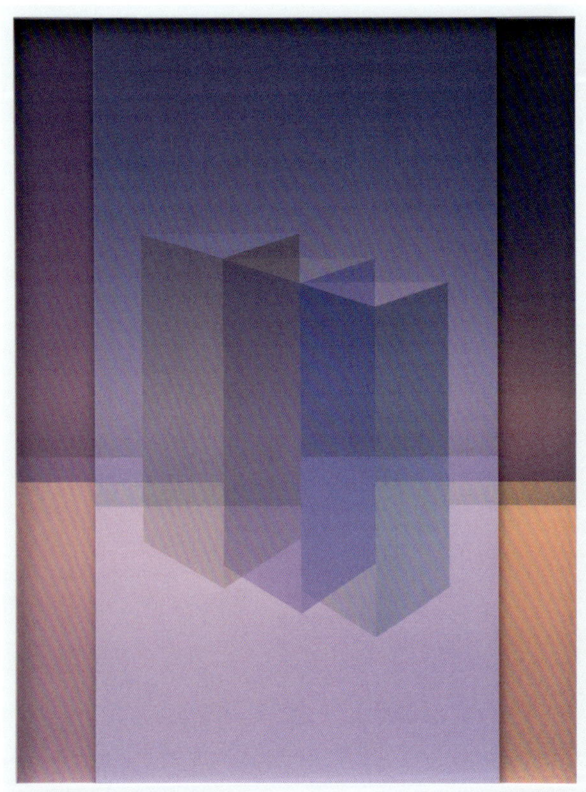

Electric Prism III, 2015

and unfixed, implying a sense of transference or movement caught at a moment of stasis. The still image is intended to feel as though it will continue to shift and re-form anew. And with this it is also a movement away from the "decisive moment" to one of an expanded duration. A sense of accumulation or transference is of consistent importance to the final resulting exhibition. Although quite choreographed and made of opaque and static materials such as marble, plaster, or concrete, my sculptures and installations are intended to feel ephemeral.

RM I see the circulation of your still images across different supports as unmistakably filmic. Does your concern with multiple framings, perspectives, movement, and layering express an interest in cinema? And in what ways do you see your work relating to that of your father, Stan VanDerBeek, whose collaboration with John Cage, Merce Cunningham, and Yvonne Rainer, as well as Ken Knowlton at Bell Labs, is reflective of a contemporary discourse around the interface of media, dance, film, technology, and everyday experience?

SV I am very interested in cinema. I am certain some of this is genetic, but some of it comes also from the fact that cinema and its narrative forms and cultural cues have had an outsized influence on our expectations of how images are both made and circulated. As someone who contributes to the enterprise of image production, I see an ethical responsibility to question the reception of images. I would need a lot more space to address my father's ongoing influence on my approach as an artist—I often

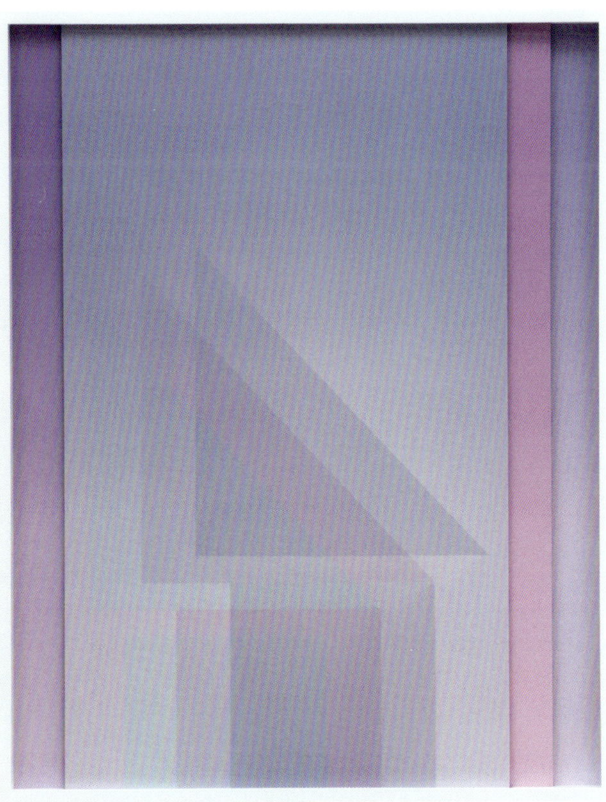

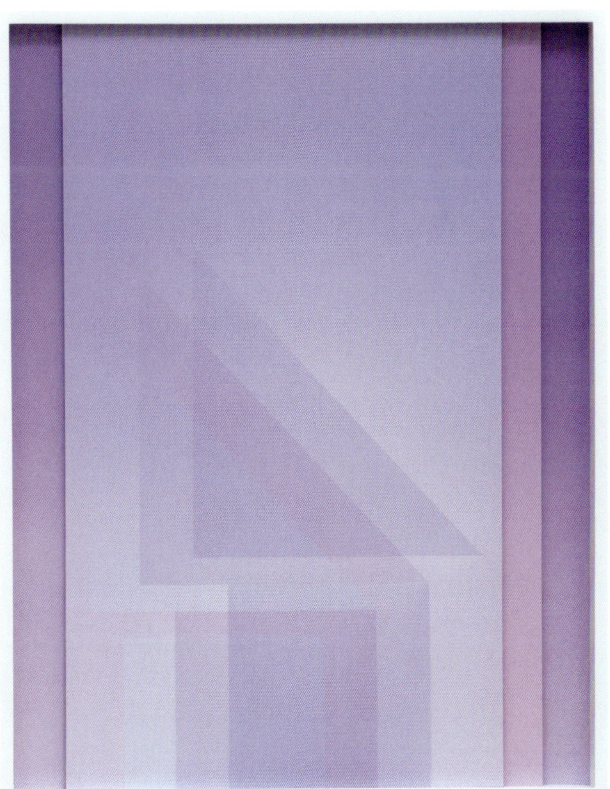

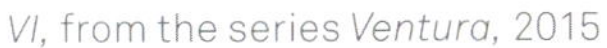

VI, from the series *Ventura*, 2015

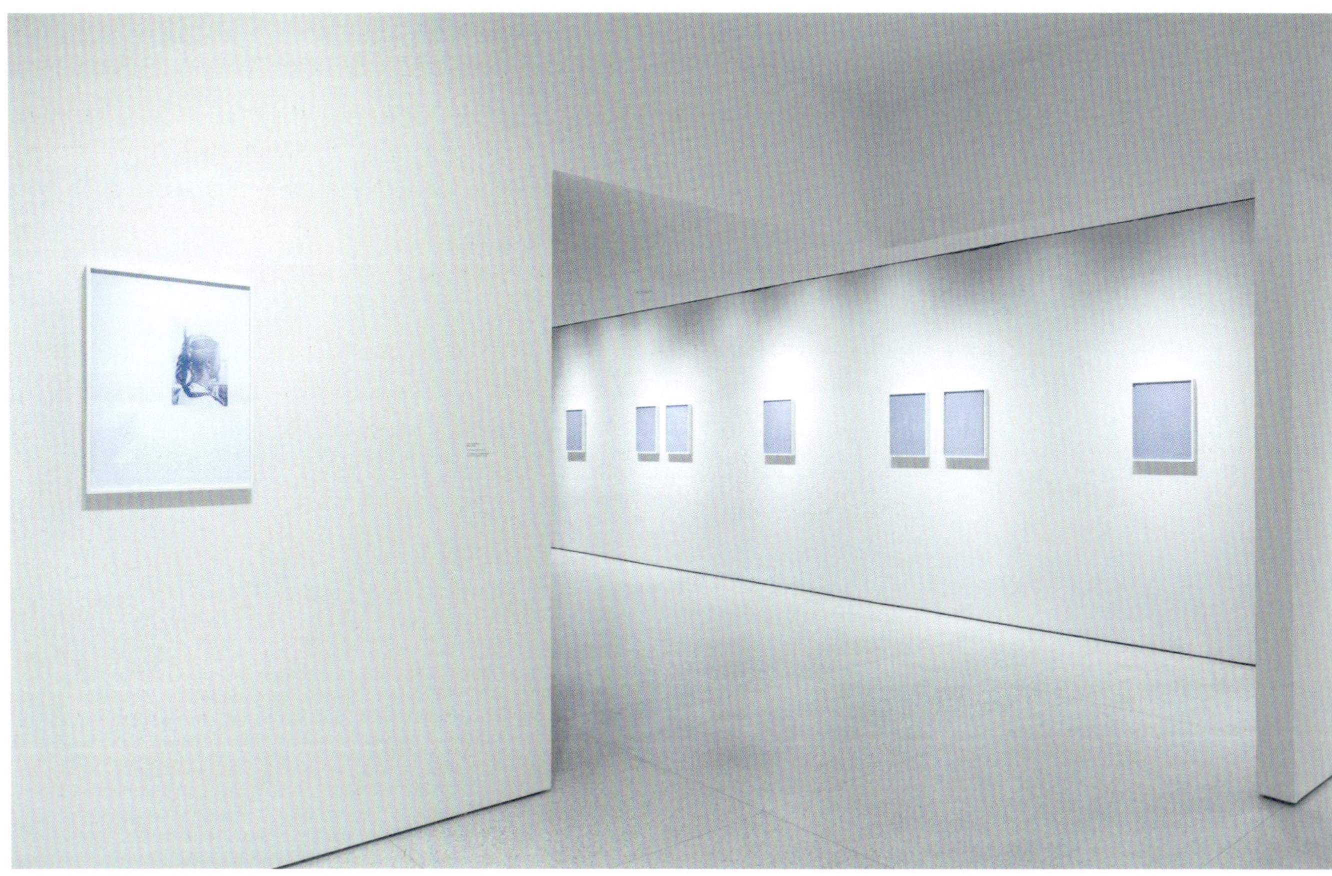

Sister, 2015, and *Crepuscule*, 2015, installation view, *Photo Poetics: An Anthology*, Guggenheim Museum of Art, New York, 2015

wish he was present to see the shape of things now. As an early voice in the debates on multimedia art, I think he would have much to say. I continue to be inspired by his prescience and forethought as an artist who was advancing important questions about the complex relationship between art and communication technology. To return to the question, what impact do you think the moving image and filmic techniques have had upon our understanding of time, memory, and the still image?

RM Sigmar Polke once said that a negative is never finished, implying that a photograph is not determined by the decisive moment (releasing the shutter), but by a series of expanded, unfinished temporalities. This has a lot to do with cinema. Polke subverted conventional darkroom techniques to a degree that was virtually unprecedented. He experimented with multiple exposures, reversed tonal values, blurring, under- and over-exposures. He pushed the reproduced image toward disintegration. He then applied the lessons he learned in the darkroom to painting, turning a static image into something closer to a slow-motion film.

I'd say that the cinematic in photography is in fact rather diverse. It appears under the format of film stills in the work of Cindy Sherman, Lorna Simpson, and Richard Prince. It can take a directorial address in the case of Philip-Lorca diCorcia, Stan Douglas, and Jeff Wall. It manifests itself in montage processes, as in your case. In split screens, multiple slide projections, photo-texts, storyboards, sequences, and narrativity in the work of Nobuyoshi Araki, Nan Goldin, and Paul Graham. There is also time-lapse photography, which is distinctly cinematic. I'm thinking here of Rineke Dijkstra, for instance. And there are various other means of temporalizing photography. Zoe Leonard's pre-photographic camera obscuras materialize a film in flux, unfolding in the present. Liz Deschenes's photograms reflect their environment, change over time as they oxidize, acquire a history of where they have been exhibited. We are talking about works that engage duration and the viewer's attention over prolonged periods of time. It's a cinematic, literary, or poetic form of observation.

SV Poetry for me is a sequence of acute observations that are then distilled down to their most essential form. The work of certain writers, such as E. E. Cummings or Anne Carson, instills a desire on my part for succinct essential gestures, long looking, and a refusal of prescriptive closure, allowing the universe in.

I translate Polke another way. A negative for me is never finished because I often work, re-work, and return to images, frequently making them into new works or incorporating them into larger installations. Similarly, I repurpose and reuse sculptural objects in my still-life images and exhibitions, and I enjoy the effect that this layering, repetition, or echoing has within the larger body of my work.

My most recent work, *Crepuscule* (2015), for example, is a response to a poem by E. E. Cummings of the same name. Mirroring its title, the images rest on the edge of indiscernibility. Triangular prisms and semicircular plaster casts are layered photographically and physically within a series of nine images in which one form slowly transforms into the next through very subtle shifts in transparent pale colors. The forms are elusive, both appearing and disappearing within the atmosphere that surrounds them. The images continually shift between the concrete and the abstract in an attempt to emulate the way that "Crepuscule" and other of Cummings's poems move so meaningfully between recognizable subjects and events, as well as dreams and the imagination, to get at this varied, complex, and compelling rendering of life.

Poetry is for me the gathering, forming, and un-forming of meaning. Its intentions are at once finite and infinite. And the fluidity of verse to move amongst the strata of existence via a few well-chosen and well-placed words is hard to beat.

Roxana Marcoci is Senior Curator in the Photography Department at The Museum of Modern Art, New York.

1 Giorgio Agamben, *Potentialities: Collected Essays in Philosophy*, ed. and trans. Daniel Heller-Roazen (Stanford University Press, 1999), p. 95.
2 Ibid.
3 Roxana Marcoci, ed., *The Original Copy: Photography of Sculpture, 1839 to Today*, exh. cat. The Museum of Modern Art (New York, 2010), p. 16.
4 Jeff Wall, "Photography and Liquid Intelligence," in *Jeff Wall: Complete Edition* (London, 2009), p. 218.
5 Scott Burton, "My Brancusi," *Artist's Choice*, exh. brochure The Museum of Modern Art (New York, 1989), n.p.
6 "Sara VanDerBeek: Los Angeles Synthesis," *Art Babble*, http://www.artbabble.org/video/hammer/sara-vanderbeek-los-angeles-synthesis (accessed January 17, 2016).
7 Sarah Charlesworth and Sara VanDerBeek, "A Space in Between," *Flash Art* 45, no. 285 (July–September 2012), pp. 80–83.
8 Etienne Hatt, "The Movement of Memory: An Interview with Sara VanDerBeek," *ArtPress* (February 27, 2015).

> Installation view, *Sara VanDerBeek*, Museum of Contemporary Art, Cleveland, 2014

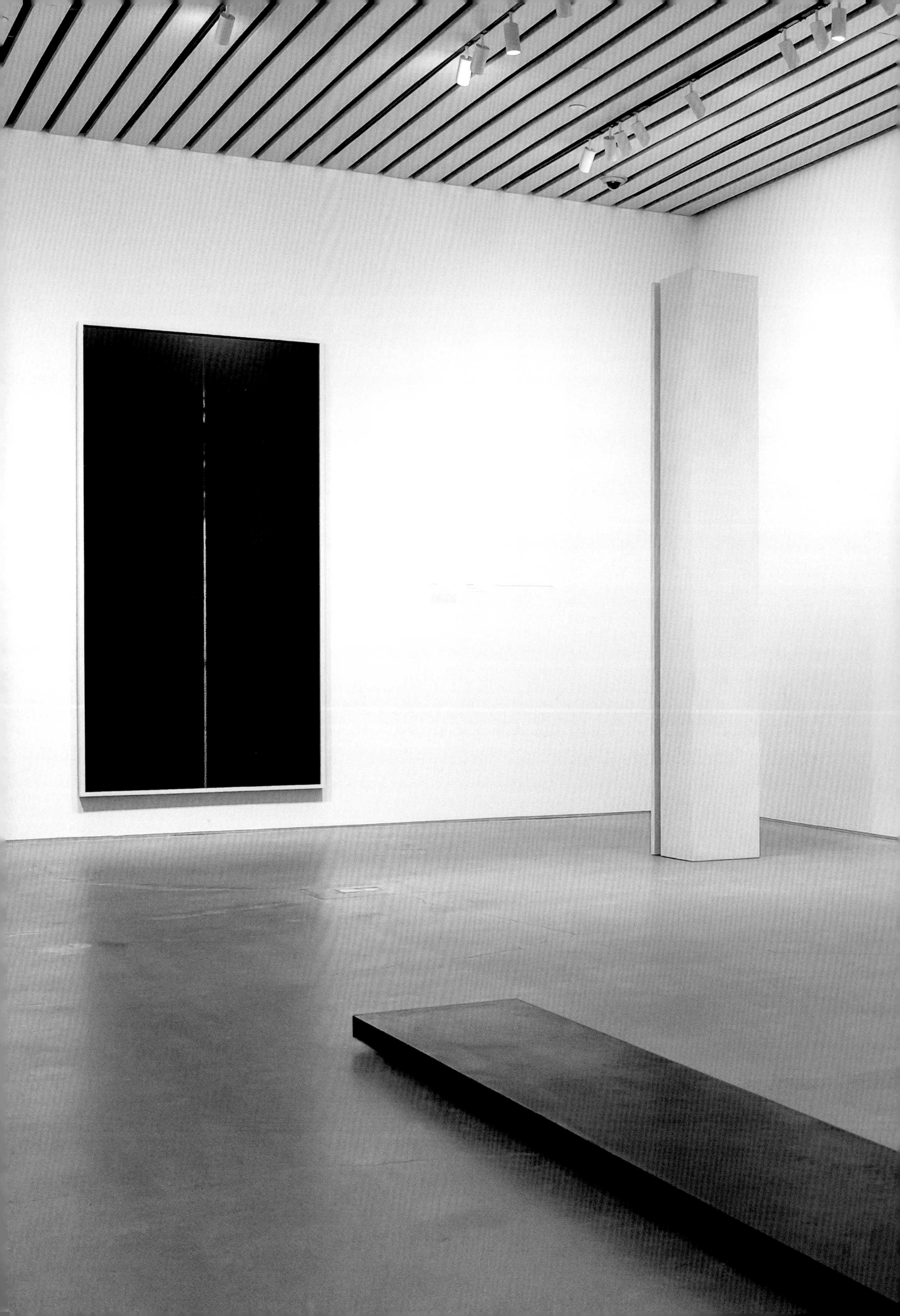

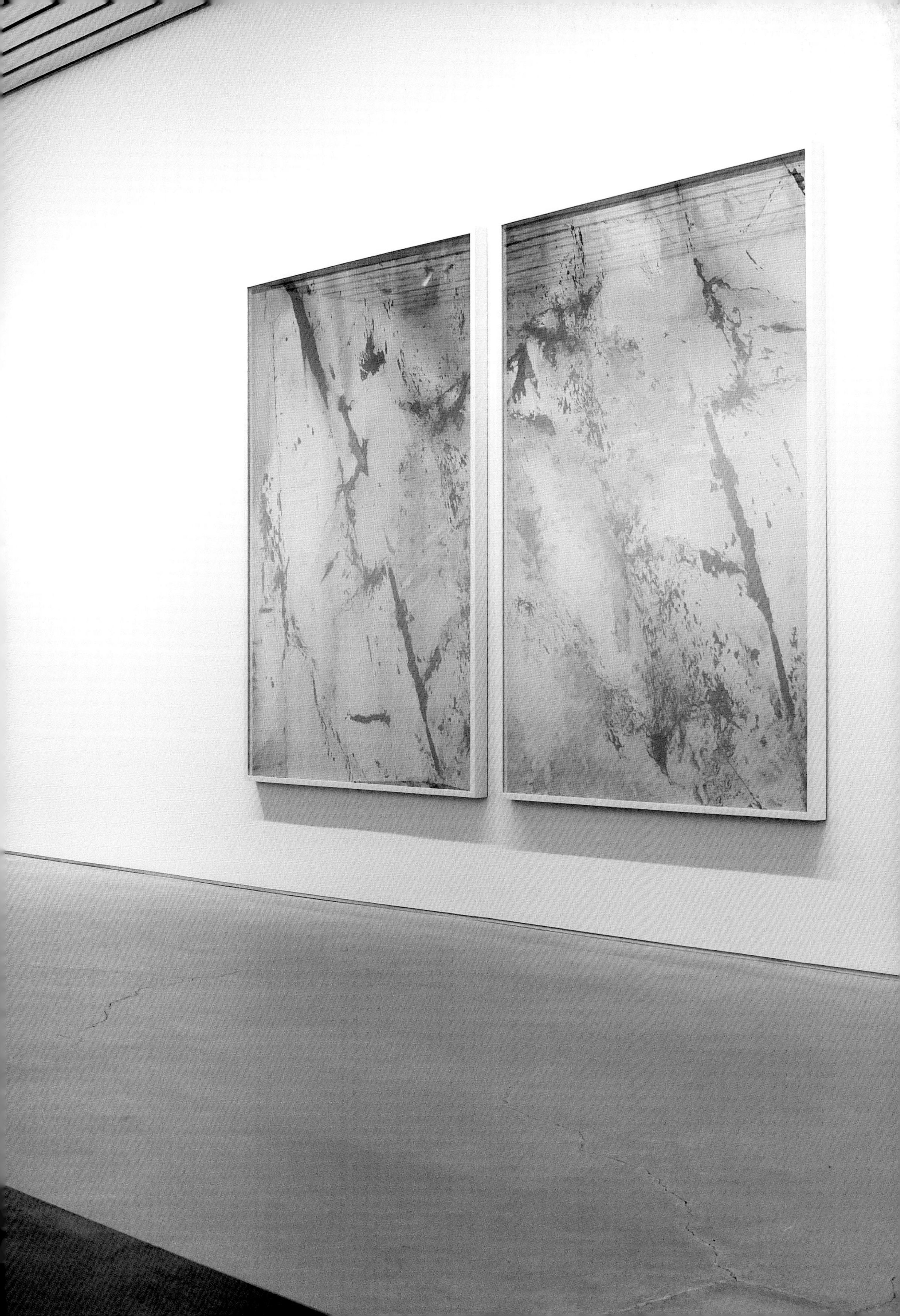

Chain, 2014

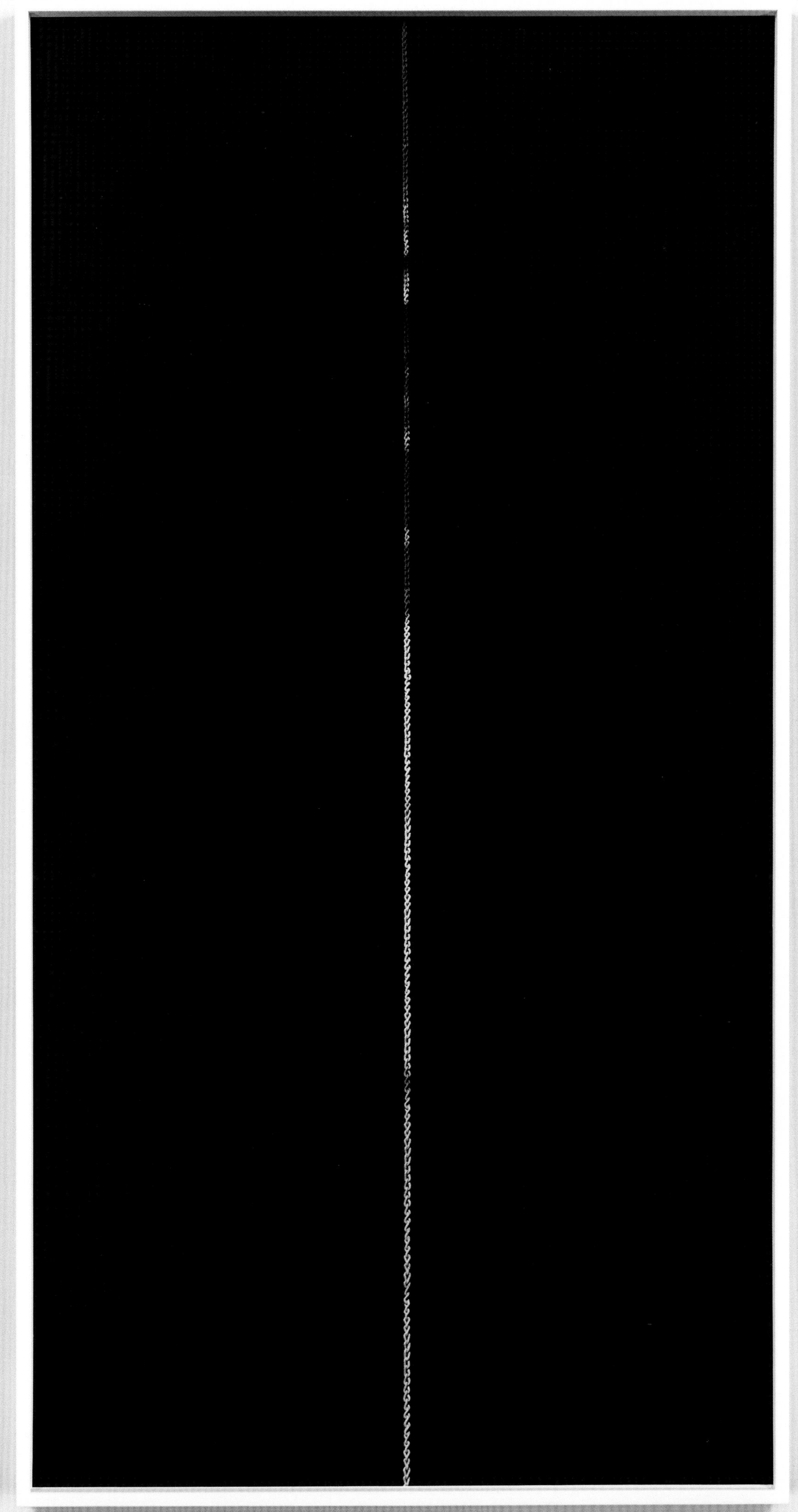

Half Moon, 2014

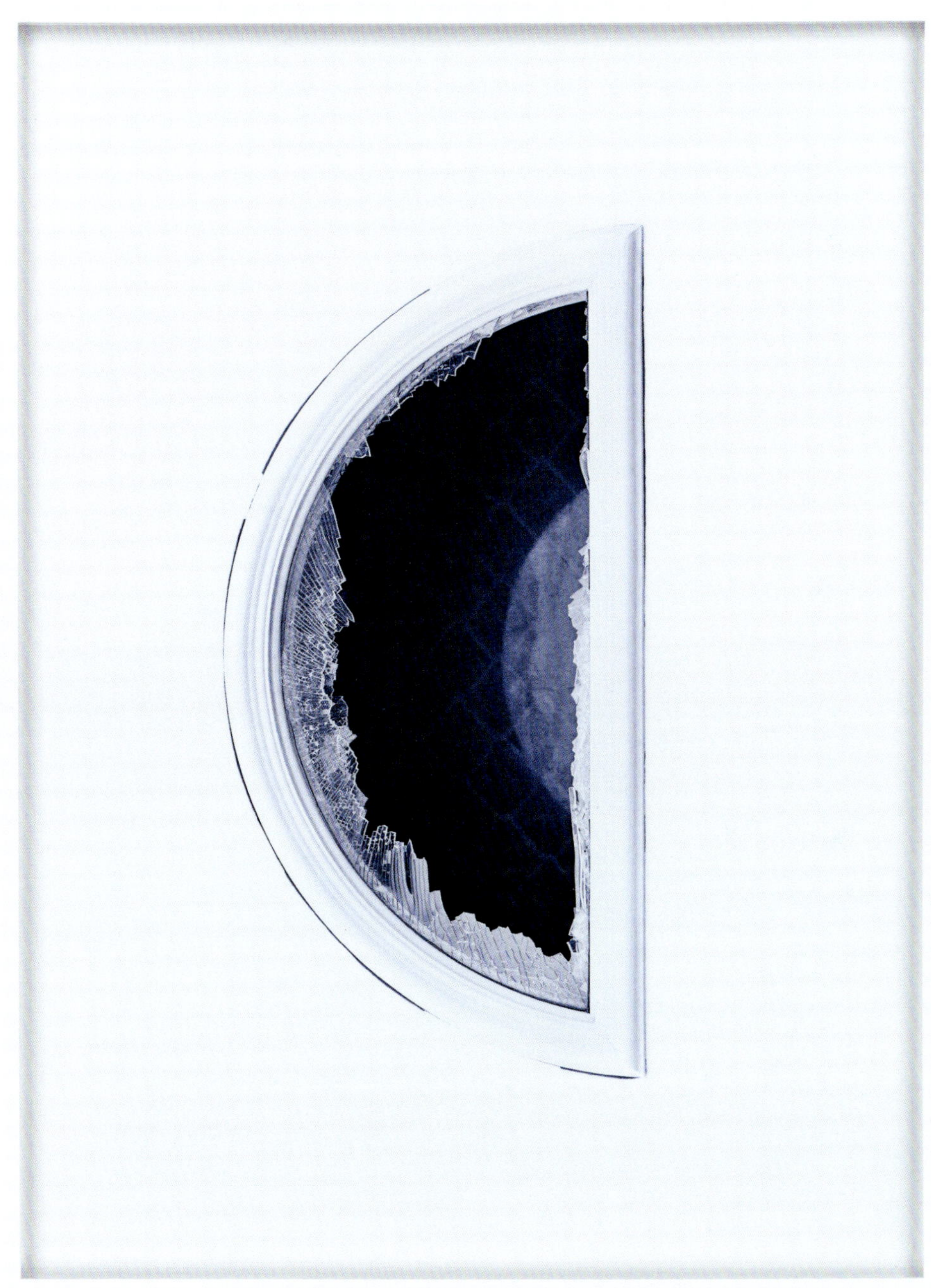

 Shadow/Sun/Moon/Sea, 2015 > *The Sea,* 2015, installation view, *Sensory Spaces 6,* Museum Boijmans Van Beuningen

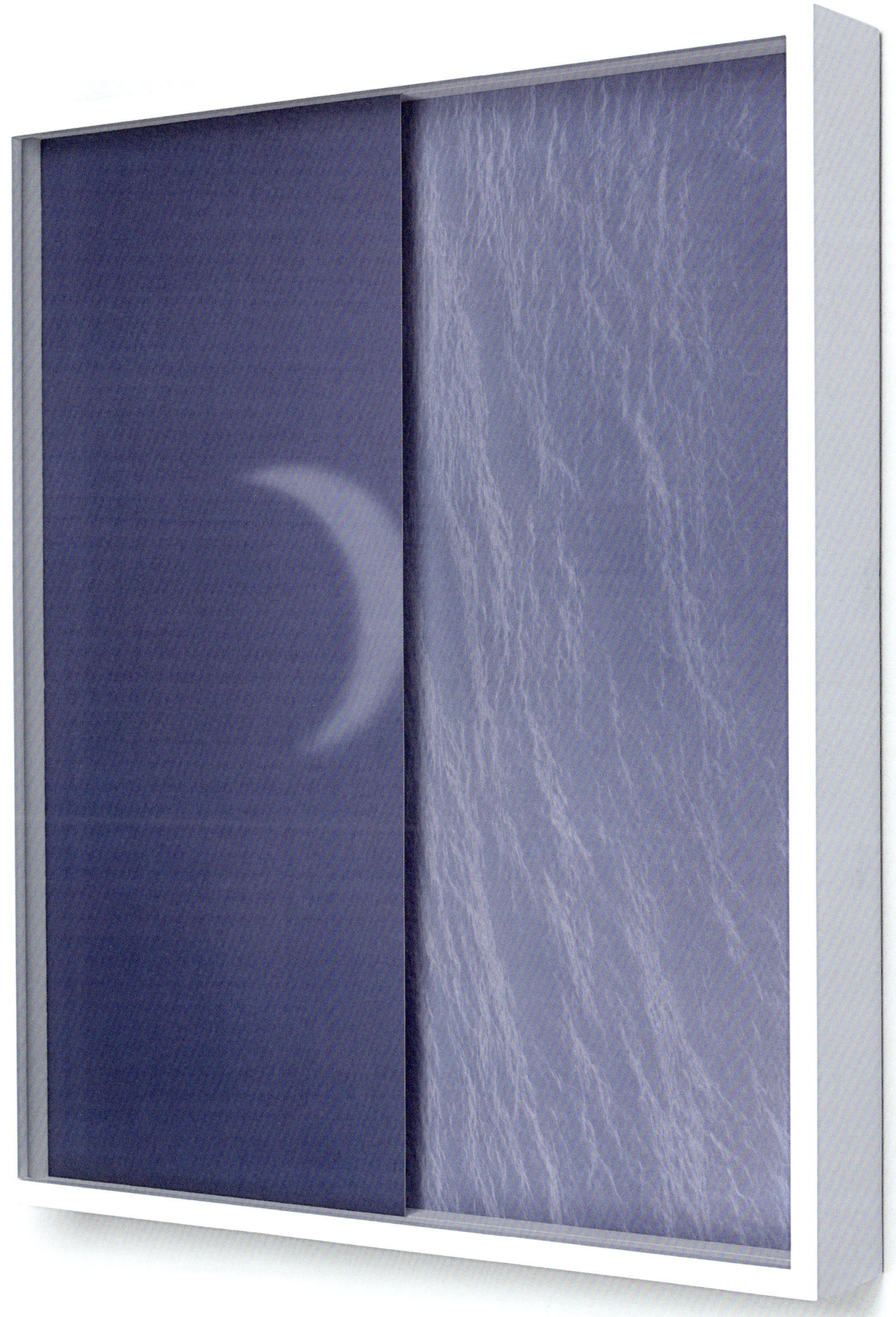

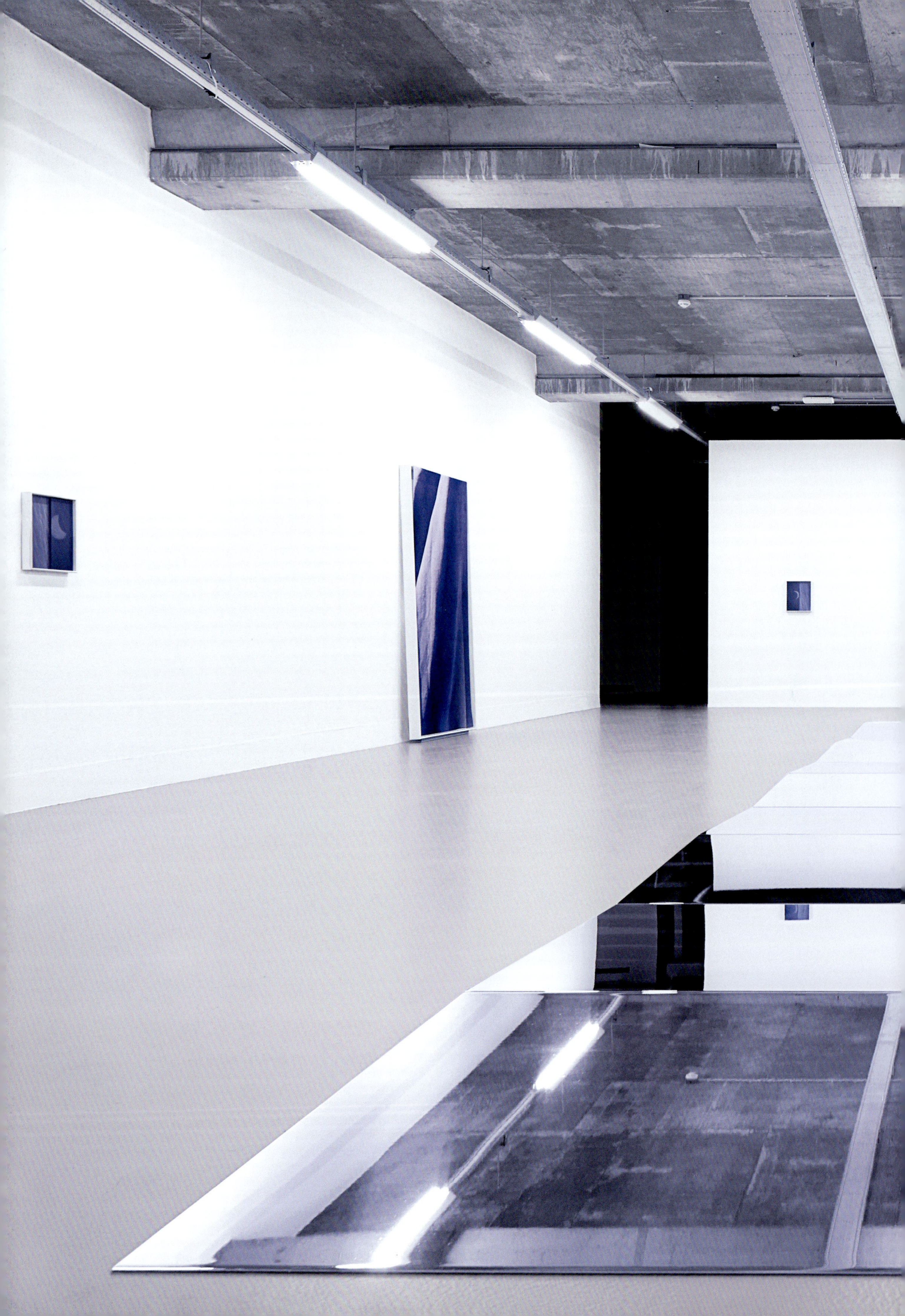

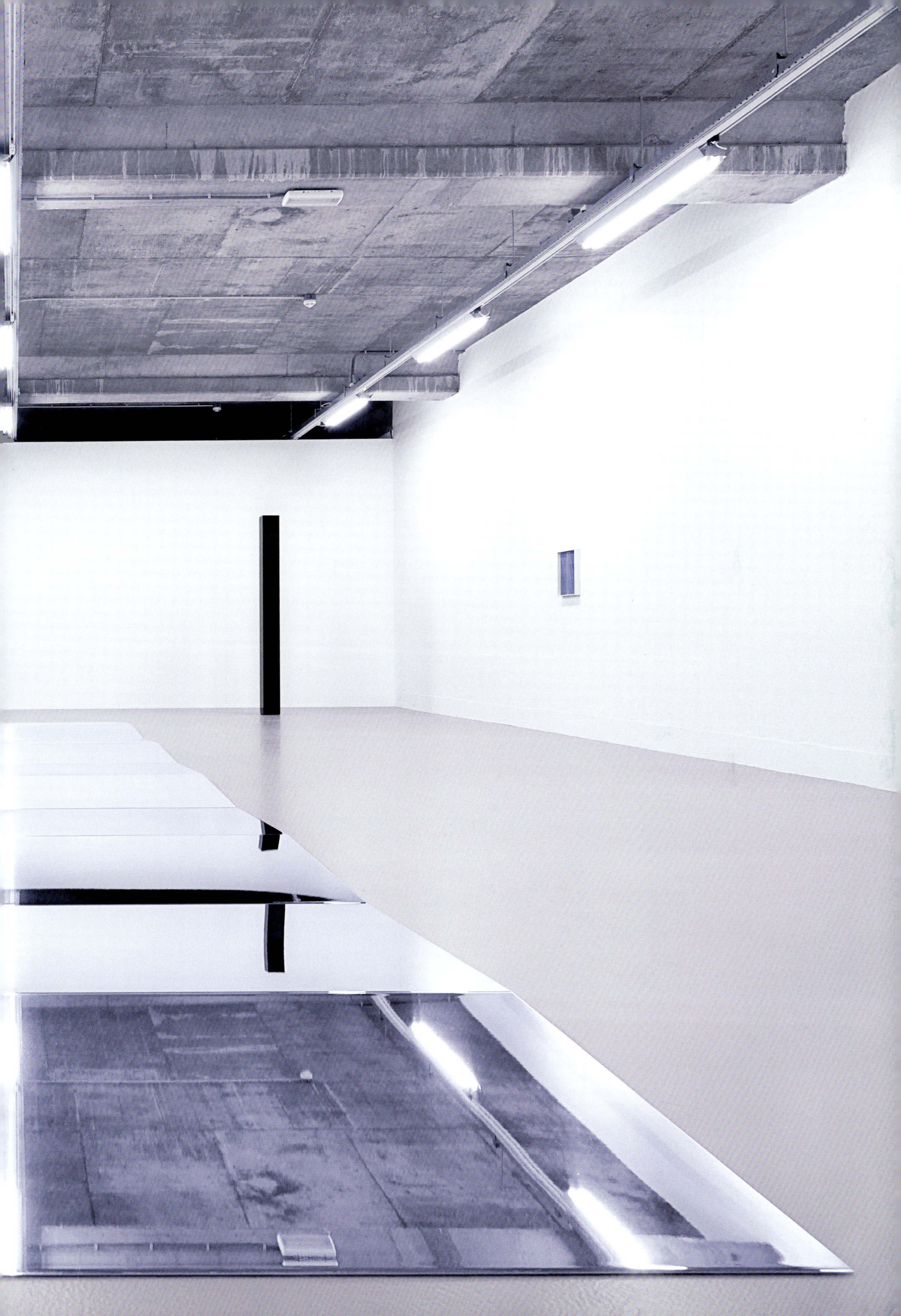

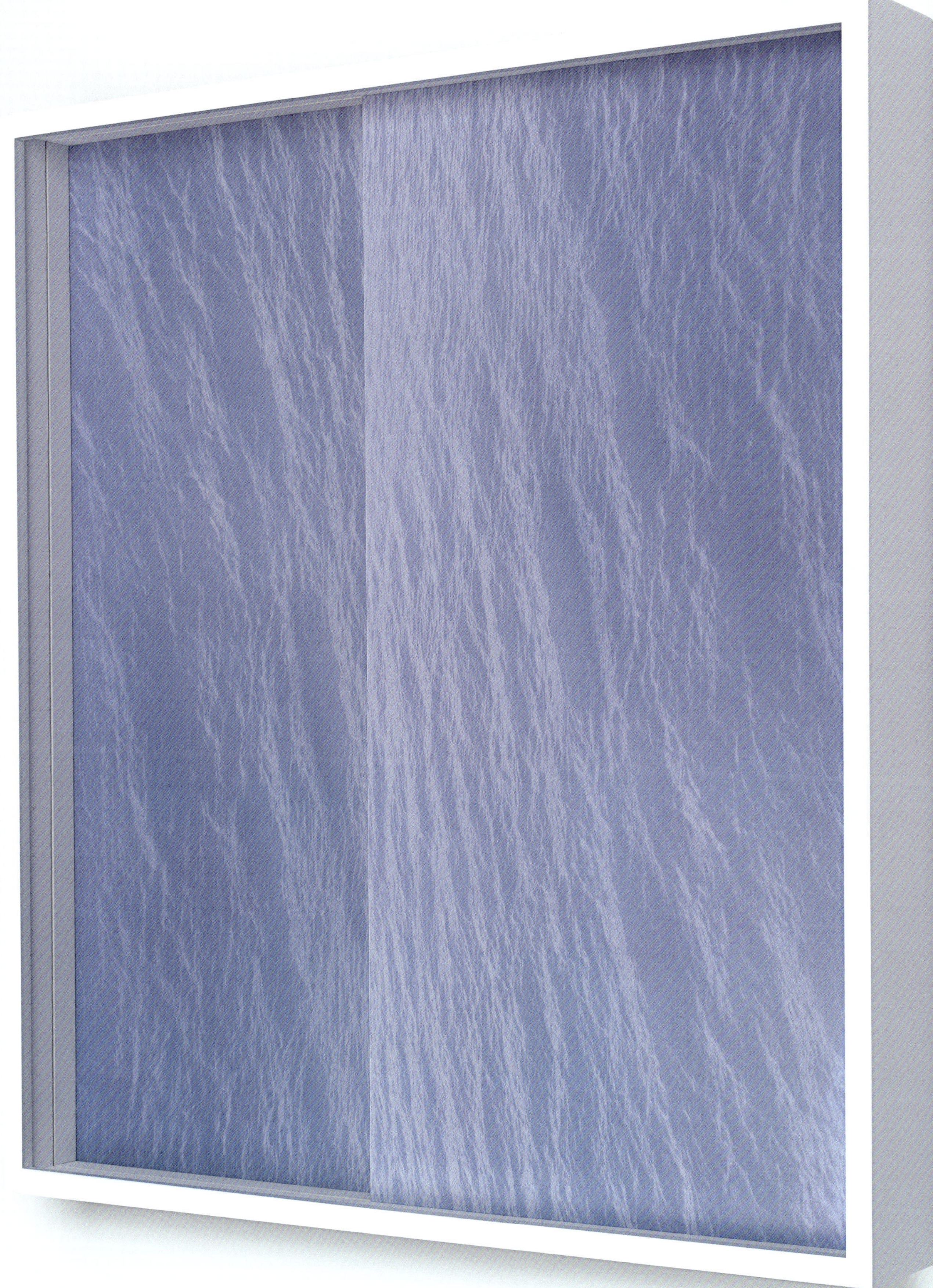

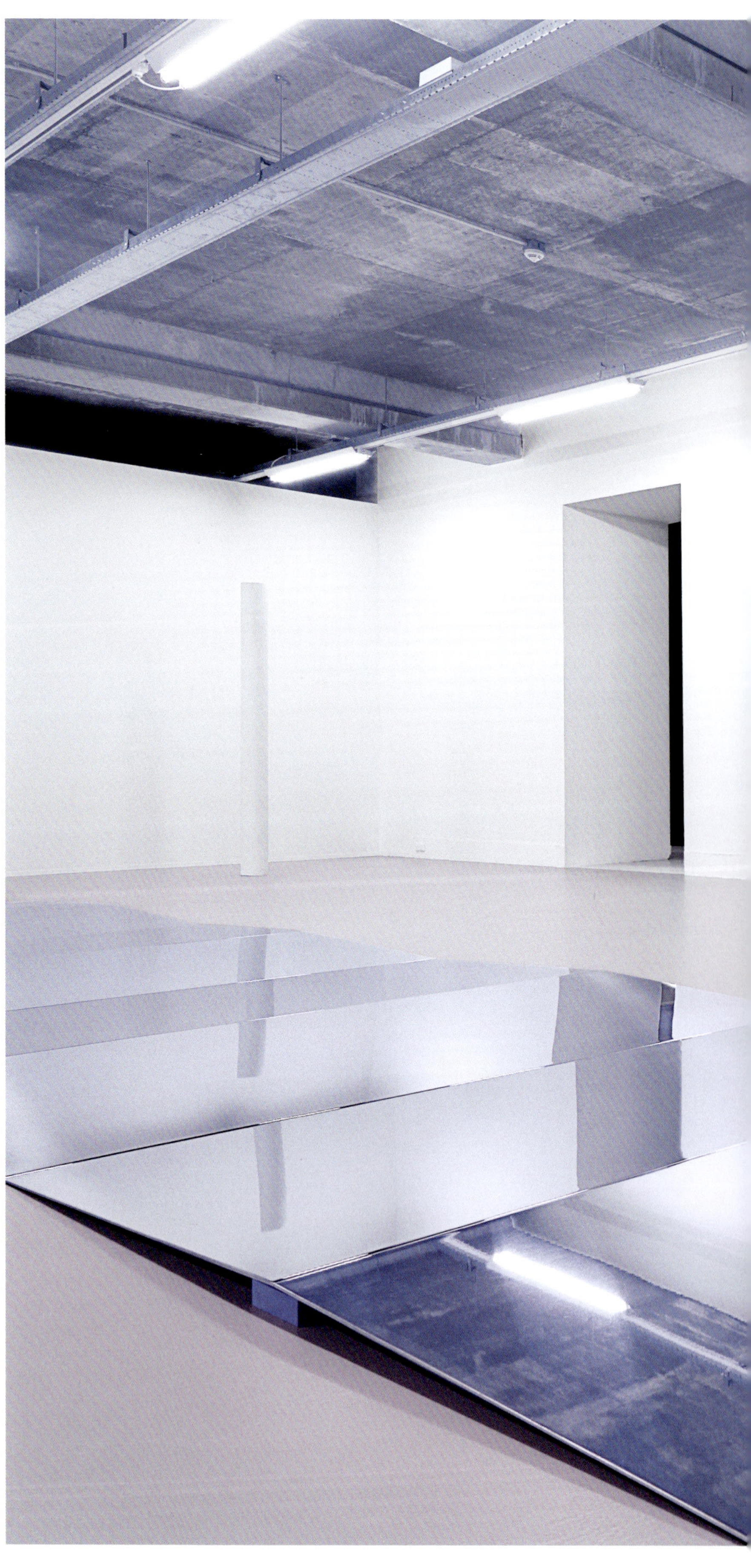

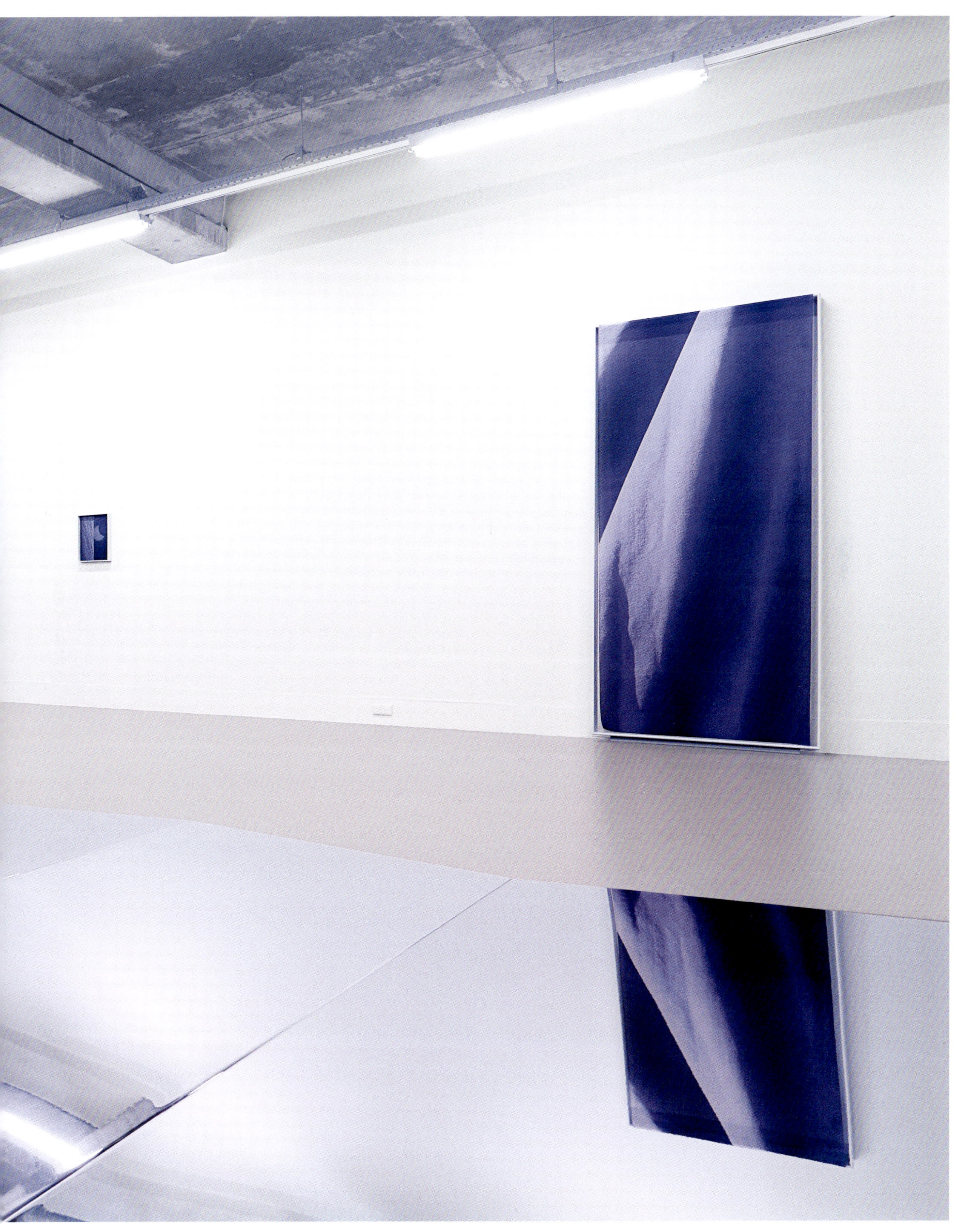

Sky Cloth, East, 2015, installation view, *Sensory Spaces 6*, Museum Boijmans Van Beuningen, Rotterdam, 2015

Marble Moon, 2015

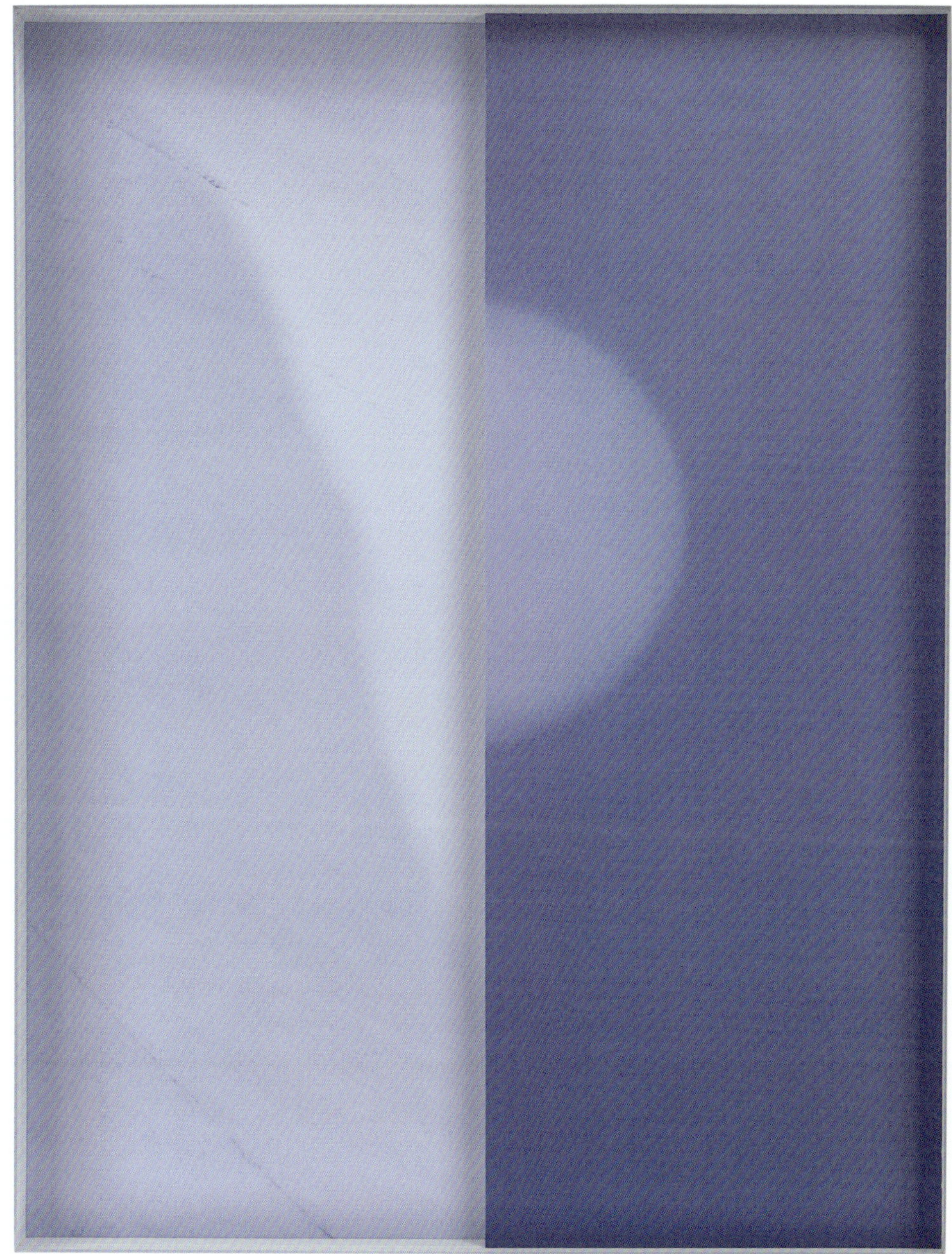

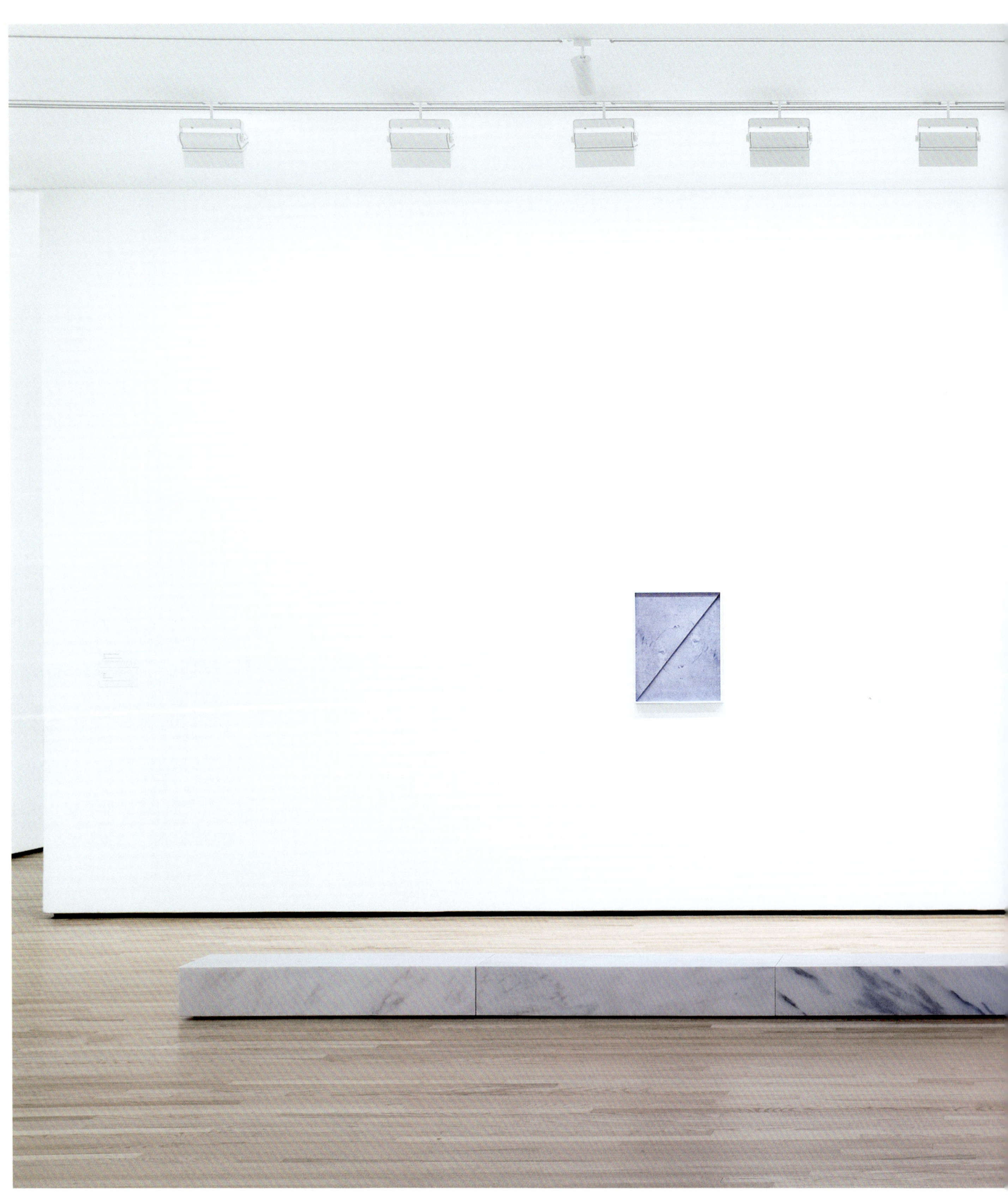

 Installation view, *Front Room: Sara VanDerBeek*, Baltimore Museum of Art, Baltimore, 2015

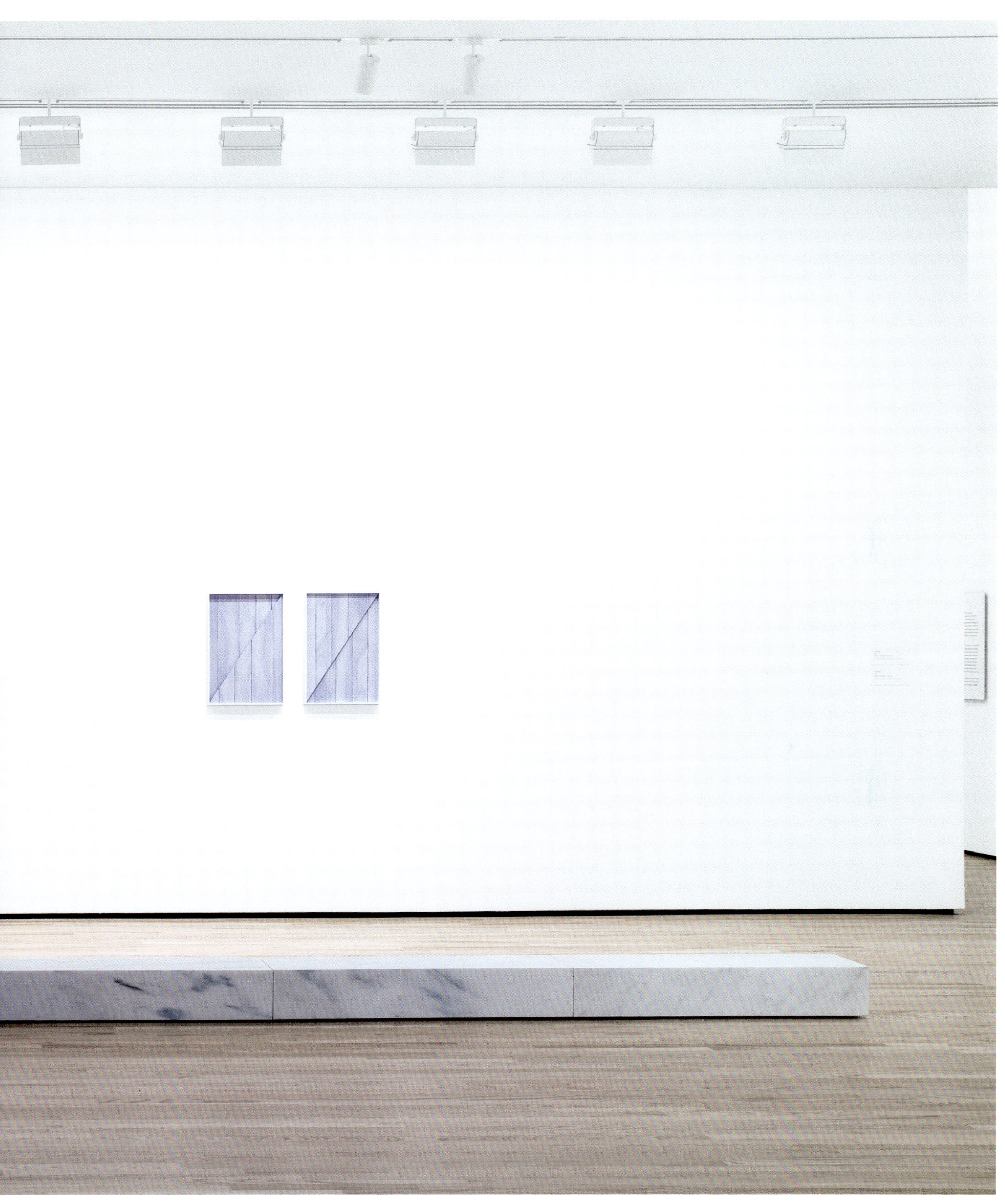

Second Chance, 2015

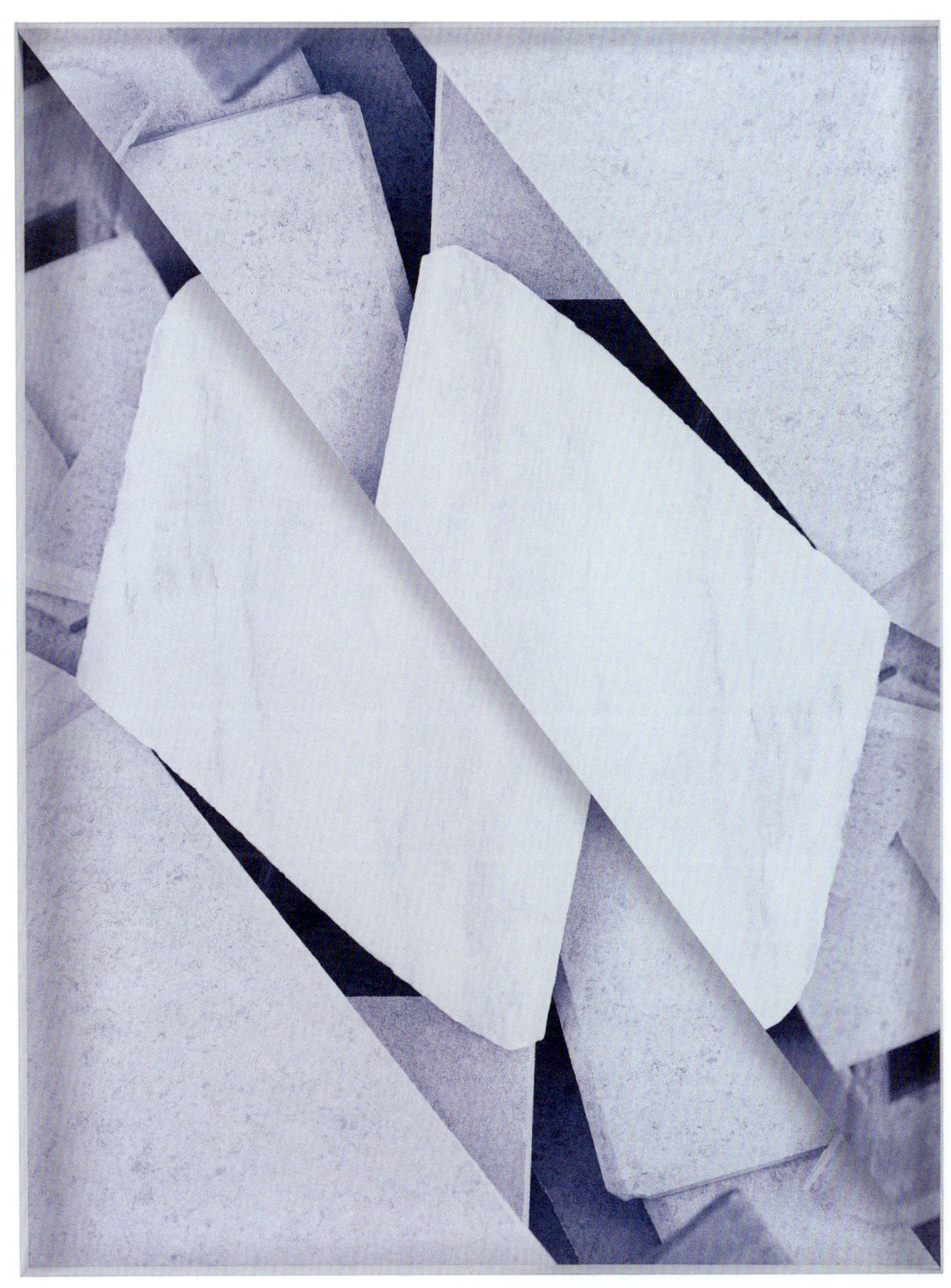

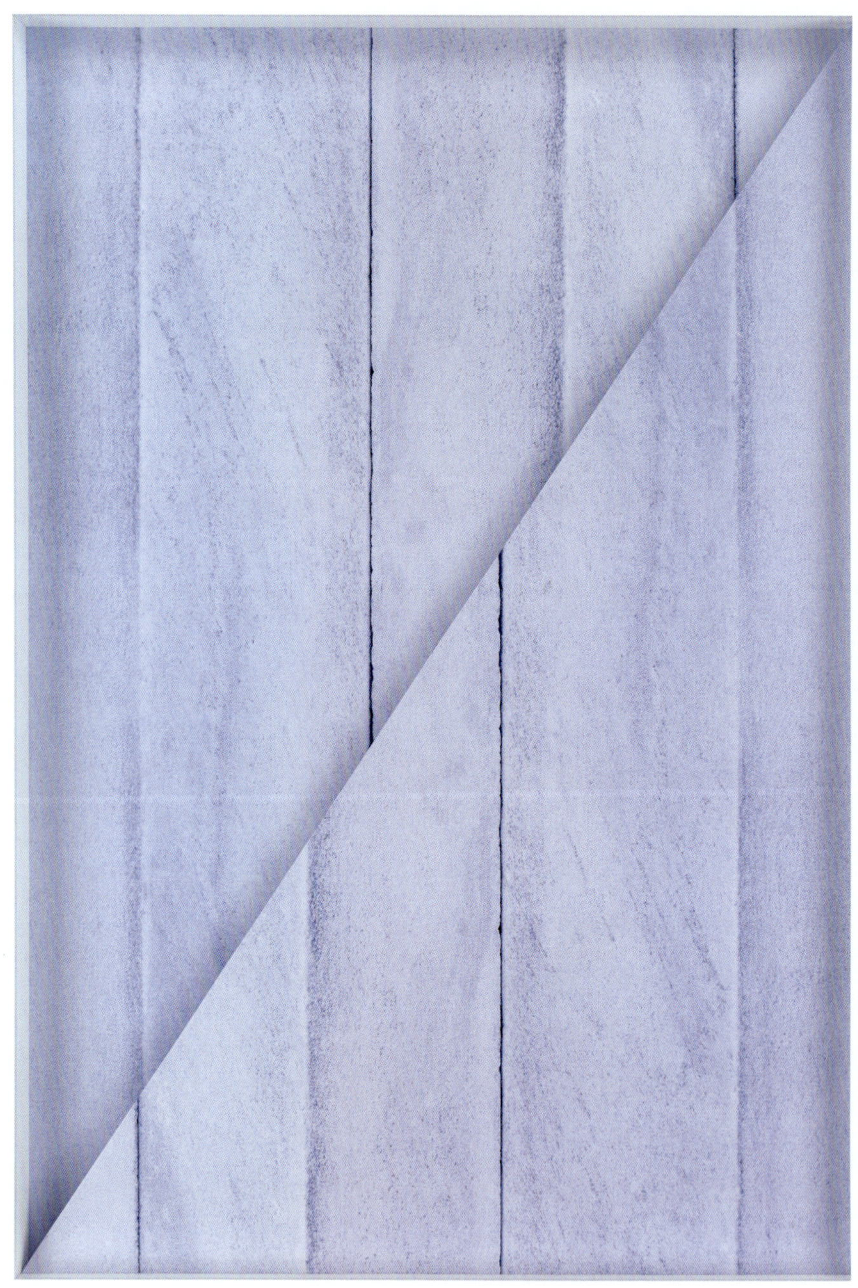

Threshold I and *II*, 2015

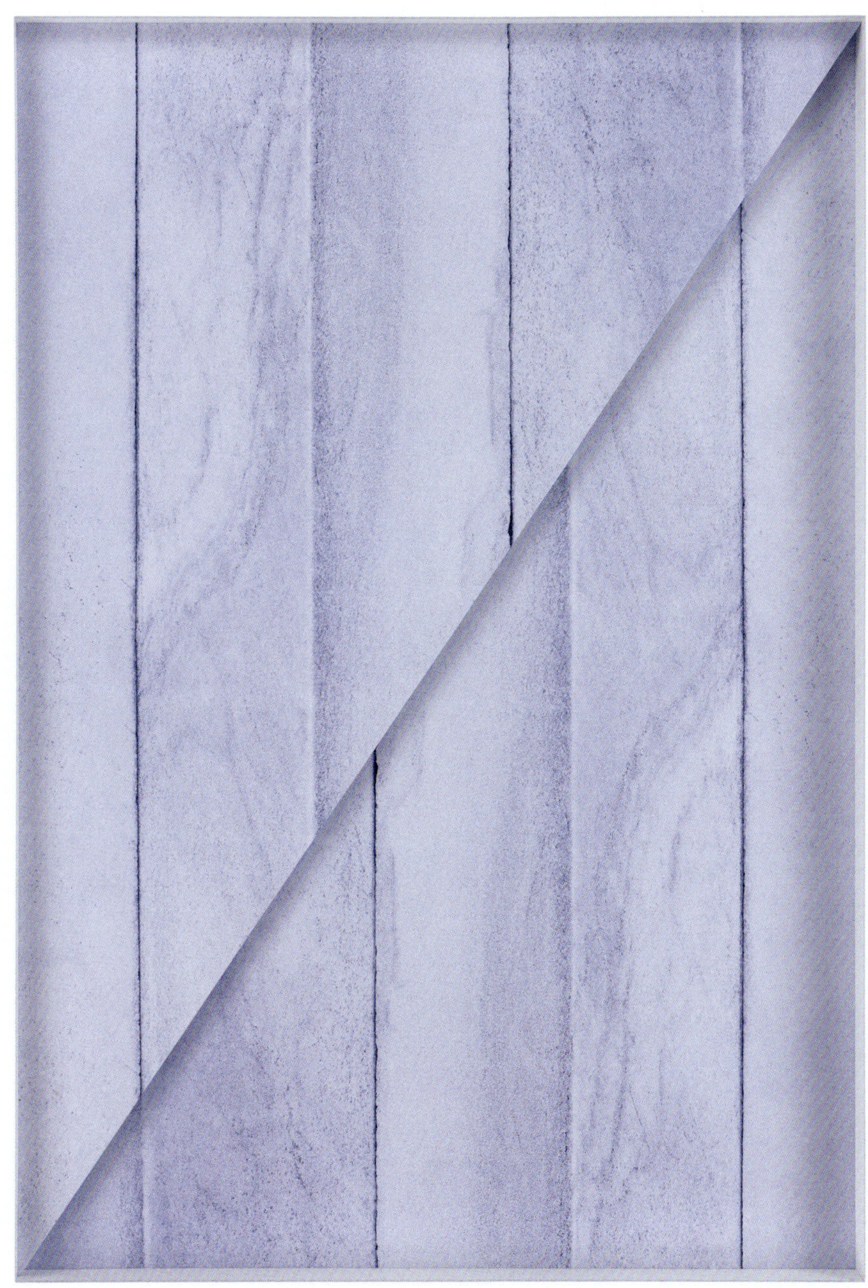

Chance, 2015

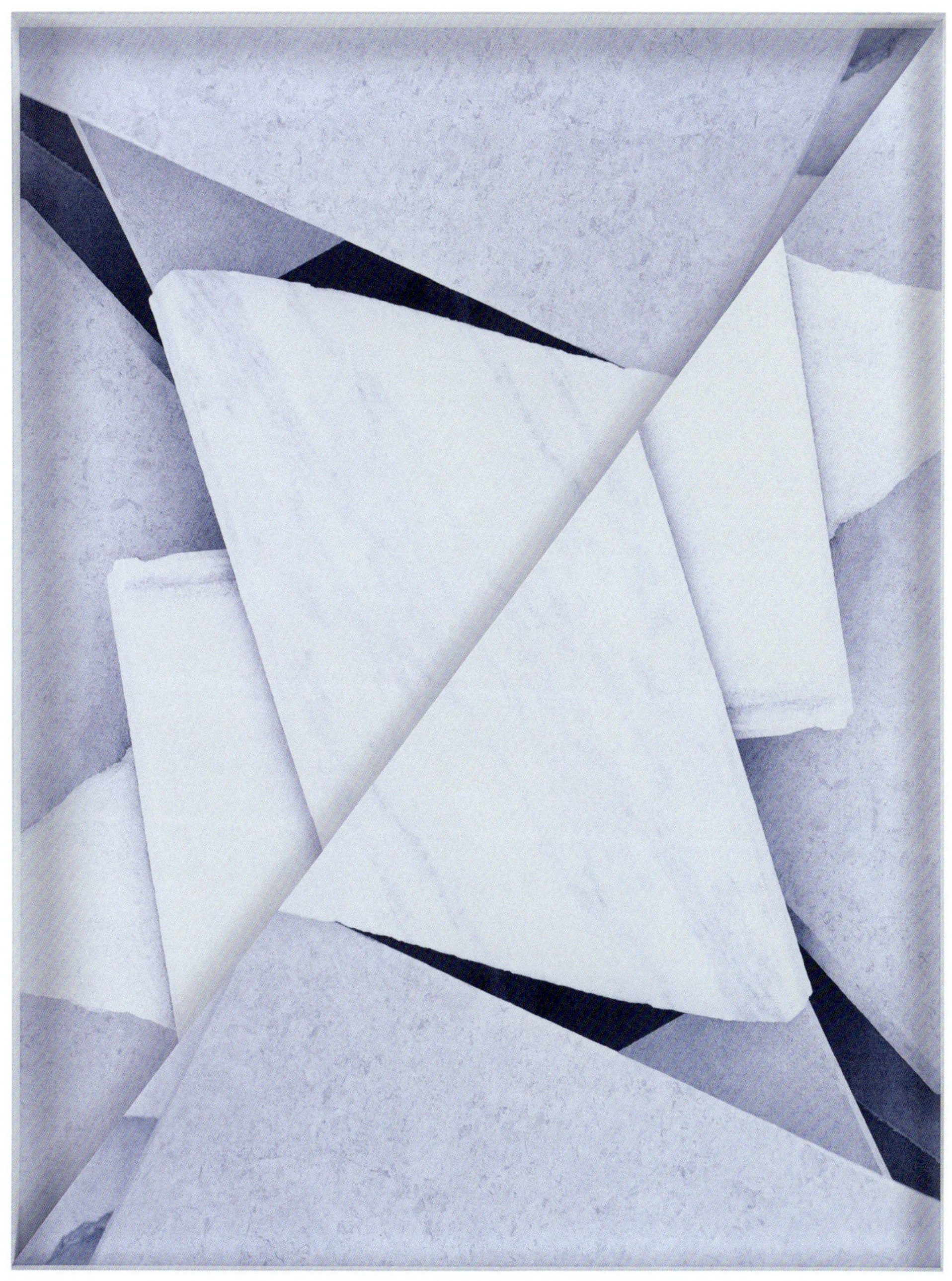

III, from the series *Ventura*, 2015

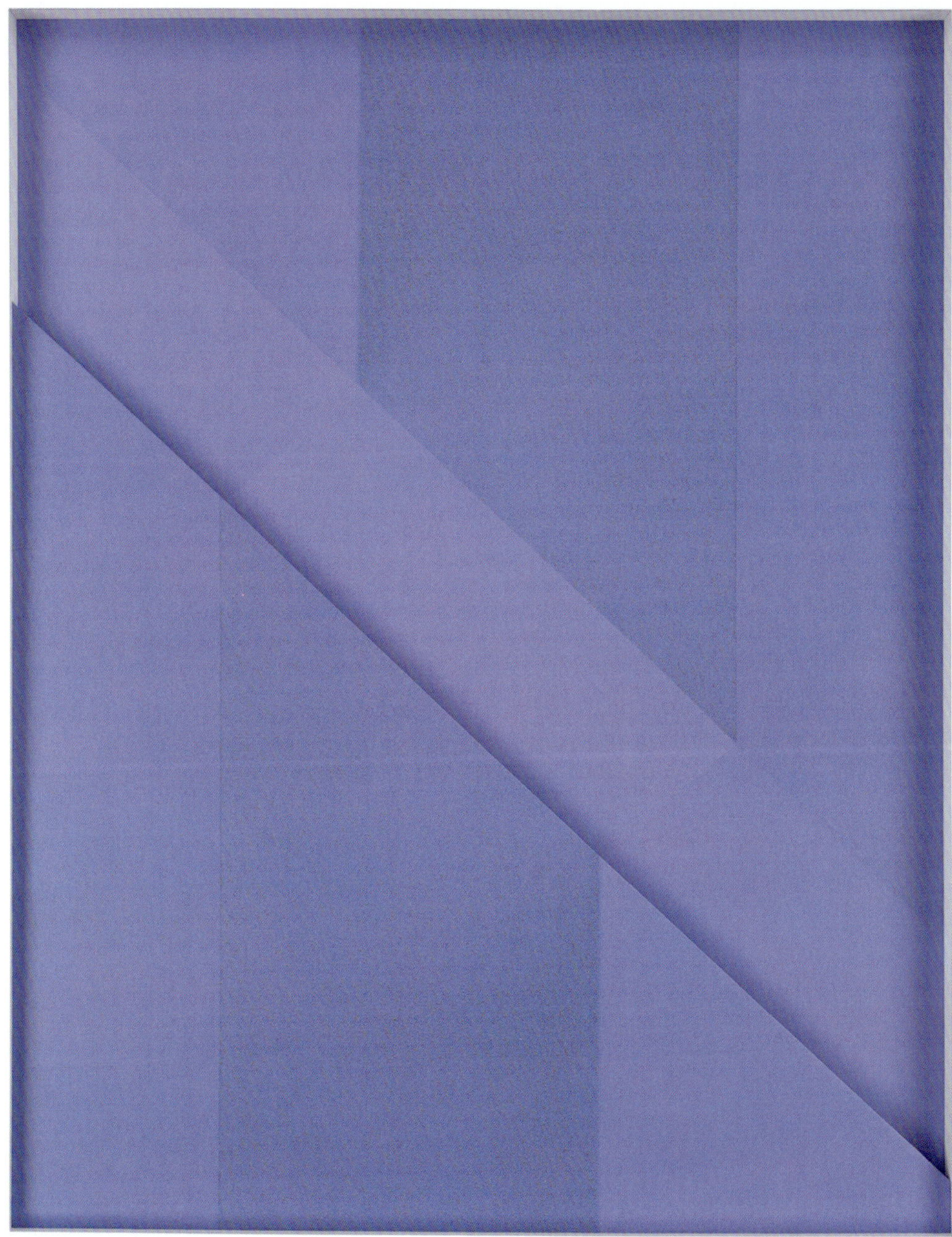

I and *II*, from the series *Ventura*, 2015

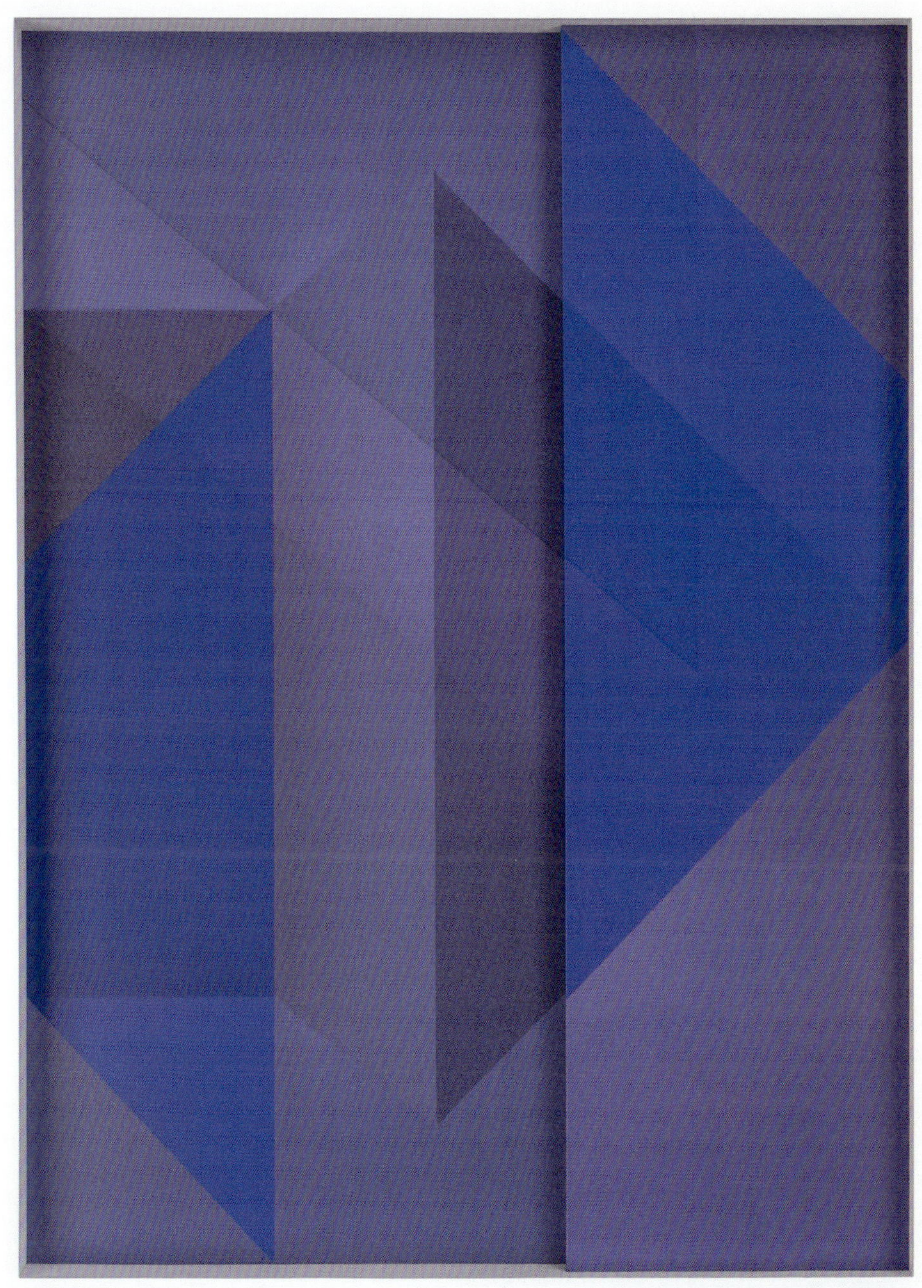

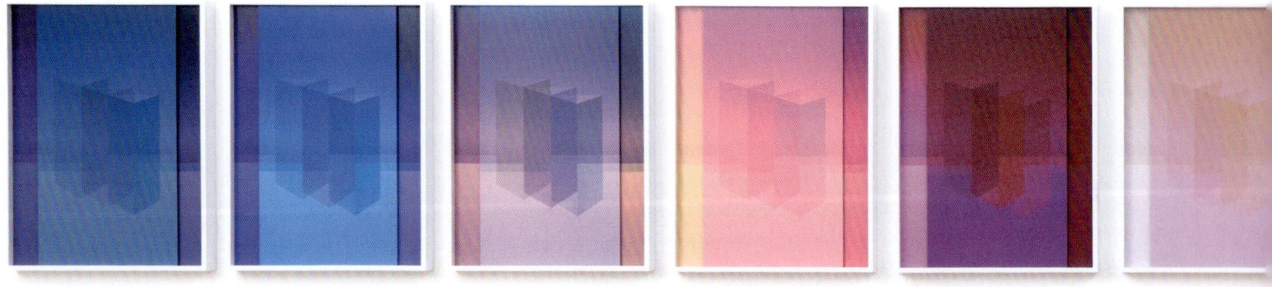

Electric Prisms I–XII, 2015, installation view, *Electric Prisms, Concrete Forms*, The Approach, London, 2015

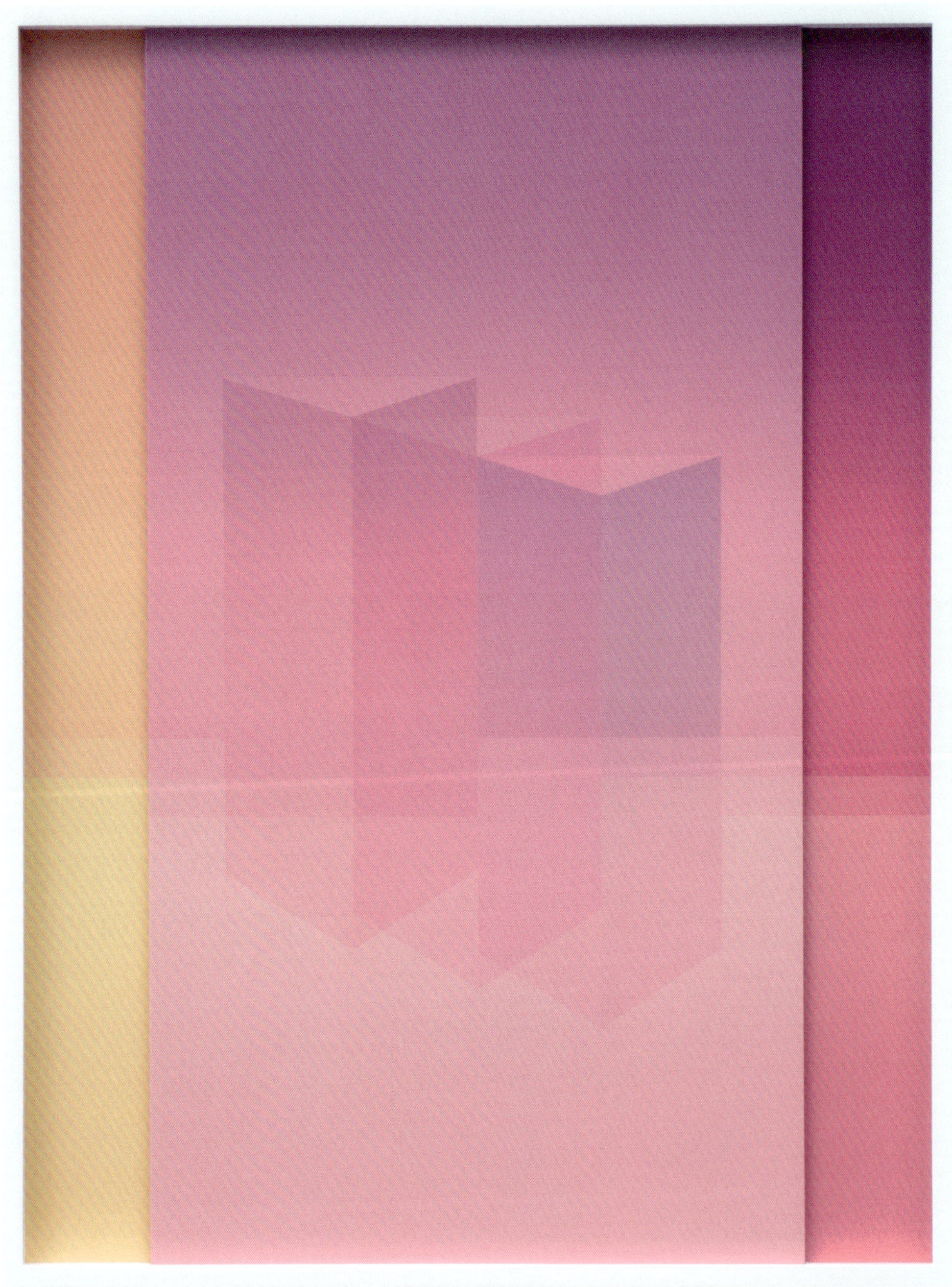

Electric Prisms IV and *V*, 2015

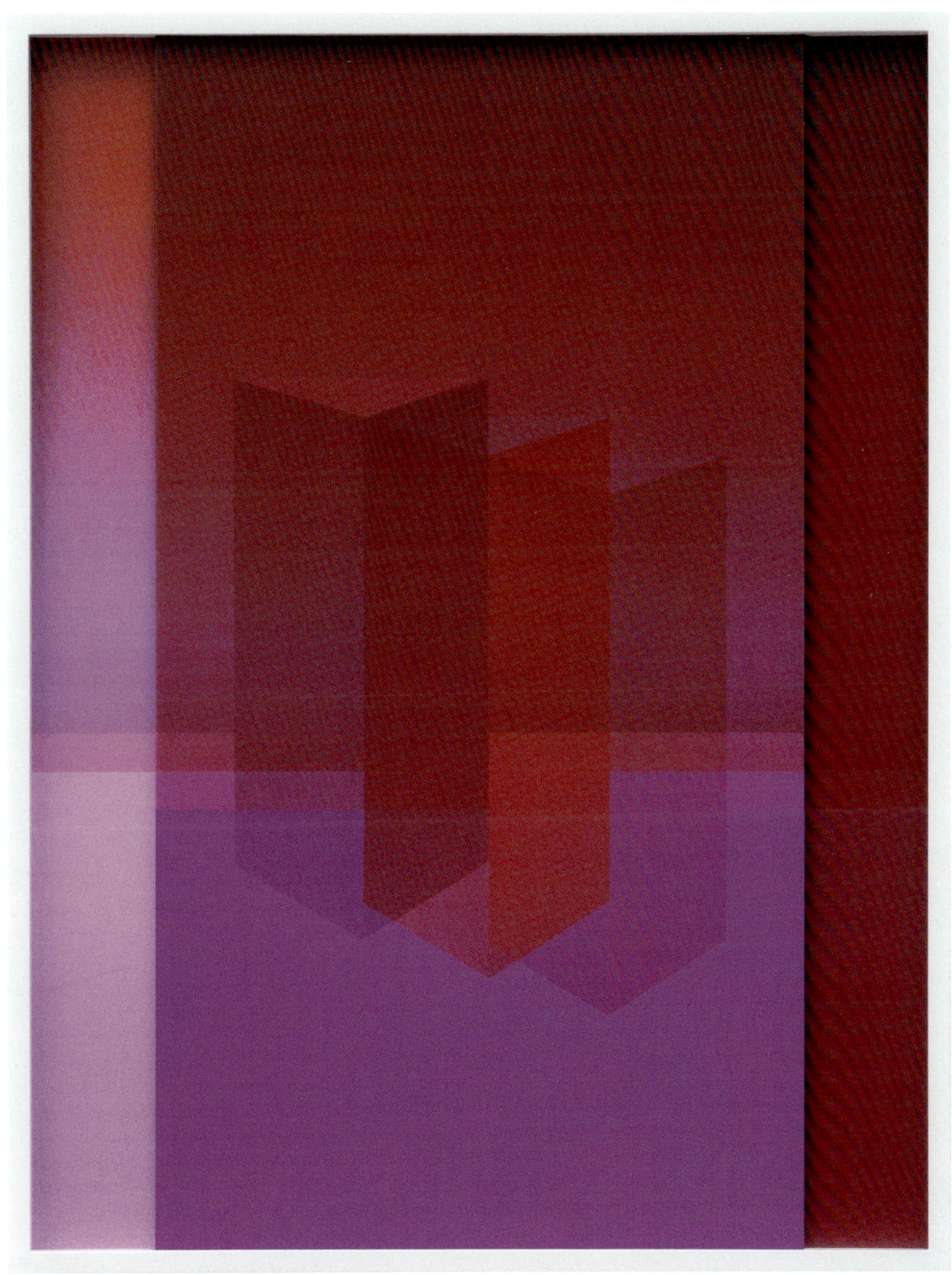

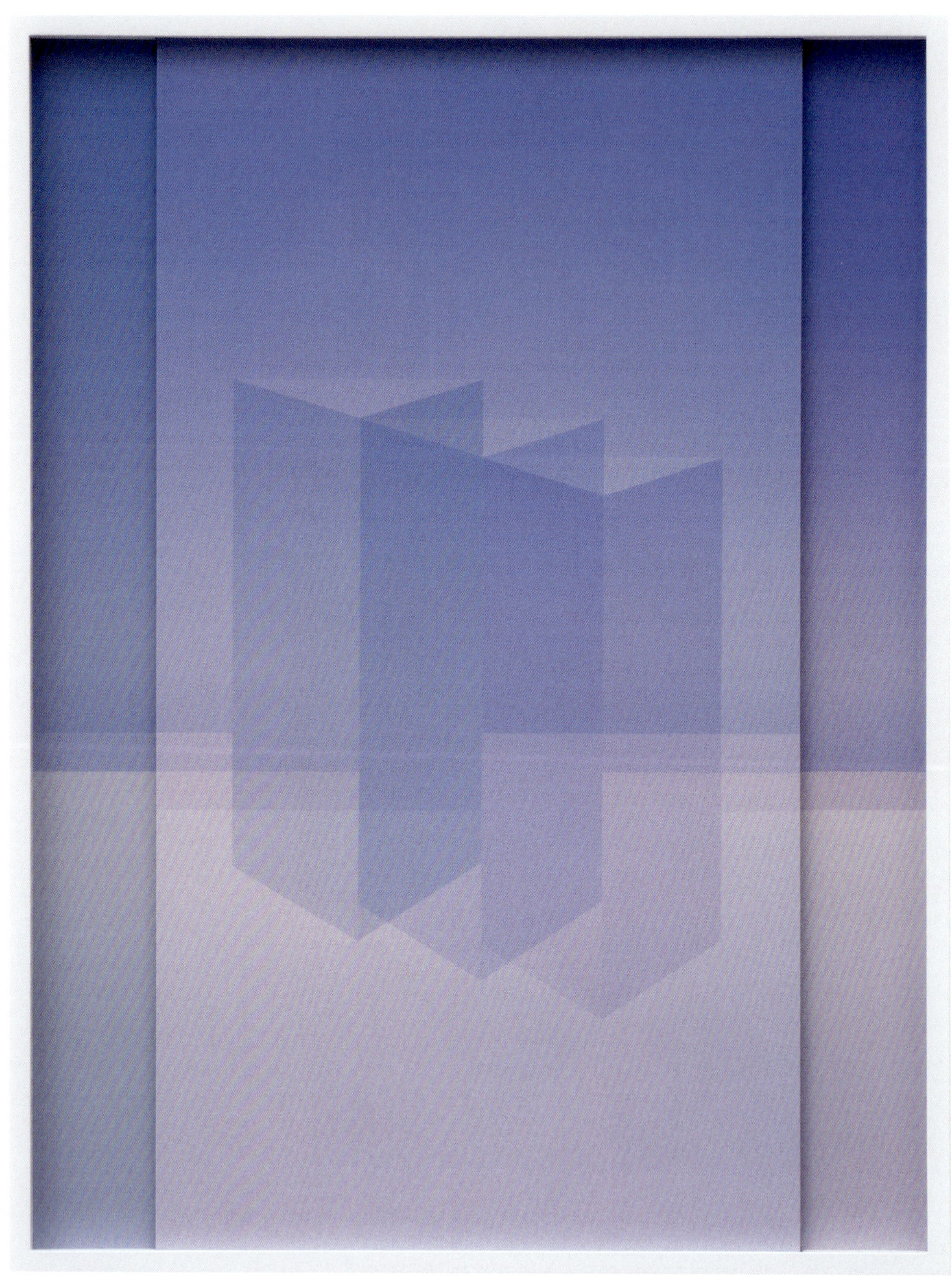

Electric Prisms X and *XII*, 2015

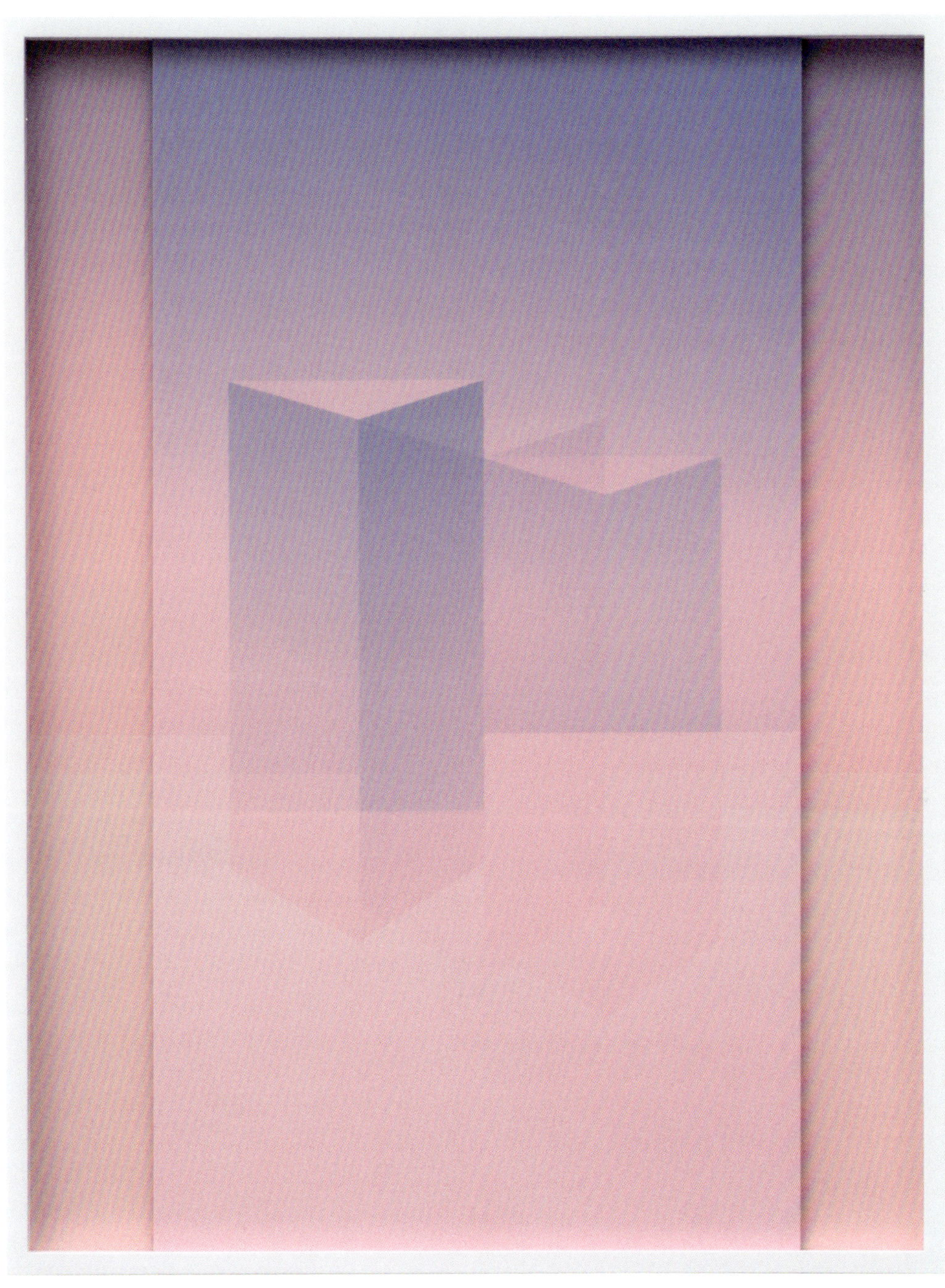

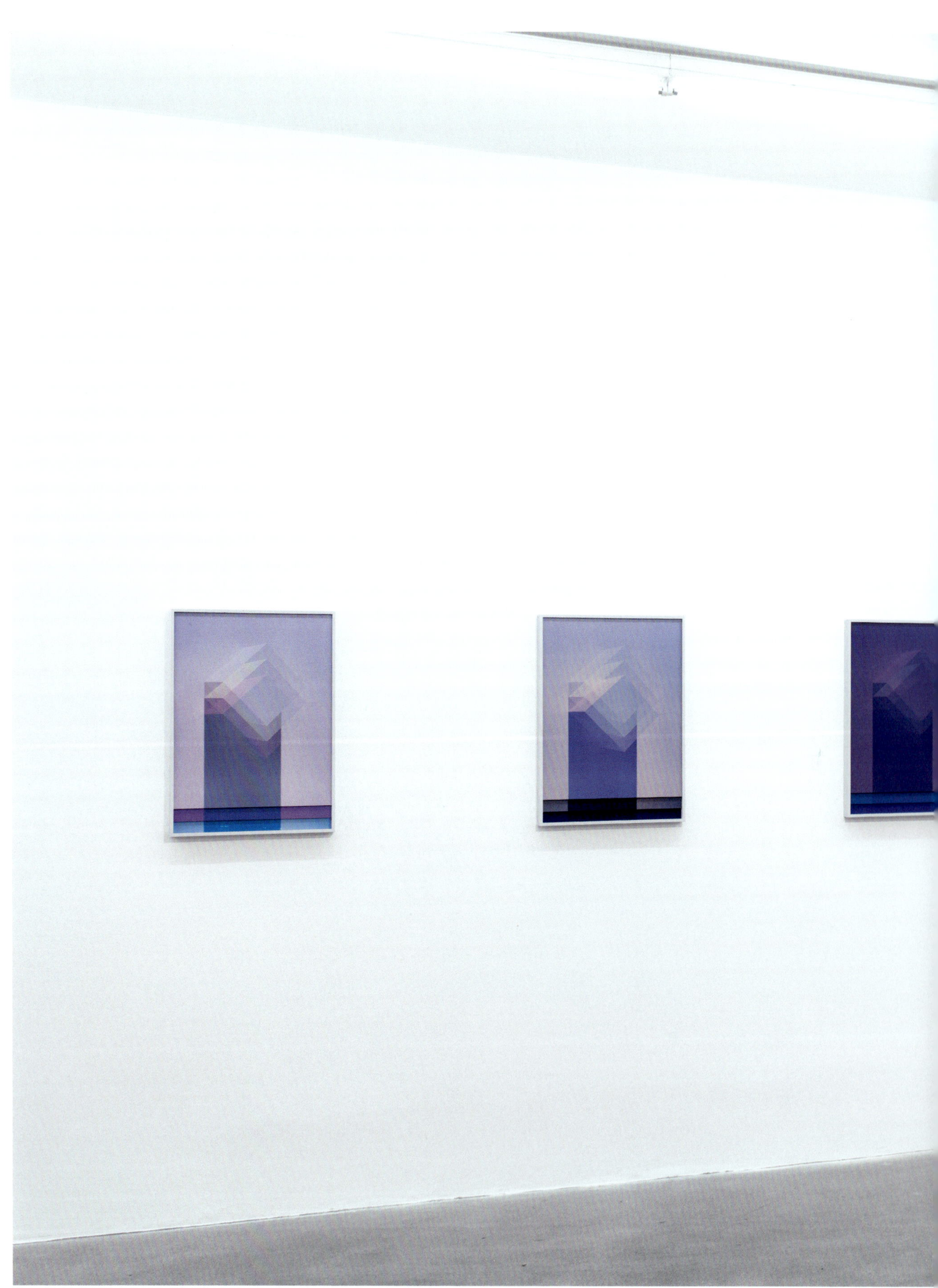

 Concrete Forms IV–IX, 2016, installation view, *DREAMING MIRRORS DREAMING SCREENS,* Sprüth Magers, Berlin, 2016

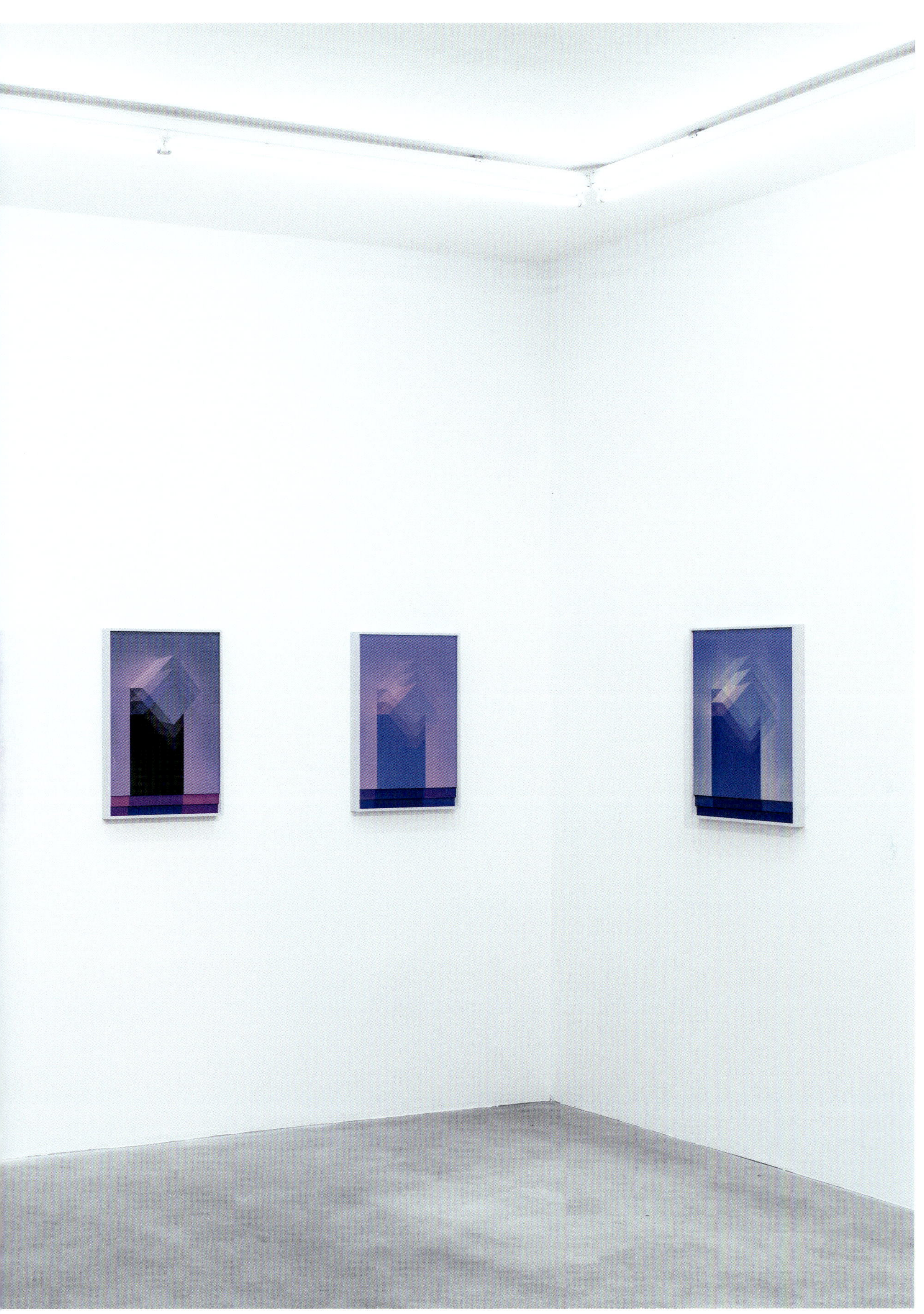

Concrete Form IV, 2016

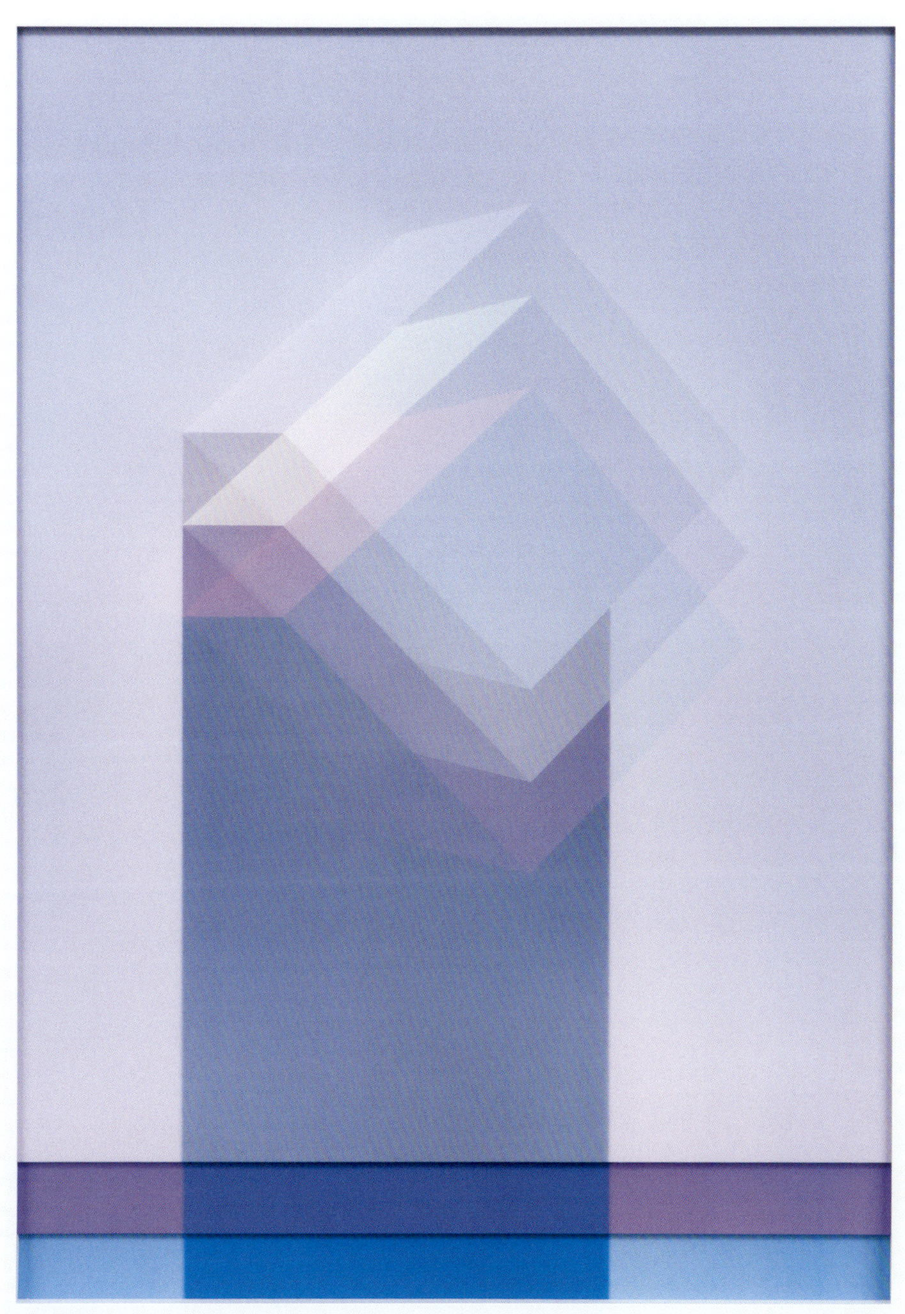

Crepuscule, 2015 (detail)

Crepuscule, 2015 (detail)

Crepuscule, 2015 (detail)

Crepuscule, 2015 (detail)

Crepuscule, 2015 (detail)

> *Crepuscule*, 2015, installation view, *Photo Poetics: An Anthology*, Guggenheim Museum of Art

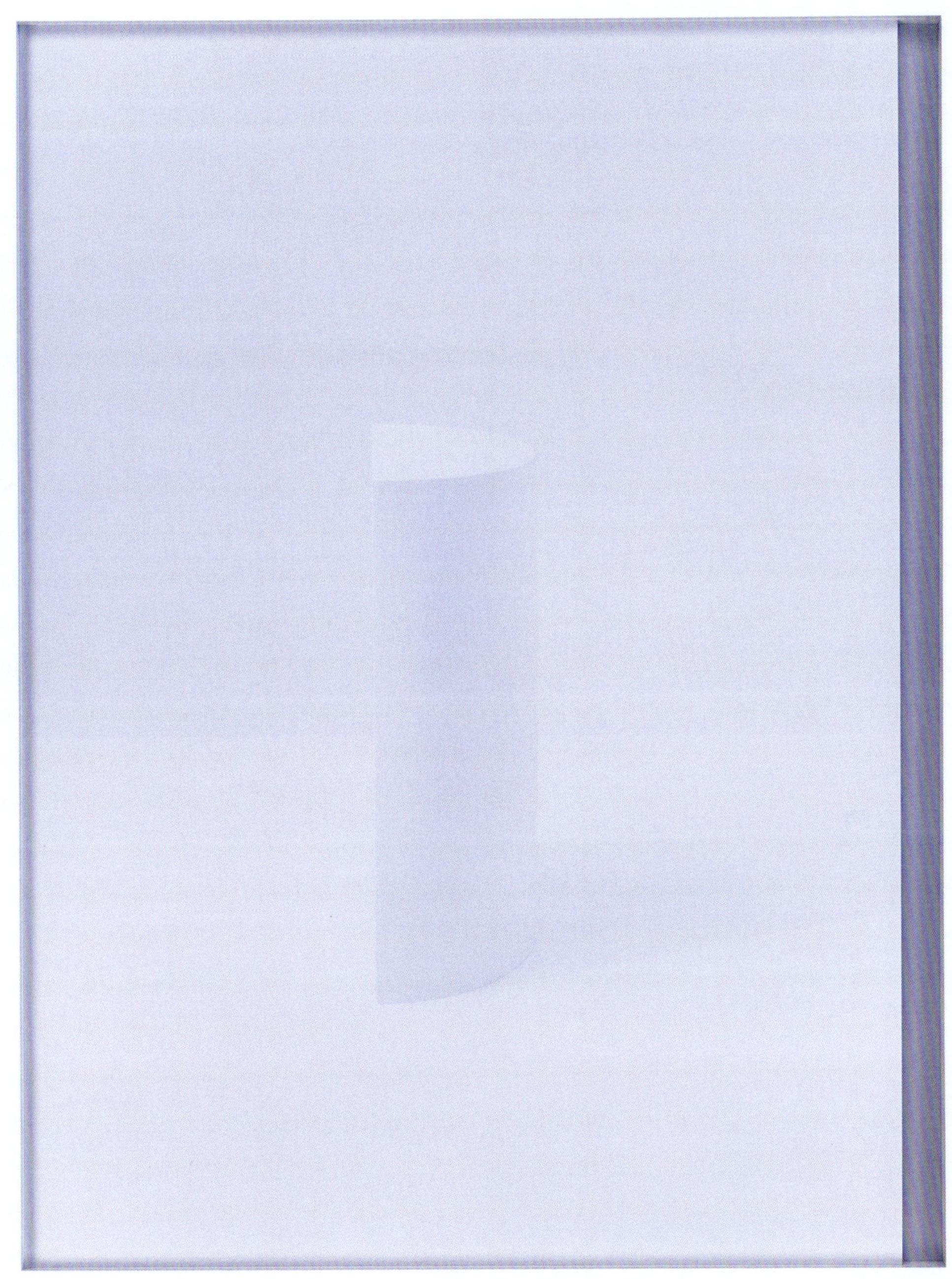

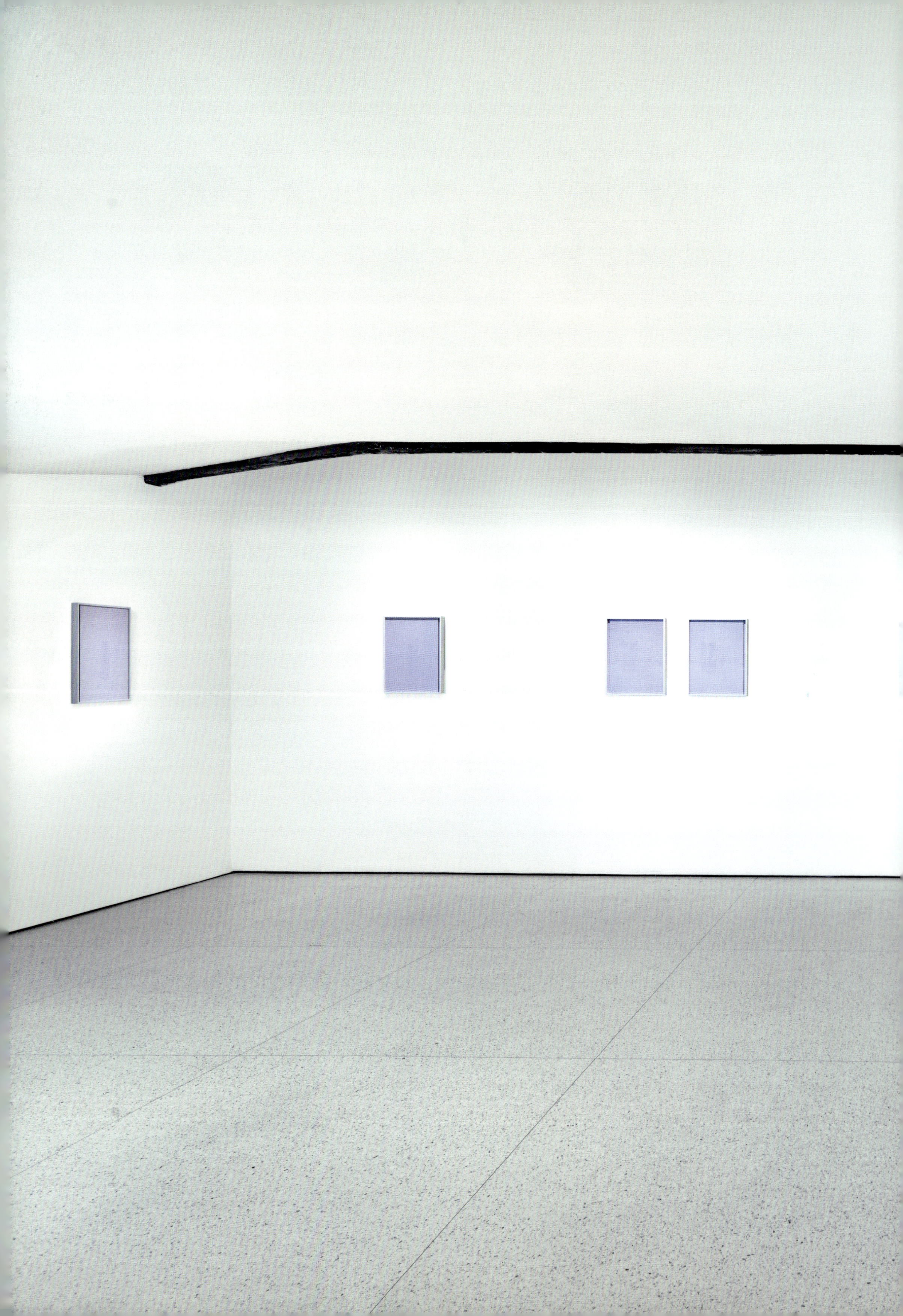

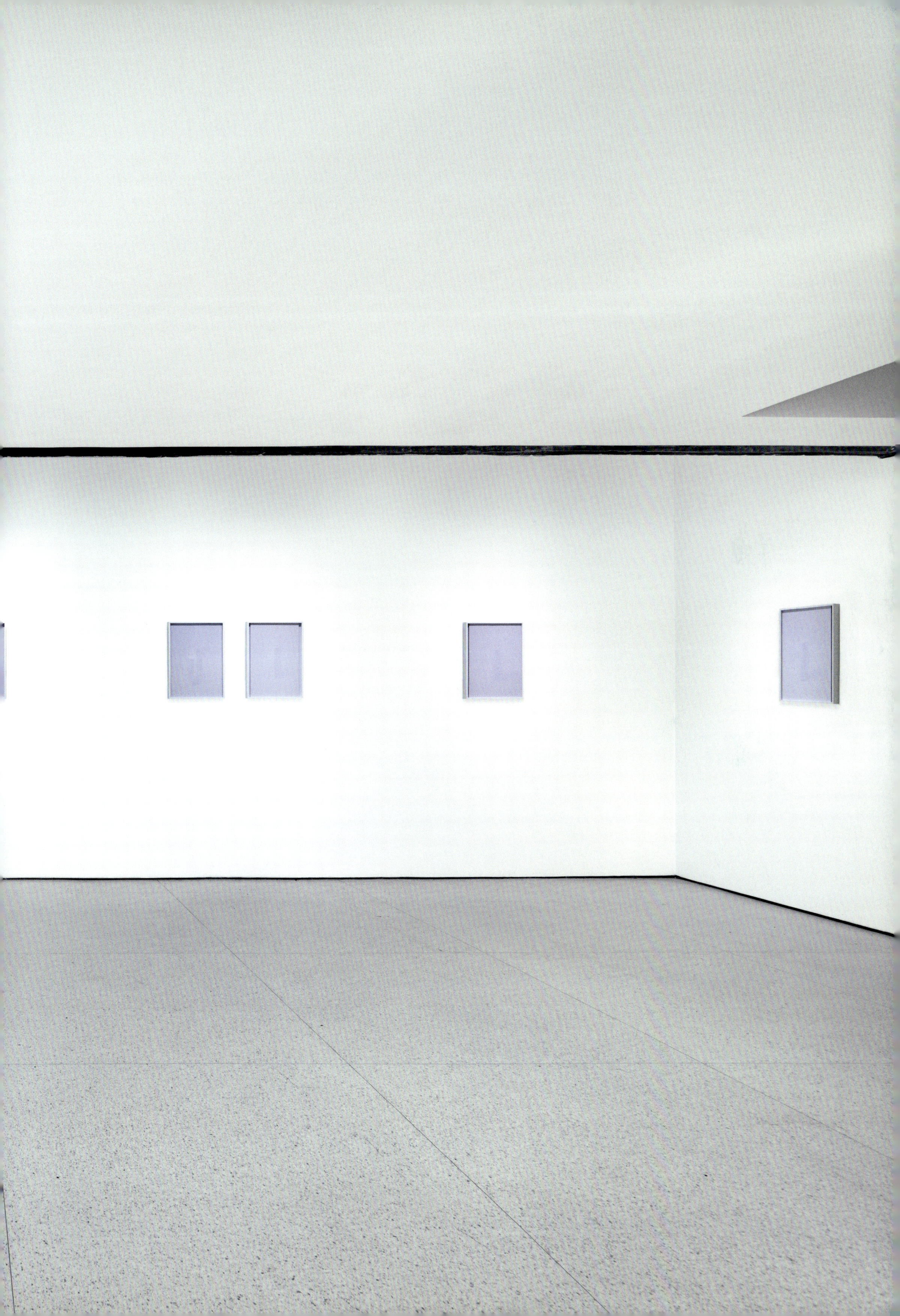

List of Works

All images courtesy of the artist and Metro Pictures, New York, unless otherwise noted.

Horses, 2006
Digital C-print, 20 x 24 in. (50.8 x 60.9 cm)
Fig. p. 5

A Different Kind of Idol, 2006
Digital C-print, 20 x 16 in. (50.8 x 40.6 cm)
Fig. p. 7

Ziggurat, 2006
Digital C-print, 40 x 30 in. (101.6 x 7602 cm)
Fig. p. 9

Decorations in a Notebook, 2006
Digital C-print, 24 x 20 in. (61 x 50.8 cm)
Fig. p. 11

A Reoccurring Pattern, 2006
Digital C-print, 30 x 40 in. (76.2 x 101.6 cm)
Fig. p. 13

Walpurgisnacht, 2007
Digital C-print, 20 x 16 in. (50.8 x 40.6 cm)
Fig. p. 15

The Principle of Superimposition II, 2008
Digital C-print, 65 x 44 1/2 in. (163.8 x 113 cm)
Fig. p. 17

A Composition for Detroit, 2009
Four digital C-prints, 65 x 48 in.
(165.1 x 121.9 cm) each
New Photography, installation view, 2009
The Museum of Modern Art, New York
Fig. pp. 18–19

Blue Eclipse, 2010
Digital C-print, 20 x 14 in. (50.8 x 35.6 cm)
Fig. p. 21

Treme School Window, 2010
Digital C-print, 20 x 15 1/4 in. (50.8 x 38.7 cm)
Fig. p. 22

Treme, 2010
Digital C-print, 20 x 15 3/4 in. (50.8 x 40 cm)
Fig. p. 23

Universe, 2010
Digital C-print, 20 x 14 3/4 in. (50.8 x 37.5 cm)
Fig. p. 25

Foundation, Rocheblave Street, 2010
Digital C-print, 20 x 15 3/4 in. (50.8 x 40 cm)
Fig. p. 26

Foundation, Reynes Street, 2010
Digital C-print, 20 x 15 3/4 in. (50.8 x 40 cm)
Fig. p. 27

Temple, 2010
Digital C-print, 20 x 15 3/4 in. (50.8 x 40 cm)
Fig. p. 29

Foundation, Alabo Street, 2010
Digital C-print, 20 1/2 x 16 1/2 in.
(52.1 x 41.9 cm)
Fig. p. 30

Foundation, Deslonde Street I, 2010
Digital C-print, 20 x 15 3/4 in. (50.8 x 40 cm)
Fig. p. 31

Blue Caryatid at Dusk, 2010
Digital C-print, 20 x 16 in. (50.8 x 40.6 cm)
Fig. p. 33

The Sleepers, 2010
Seventeen digital C-prints,
dimensions variable
To Think of Time, installation view, 2010
Whitney Museum of American Art,
New York
Fig. pp. 34–35

Caryatid, 2010
Digital C-print, 75 x 49 1/8 in.
(90.5 x 124.8 cm)
Knight's Move, installation view, 2010
SculptureCenter, New York
Fig. p. 36

Turned Stairs/Stars, 2014
Oak, marble dust gesso, digital C-print,
blue glass, sculpture: 96 x 131 x 10 1/2 in.
(243.8 x 332.7 x 26.7 cm), digital C-print:
24 x 16 in. (61 x 40.6 cm)

The Blue of Distance, installation view, 2015
Aspen Museum of Art, Colorado
Photo: Tony Prikryl
Fig. p. 38

Alhambra I, 2014
Two digital C-prints, Mirona glass,
78 x 48 in. (198.1 x 121.9 cm) each
Fig. p. 39

Setting Sky, 2014
Pigmented concrete, 108 x 12 x 12 in.
(274.3 x 30 1/2 x 30 1/2 cm)
Fig. p. 40

Hammer Projects, installation view, 2011
Hammer Museum, Los Angeles
Photo: Brian Forrest
Figs. pp. 43–48

Sculpture: *Four Directions*, 2011
Patinated steel with mica, 84 x 12 x 12 in.
(213.4 x 30.5 x 30.5 cm)
Fig. p. 44

Sculpture left: *The Visible West*, 2011
Painted aluminum, fringe, 108 x 72 x 1.5 in.
(274.3 x 182.9 x 3.8 cm)
Fig. p. 45

Sculpture left: *Feathers*, 2011
Steel, Macaw feathers, fiberglass-reinforced
plaster, 66 x 18 x 13 in. (167.6 x 45.7 x 33 cm)
Fig. p. 47

Sculpture in foreground: *Star Map*, 2011
Plaster, metal, found materials,
48 x 12 x 13 in. (121.9 x 30.5 x 33 cm)
Fig. p. 48

Sonya Flores, 2011
Digital C-print, 16 1/4 x 12 1/4 in.
(41.3 x 31.1 cm)
Fig. p. 49

Western Costume, Isis, 2011
Digital C-print, 20 x 15 1/2 in. (50.8 x 39.4 cm)
Fig. p. 51

Western Costume, Aurora, 2011
Digital C-print, 20 x 16 1/2 in. (50.8 x 41.9 cm)
Fig. p. 53

Installation view, 2012
The Approach, London
Courtesy of the artist and The Approach, London
Fig. pp. 54–55

Top: *Baltimore Dancers, Nine,* 2012
Digital C-print, 8 x 6 in. (20.3 x 15.2 cm)
Bottom: *Baltimore Dancers, Ten,* 2012
Digital C-print, 8 x 6 in. (20.3 x 15.2 cm)
Fig. p. 57

Sara VanDerBeek, installation view, 2012
Fondazione Memmo, Rome
Courtesy of Fondazione Memmo Arte Contemporanea, Rome
Fig. pp. 58–59

Mask, 2012
Digital C-print, 84 x 48 in. (213.4 x 121.9 cm)
Fig. p. 61

Sara VanDerBeek, installation view, 2012
Fondazione Memmo, Rome
Courtesy of Fondazione Memmo Arte Contemporanea, Rome
Fig. pp. 62–63

Caracalla, 2012
Digital C-print, 20 x 15 3/4 in. (50.8 x 40 cm)
Fig. p. 65

Installation view, 2013
Metro Pictures, New York
Fig. pp. 66–67

Pink Nude, Blue, 2013
Digital C-print with blue and pink Plexiglas, 80 x 48 in. (203.2 x 121.9 cm)
Fig. p. 69

Installation view, 2013
Metro Pictures, New York
Fig. pp. 70–71
Sculpture: *XXVI,* 2013
Concrete and latex paint, 2 x 144 x 12 in. (30.5 x 365.8 x 30.5 cm)
Photographs: *Roman Women VIII,* 2013
Two digital C-prints, 20 x 16 in. (50.8 x 40.6 cm) each

Roman Women I, 2013
Digital C-print, 20 x 16 in. (50.8 x 40.6 cm)
Fig. p. 73

Parallel, 2013
Two digital C-prints, 20 x 15 3/4 in. (50.8 x 40 cm)
Figs. pp. 74, 75

Roman Woman VII, 2013
Digital C-print, 20 x 16 in. (50.8 x 40.6 cm)
Fig. p. 77

Roman Women VIII, 2013
Two digital C-prints, 20 x 16 in. (50.8 x 40.6 cm) each
Figs. pp. 78, 79

Roman Women IX, 2013
Digital C-print, 20 x 16 in. (50.8 x 40.6 cm)
Fig. p. 81

Shift, 2014
Digital C-print, 24 x 16 in. (61 x 40.6 cm)
Fig. p. 83

Pyramid Steps, Day, 2014
Digital C-print, 24 x 18.5 in. (61 x 47 cm)
Fig. p. 85

Synthetic Geometry, 2014
Two digital C-prints, 24 x 19 in. (61 x 48.3 cm) each
Figs. pp. 86, 87

Ancient Solstice, 2014
Digital C-print, 24 x 17 3/4 in. (61 x 45.1 cm)
Fig. p. 89

Mimbre, 2014
Digital C-print, 24 x 18 in. (61 x 45.7 cm)
Fig. p. 91

Delaunay, 2008
Digital C-print, 40 x 40 in. (101.6 x 101.6 cm)
Fig. p. 92

Chorerra, 2014
Digital C-print, 24 x 18 1/4 in. (61 x 46.4 cm)
Fig. p. 94

Top: *Lunar Calendar,* 2014
Oak, glass, plaster, paint, digital C-print, table: 30 x 72 x 24 in. (76.2 x 182.9 x 61 cm); two hexagon sculptures: 10.5 x 12 x 24 in. (26.7 x 30.5 x 61 cm) and 10.5 x 12 x 12 in. (26.7 x 30.5 x 30.5 cm); photograph: 24 x 18 in. (61 x 45.7 cm)
Courtesy of the artist and Altman Siegel Gallery, San Francisco
Fig. p. 95

After, 2009
Digital C-print, 60 x 40 in. (152.4 x 101.6 cm)
Fig. p. 97

To Think of Time, installation view, 2010
Whitney Museum of American Art, New York
Fig. p. 101

Four Photographers, 2008 (detail)
Digital C-print, 18 x 21 in. (45.7 x 53.3 cm)
Fig. p. 104

Four Photographers, 2008
Six digital C-prints, 18 x 21 in. (45.7 x 53.3 cm) each
Courtesy of The Approach, London
Fig. p. 105

Hammer Projects, installation view, 2011
Hammer Museum, Los Angeles
Photo: Brian Forrest
Fig. p. 106

Sensory Spaces 6, installation view, 2015
Museum Boijmans Van Beuningen, Rotterdam
Photo: Studio Hans Wilschut
Fig. p. 108

Western Costume, Aurora, 2011
Digital C-print, 20 x 16 1/2 in. (50.8 x 41.9 cm)
Hammer Projects, installation view, 2011
Hammer Museum, Los Angeles
Fig. p. 109

Metal Mirror VII (Magia Naturalis), 2013
Digital C-print and Mirona glass, 96 x 48 in. (243.8 x 121.9 cm)
Fig. p. 110

Sonya Flores, Fancy Shawl Dance, 2011
Digital C-print 6 x 8 in. (15.2 x 20.32 cm)
Fig. p. 113

Orpheus, 2015
Two digital C-prints, one mounted on aluminum, foreground triangle on dibond, 16 x 12 1/4 in. (40.6 x 31.1 cm)
Fig. p. 115

Modern Symbols, 2015 (detail)
Marble, fiberglass-reinforced plaster, two wooden pedestals, triangle one: 13/16 x 7 7/8 x 1 1/6 in. (30 x 20 x 3 cm); triangle two: 1 1/8 x 8 x 8 in. (2.9 x 20.3 x 20.3 cm); triangle three: 12 1/4 x 8 x 1 1/2 in. (31.1 x 20.3 x 3.8 cm); triangle four: 1 1/8 x 8 x 8 in. (2.9 x 20.3 x 20.3 cm); pedestals: 54 x 1 x 12 in. (137.2 x 2.5 x 30.5 cm) and 36 1/8 x 12 x 12 in. (91.8 x 30.5 x 30.5 cm)
Fig. p. 116

Front Room: Sara VanDerBeek, installation view, 2015
Baltimore Museum of Art, Maryland
Fig. p. 117

Electric Prism III, 2015
Two digital C-prints
20 x 14 3/4 in. (50.8 x 37.5 cm)
Fig. p. 118

VI, from the series *Ventura*, 2015
Six digital C-prints, 20 x 15 1/4 in.
(50.8 x 38.7 cm)
Fig. p. 119

Sister, 2015
Digital C-Print, 24 x 18 in.
Crepuscule, 2015
Nine framed works, each containing
two digital C-prints, dimensions variable
Photo Poetics: An Anthology,
installation view, 2015
Guggenheim Museum of Art, New York
© Solomon R. Guggenheim Museum,
New York. Photo: David Heald
Fig. p. 120

Sara VanDerBeek, installation view, 2014
Museum of Contemporary Art, Cleveland
Photo: Tim Safranek
Fig. pp. 122–23
Photographs: *Alhambra II*, 2014
Two digital D-prints with Mirona glass,
78 x 48 in. (198.1 x 121.9 cm)

Chain, 2014
Digital C-print, 96 x 48 in. (243.8 x 121.9 cm)
Fig. p. 125

Half Moon, 2014
Digital C-print, 24 x 17.25 in. (61 x 43.8 cm)
Fig. p. 127

Shadow/Sun/Moon/Sea, 2015
Two digital C-prints, one mounted on
aluminum, one on glass, 16 1/2 x 13 1/2 in.
(41.9 x 34.3 cm)
Fig. p. 129

Sensory Spaces 6, installation view, 2015
Museum Boijmans Van Beuningen,
Rotterdam
Photo: Studio Hans Wilschut
Fig. pp. 130–31
Sculpture in foreground: *The Sea*, 2015
Twelve sheets of polished aluminum,
ten stained pine supports, metal
dimensions: 48 x 96 in. (121.9 x 243.8 cm);
ten support dimensions: 1 3/4 x 96 x 6 in.
(4.4 x 121.9 x 15.2 cm); six support dimensions:
1 3/4 x 95 1/2 x 6 in. (4.4 x 242.6 x 15.2 cm)

Sea/Eternal, 2015
Two digital C-prints, one mounted on
aluminum, one on glass, 16 1/2 x 14 1/2 in.
(41.9 x 36.8 cm)
Fig. p. 133

Sensory Spaces 6, installation view, 2015
Museum Boijmans Van Beuningen,
Rotterdam
Photo: Studio Hans Wilschut
Fig. pp. 134–35
Photographic work on the right:
Sky Cloth, East, 2015
Dye sublimation print on fabric, wood,
96 x 48 in. (21.9 x 243.8 cm)

Marble Moon, 2015
Two digital C-prints, one print mounted on
aluminum, one on glass, 16 1/2 x 12 1/2 in.
(41.9 x 31.8 cm)
Fig. p. 137

Front Room: Sara VanDerBeek,
installation view, 2015
Baltimore Museum of Art, Maryland
Fig. pp. 138–39

Second Chance, 2015
Two digital C-prints, one mounted on
aluminum, foreground triangle on dibond,
24 1/2 x 18 1/4 x 2 in. (62.2 x 46.4 x 5.1 cm)
Fig. p. 141

Threshold I, 2015
Two digital C-prints, one mounted on
aluminum, foreground triangle on dibond,
24 x 16 x 2 in. (61 x 40.6 x 5.1 cm)
Fig. p. 142

Threshold II, 2015
Two digital C-prints, one mounted on
aluminum, foreground triangle on dibond,
24 3/4 x 16 3/4 x 2 in. (62.9 x 42.5 x 5.1 cm)
Fig. p. 143

Chance, 2015
Two digital C-prints, one mounted on
aluminum, foreground triangle on dibond,
24 1/2 x 18 1/4 x 2 in. (62.2 x 46.4 x 5.1 cm)
Fig. p. 145

III, from the series *Ventura*, 2015
Two digital C-prints, 24 x 18 in. (61 x 45.7 cm)
Fig. p. 147

I, from the series *Ventura*, 2015
Two digital C-prints, 24 x 18 in. (61 x 45.7 cm)
Fig. p. 148

II, from the series *Ventura*, 2015
Two digital C-prints, 24 x 18 in. (61 x 45.7 cm)
Fig. p. 149

Electric Prisms I–XII, 2015
Twelve framed individual works, each made
up of two digital C-prints, 20 x 14 3/4 in.
(50.8 x 37.5 cm) each
Electric Prisms, Concrete Forms,
installation view, 2015
The Approach, London
Courtesy the artist and The Approach,
London
Fig. pp. 150–51

Electric Prism IV, 2015
Two digital C-prints, 20 x14 3/4 in.
(51.9 x 40.2 cm)
Fig. p. 152

Electric Prism V, 2015
Two digital C-prints, 20 x 14 3/4 in.
(51.9 x 40.2 cm)
Fig. p. 153

Electric Prism X, 2015
Two digital C-prints, 20 x 14 3/4 in.
(50.8 x 37.5 cm)
Fig. p. 154

Electric Prism XII, 2015
Two digital C-prints, 20 x 14 3/4 in.
(50.8 x 37.5 cm)
Fig. p. 155

Concrete Forms IV–IX, 2016
Six digital C-prints, 26 x 18 in.
(66.8 x 46.2 x 4.4 cm) each
DREAMING MIRRORS DREAMING SCREENS,
installation view, 2016
Sprüth Magers, Berlin
Fig. pp. 156–57

Concrete Form IV, 2016
Digital C-print, 20 x 14 1/2 in.
(66.8 x 46.2 x 4.4 cm)
Fig. p. 159

Crepuscule, 2015 (detail)
Nine framed works, each containing two
digital C-prints, 20 x 14 in. (50.8 x 35.6 cm)
Figs. pp. 161, 163, 165, 166, 167, 169

Crepuscule, 2015
Nine framed works, each containing two
digital C-prints, dimensions variable
Photo Poetics: An Anthology,
installation view, 2015
Guggenheim Museum of Art, New York
Fig. pp. 170–71

Acknowledgments

Many thanks to Matthew Dipple, my parents Louise and Stan VanDerBeek, my siblings and my larger family, my friends, Camerawork, Guild & Greyshkul, Gloria Sutton, Roxana Marcoci, Ina Blom, Helene Winer, Janelle Reiring, Allison Card, Alexander Ferrando, Metro Pictures, Claudia Altman Siegel, Altman Siegel Gallery, Emma Robertson, Jake Miller, The Approach, Pochron Studios, East Frames, Sarah Charlesworth, my teachers, my students, and all the generous individuals and institutions who have supported my work.

Editor
Gloria Sutton

Copyeditor
Dawn Michelle d'Atri

Graphic design and typesetting
Gabriele Sabolewski, Hatje Cantz

Project management
Sonja Altmeppen, Hatje Cantz

Production
Heidrun Zimmermann, Hatje Cantz

Reproductions
perfect image, Ostfildern

Typeface
Akkurat, Celeste

Paper
Magno Satin, 150 g/m^2

Printing
Offsetdruckerei Karl Grammlich, Pliezhausen

Binding
Josef Spinner Grossbuchbinderei GmbH, Ottersweier

Published by
Hatje Cantz Verlag
Zeppelinstrasse 32
73760 Ostfildern
Germany
Tel. +49 711 4405-200
Fax +49 711 4405-220
www.hatjecantz.com
A Ganske Publishing Group company

Hatje Cantz books are available internationally at selected bookstores.
For more information about our distribution partners, please visit our website at www.hatjecantz.com.

Trade edition
ISBN 978-3-7757-4108-8

Printed in Germany

Cover illustration
Concrete Form IV, 2016 (fig. p. 159)